Home Cooking

CONTENTS

FOR THE PROUD COOK

America's Best Homemade Recipes!

OVER 600 FAMILY-PROVEN RECIPES!

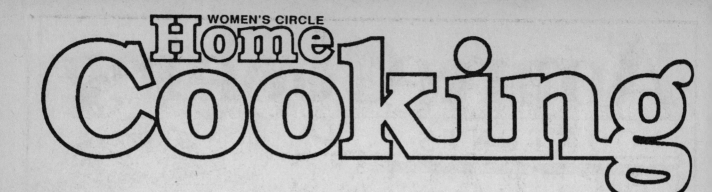

WOMEN'S CIRCLE
Home Cooking

EDITOR
JUDI K. MERKEL

PRODUCTION
PATRICIA ELWELL
BEVERLY WEILAND
DARLENE ZEHR

PHOTOGRAPHY
RHONDA DAVIS
MARY JOYNT
NANCY SHARP

PUBLISHERS
CARL H. MUSELMAN
ARTHUR K. MUSELMAN

CHIEF EXECUTIVE OFFICER
JOHN ROBINSON

MARKETING DIRECTOR
SCOTT MOSS

(219) 589-8741
FAX: (219) 589-8093

Women's Circle Home Cooking cookbook is a collection of recipes obtained from *Women's Circle Home Cooking* magazine, published by House of White Birches, 306 East Parr Road, Berne, Indiana 46711.

Exclusively distributed by:

P.S.I. & Associates, Inc.
13322 SW 128th St.
Miami, Florida 33186
(305) 255-7959

Printed In The USA

27960

Appetizers
APPEALING

SAUSAGE BALLS
Makes 4 dozen

1 pound hot sausage, at room
  temperature
10 ounces extra-sharp Cracker
  Barrel cheese, grated
3 cups Bisquick mix

Mix Bisquick and grated cheese; add sausage. Blend well. Shape into small balls. Freeze on cookie sheet. Store in a plastic bag in the freezer. Place frozen balls on greased cookie sheet. Bake at 300 degrees for 35-45 minutes. Serve hot.

Marcella Swigert, Monroe City, Mo.

CHINESE ROLL-UPS WITH HOT MUSTARD SAUCE
Makes 10

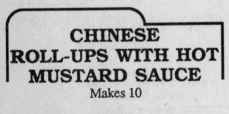

1 pound ground beef
1 can water chestnuts, chopped
2 tablespoons chopped onion
1 package onion and mushroom
  soup mix
1 tablespoon beef bouillon
1 can bean sprouts, drained
3 packages crescent rolls
1/4 cup prepared mustard
1/4 cup mayonnaise
1 clove garlic, chopped
1/4 teaspoon hot sauce
2 teaspoons horseradish

Brown ground beef. Add next 5 ingredients. Simmer for 5 minutes. Remove from heat. Place 1 tablespoon meat mixture in center of each crescent triangle. Pull corners over meat mixture; pinch together to seal.

Place on baking sheet. Bake at 350 degrees for 15 minutes, or until browned. Combine remaining ingredients; mix well. Refrigerate until serving time. Serve hot mustard sauce over roll-ups while still warm. May be frozen for use later.

Marcella Swigert, Monroe City, Mo.

MUSHROOM MUNCHIES

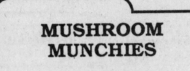

1/4 cup vegetable oil
1/4 cup vinegar with lemon
1 tablespoon sugar
1/2 teaspoon onion powder
1/4 teaspoon garlic powder
Pinch of oregano
1 (10-ounce) can whole mushrooms, drained

Mix ingredients together in small bowl. Add mushrooms and marinate for 1 hour. Toothpicks will assist with serving or snacking of the whole mushrooms.

Millicent Corkum, St. John's, Newfoundland, Canada

FANCY DOGS
Serves 12

1 (6-ounce) jar mustard
1 (6-ounce) jar currant jelly
1 pound hot dogs, cut diagonally

Combine mustard and jelly in fondue pot; mix well. Heat to boiling point. Add cut hot dogs. Heat until warm. Place over fondue flame, stirring occasionally.

Marcella Swigert, Monroe City, Mo.

NUTTY BLEU CHEESE DIP
Makes 2 cups

1 cup mayonnaise
1 (8-ounce) container sour cream
1/4 cup (1 ounce) bleu cheese,
  crumbled
1 tablespoon finely chopped onion
2 teaspoons instant beef bouillon
1/2 to 3/4 cup walnuts, coarsely
  chopped
Assorted fresh vegetables

In medium bowl, combine mayonnaise, sour cream, bleu cheese, onion, and bouillon; mix well. Stir in nuts; cover and chill. Stir before serving. Garnish as desired. Serve with vegetables. Refrigerate leftovers.

Agnes Ward, Erie, Pa.

QUICK PEANUTTY POPCORN BALLS
Makes 8 (2-1/2-inch) balls

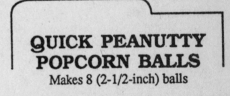

1/2 cup light corn syrup
1/4 cup sugar
3/4 cup peanut butter
2 quarts plain popped corn

In a saucepan mix corn syrup and sugar. Cook over medium heat; stir constantly until mixture comes to a boil and sugar is completely dissolved. Remove from heat. Stir in peanut butter until smooth. Immediately pour mixture over popcorn in large bowl. Stir until well-coated. Grease hands and shape into 8 (2-1/2-inch) balls.

Vickie Vogt, Kewaskum, Wis.

FAVORITE SPOON BREAD

Serves 8

1 1/3 teaspoons sugar
1 1/2 teaspoons salt
1 cup cornmeal, sifted
1 1/3 cups water, boiling (cool 5 minutes)
1/4 cup butter *or* margarine
3 eggs, lightly beaten
1 1/4 cups milk
1 teaspoon baking powder

Preheat oven to 350 degrees. Mix together sugar, salt and cornmeal. Pour water over meal mixture, stirring constantly. Mix in butter; let stand until cooled; add eggs, milk and baking powder, blending well.

Pour into buttered pan (2-quart). Place in shallow pan of hot water. Bake in a 350-degree oven for 35 minutes, or until crusty. Spoon out; serve.

This spoon bread has a light texture, soft center, and crusty top. Most delicious!

Jeanie Blass, Richmond, Va.

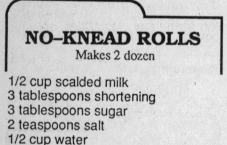

NO–KNEAD ROLLS

Makes 2 dozen

1/2 cup scalded milk
3 tablespoons shortening
3 tablespoons sugar
2 teaspoons salt
1/2 cup water
1 cake yeast *or* 1 package active dry yeast
1 egg
3 cups all-purpose flour
Melted shortening

Blend together milk, 3 tablespoons shortening, sugar, and salt. Cool to lukewarm by adding water. Add yeast, and mix well. Add egg. Add flour, gradually, mixing until dough is well-blended. Place in greased bowl. Brush top with melted shortening and allow to rise until light. Knead dough a few times to make smooth ball. Form into desired shapes and bake in 400-degree oven for 15-25 minutes or until golden brown. Easy and very tasty.

Agnes Ward, Erie, Pa.

POPPY SEED BREAD

1 package Duncan Hines Yellow Cake Mix
1 package toasted coconut instant pudding (Royal brand)
1/4 cup (scant) poppy seeds
4 eggs
1 cup hot water
1/2 cup Crisco oil

Mix well; pour into 2 well-greased loaf pans 9x5-1/2x2 1/2-inches. Bake at 350 degrees for 40-50 minutes. This is a very moist bread!

This is very delicious spread with Philadelphia Cream Cheese, plus makes a nice bread to serve along with fruit salad!

Alberta Wiley, Zionsville, Ind.

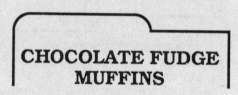

CHOCOLATE FUDGE MUFFINS

1 cup butter or margarine
4 squares semisweet chocolate
1-1/2 cups white sugar
1 cup flour
1/4 teaspoon salt
4 eggs, beaten
1 teaspoon vanilla

In a saucepan over low heat, combine margarine and chocolate. Melt, stirring frequently, so the chocolate does not burn or stick.

In a bowl, combine sugar, flour and salt. Stir in chocolate mixture. Beat eggs, then add them to batter with the vanilla. Stir until eggs are well-blended, but do not beat the mixture. Line muffin tins with paper liners. Fill each one about two-thirds full. Bake at 300 degrees for 30–40 minutes. Check to see if muffins are done by inserting a toothpick in one near the center of the muffin. If the toothpick does not come out clean, bake for another 5 minutes. Let muffins cool 5 minutes before removing them from the pan. These taste much like brownies. Keep any leftovers in a covered container, then rewarm them.

Lillian Smith, Montreal, Quebec, Canada

CRANBERRY BANANA NUT BREAD

2 cups flour
3 teaspoons baking powder
1/2 teaspoon salt
1/2 teaspoon cinnamon
1 cup fresh cranberries, ground
1 teaspoon grated orange rind
1 cup mashed very ripe bananas (3 large)
1/2 cup milk
4 tablespoons butter
1 cup sugar
1 egg
1 cup chopped pecans

Sift together flour, baking powder, salt and cinnamon. Blend orange rind with ground cranberries. In 2-quart bowl, blend bananas and milk. Cream butter and sugar together; blend in egg. Sift dry ingredients alternately with banana mixture, stirring until just blended. Stir in cranberry mixture and pecans. Bake in 9x5x3-inch pan at 350 degrees for 1 hour and 15 minutes. Store at least 24 hours before slicing.

Jenni Lien, Stoughton, Wis.

BUTTERMILK CORN BREAD

3/4 cup Lysine cornmeal
1 cup white flour
3 tablespoons sugar
1 teaspoon soda
3/4 teaspoon salt
1 cup buttermilk
1 egg, beaten
2 tablespoons melted margarine

Preheat oven to 400 degrees. Stir together cornmeal, flour, sugar and salt. Set aside.

Dissolve soda in buttermilk. Add beaten egg and melted margarine; stir until mixed, then add to dry ingredients and mix well. Turn into greased 9x9-inch pan, or into greased muffin pan. Bake 20 minutes, or until golden and done.

These are delicious and healthful eating.

Irene Adney, Eureka Springs, Ark.

CHEESE DIP
Makes 3-1/2 cups

2 cups sour cream
1-1/2 cups shredded Cheddar
  cheese
1/4 cup sliced pimiento-stuffed
  olives
1/2 teaspoon salt
1/4 teaspoon sage

Blend sour cream with remaining ingredients. Serve chilled. Especially good with saltine crackers!

Lucy Dowd, Sequim, Wash.

FRUIT DIP
Make 3 cups

2 cups sour cream
1/4 cup drained crushed pineapple
2/3 cup chopped red apples
1/2 teaspoon curry powder
1/2 teaspoon garlic salt
Apple slices for garnish

Blend sour cream with apple, pineapple, curry powder, and garlic salt. Place in bowl and chill. Garnish with sliced apples around outer edge of bowl.

Good with corn chips or shredded wheat wafers.

Lucy Dowd, Sequim, Wash.

FRESH MUSHROOM DIP

1-8 ounce package cream cheese,
  softened
2 tablespoons snipped ripe olives
2 tablespoons snipped parsley
3/4 teaspoon seasoned salt
4 drops bottled hot pepper sauce
1/2 cup sour cream
1/2 pound fresh mushrooms, finely
  chopped

Combine cream cheese and seasonings; fold in sour cream and chill. Stir in mushrooms just before serving.

Marcella Swigert, Monroe City, MO

DIPPETY DOO DIP

1 squeeze tube of hickory smoked
  cheese
1 cup sour cream
1 can bean with bacon soup (undiluted)
2 or 3 minced green onions (use all)

Combine all ingredients and warm over double boiler or in Microwave. Mix well. Serve with tortilla chips.
You can't eat just one!

Mary Bruesehoff, Spokane, WA

SNACKIN DIPS FOR CHIPS
Serves 4

1 can (6 1/2 ounce) chunk tuna
1 envelope instant onion soup mix
1 cup dairy sour cream
1 tablespoon prepared horseradish
Parsley for garnish
Potato chips - celery sticks - cherry
  tomatoes

Drain tuna. Combine tuna with soup mix, sour cream, and horseradish. Garnish with parsley. Arrange potato chips, celery sticks, and tomatoes on platter.   **Agnes Ward, Erie, PA**

LOW CAL CLAM DIP
Makes 2 cups

1-8 ounce can minced clams
1-1/2 cups cottage cheese
1/2 teaspoon seasoned salt
2 teaspoons lemon juice
1 teaspoon Worcestershire sauce
1 tablespoon minced green onions
Assorted crisp vegetable dippers

In blender container, combine clams with liquid, cottage cheese seasoned salt, lemon juice, and Worcestershire sauce. Cover and whirl around until smooth. Stir in green onions. Cover and chill at least two hours to blend flavors. Serve with cauliflower, broccoli, and strips of carrots, zucchini, and cucumbers.

Agnes Ward, Erie, PA

BLUE CHEESE DIP

3 ounces blue cheese, crumbled
1/2 cup sour cream
1/2 cup mayonnaise
Dash of paprika
Dash of garlic powder
Assorted vegetables, cut in strips

Mix together all ingredients except vegetables and chill 2 hours to blend flavors. Serve with vegetables.

Charlotte Adams, Detroit, MI

RAW VEGETABLE DIP
Yield - 2-1/2 cups

2 cups applesauce
1/2 pint dairy sour cream
2 tablespoons minced onion
1 teaspoon Worcestershire sauce
1/2 teaspoon salt

Slowly cook applesauce abut 5 minutes to evaporate some of the liquid; chill. Combine the applesauce, sour cream, onion, Worcestershire sauce and salt. Mix well. Use as a dip for fresh, raw vegetables of your choice.

Agnes Ward, Erie, PA

CHEESE BALL

8 ounce cream cheese
6 ounce blue cheese, crumbled
6 ounce jar Old English cheese
2 tablespoons mayonnaise
Dash of garlic salt
2 tablespoons finely chopped onion
6 ounce chopped walnuts

Mix all three (3) cheeses together with an electric mixer. Add mayonnaise, garlic salt, onion, and walnuts to cheese mixture. Shape into a ball and wrap with plastic wrap. Refrigerate twenty-four (24) hours before serving. When ready to serve, sprinkle paprika.

Joanie Lopez, Beckley, WV

Beverages
FROSTY & HOT

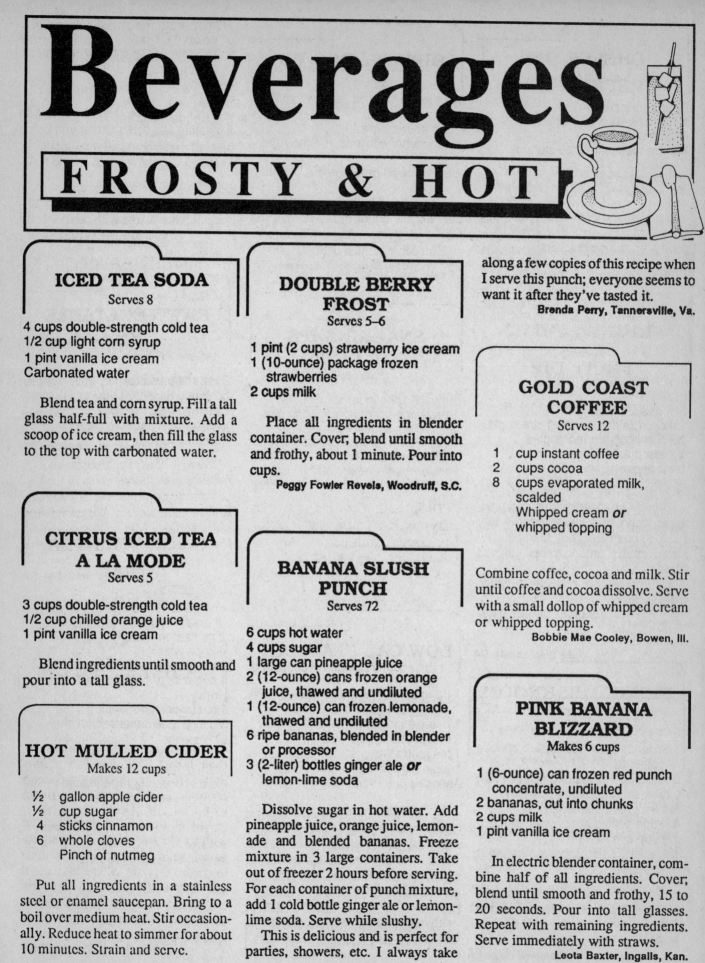

ICED TEA SODA
Serves 8

4 cups double-strength cold tea
1/2 cup light corn syrup
1 pint vanilla ice cream
Carbonated water

Blend tea and corn syrup. Fill a tall glass half-full with mixture. Add a scoop of ice cream, then fill the glass to the top with carbonated water.

CITRUS ICED TEA A LA MODE
Serves 5

3 cups double-strength cold tea
1/2 cup chilled orange juice
1 pint vanilla ice cream

Blend ingredients until smooth and pour into a tall glass.

HOT MULLED CIDER
Makes 12 cups

½   gallon apple cider
½   cup sugar
4   sticks cinnamon
6   whole cloves
    Pinch of nutmeg

Put all ingredients in a stainless steel or enamel saucepan. Bring to a boil over medium heat. Stir occasionally. Reduce heat to simmer for about 10 minutes. Strain and serve.

DOUBLE BERRY FROST
Serves 5–6

1 pint (2 cups) strawberry ice cream
1 (10-ounce) package frozen strawberries
2 cups milk

Place all ingredients in blender container. Cover; blend until smooth and frothy, about 1 minute. Pour into cups.

Peggy Fowler Revels, Woodruff, S.C.

BANANA SLUSH PUNCH
Serves 72

6 cups hot water
4 cups sugar
1 large can pineapple juice
2 (12-ounce) cans frozen orange juice, thawed and undiluted
1 (12-ounce) can frozen lemonade, thawed and undiluted
6 ripe bananas, blended in blender or processor
3 (2-liter) bottles ginger ale *or* lemon-lime soda

Dissolve sugar in hot water. Add pineapple juice, orange juice, lemonade and blended bananas. Freeze mixture in 3 large containers. Take out of freezer 2 hours before serving. For each container of punch mixture, add 1 cold bottle ginger ale or lemon-lime soda. Serve while slushy.

This is delicious and is perfect for parties, showers, etc. I always take along a few copies of this recipe when I serve this punch; everyone seems to want it after they've tasted it.

Brenda Perry, Tannersville, Va.

GOLD COAST COFFEE
Serves 12

1   cup instant coffee
2   cups cocoa
8   cups evaporated milk, scalded
    Whipped cream *or* whipped topping

Combine coffee, cocoa and milk. Stir until coffee and cocoa dissolve. Serve with a small dollop of whipped cream or whipped topping.

Bobbie Mae Cooley, Bowen, Ill.

PINK BANANA BLIZZARD
Makes 6 cups

1 (6-ounce) can frozen red punch concentrate, undiluted
2 bananas, cut into chunks
2 cups milk
1 pint vanilla ice cream

In electric blender container, combine half of all ingredients. Cover; blend until smooth and frothy, 15 to 20 seconds. Pour into tall glasses. Repeat with remaining ingredients. Serve immediately with straws.

Leota Baxter, Ingalls, Kan.

ZESTY FRUIT REFRESHER

1 cup cranberry cocktail juice
1 cup prune juice (Welch's)
2 cups apple juice

Mix all the above juices and place in refrigerator. When ready to serve, place 1/2 cup fruit juice mixture into glass tumbler and fill rest of glass with ginger ale.

M. Powell Hamilton, Ontario, Canada

FRUIT LOW-BALL

Serves 6

1 (10-ounce) package frozen peaches
1/4 cup firmly-packed light brown sugar
1/4 teaspoon cinnamon
1 quart buttermilk
1 medium orange

Thaw peaches. Combine peaches, sugar, and cinnamon in blender. Whirl at medium speed until smooth. Add buttermilk; whirl again.

To serve, pour into six 8-ounce glasses. Slice orange very thin; garnish each glass edge with an orange wheel. Top with dash of cinnamon. Very zesty and refreshing with the buttermilk!

Judie Betz, Lomita, CA

ORANGE-TOMATO COCKTAIL

Serves 6

1-1/2 cups chilled tomato juice
1 cup chilled orange juice
1 tablespoon lemon juice
1/2 teaspoon salt
1 slice onion

Blend all ingredients in blender about 30 seconds or until thoroughly mixed. Add 4 ice cubes, one at a time, and blend until mixed.

Agnes Ward, Erie, PA

PINEAPPLE SLUSH

Makes 3 cups

1 (5-1/4 ounce) can pineapple tidbits, undrained
1 medium banana, chilled
1/4 cup milk
2 cups pineapple sherbet

Combine all ingredients in container of electric blender; process until smooth.

Edna Askins, Greenville, Texas

MOCHA

Serves 8-10

2/3 cup instant cocoa mix
1/2 cup instant coffee
8 cups boiling water
Sweetened whipped cream or Cool Whip

Mix cocoa and coffee in pot or pitcher. Pour in boiling water and stir. Serve hot and topped with Cool Whip or whipped cream.

Betty Klopfenstein, Waterman, Ill.

CHOCOLATE-PEANUT-BUTTER MILK SHAKE

Makes 2 cups

2 tablespoons powdered chocolate drink mix
3 tablespoons crunchy peanut butter
1 cup milk, chilled
1 teaspoon honey
Dash cinnamon
Dash nutmeg
8 ice cubes

Place all ingredients in blender. Cover and process until frothy. Pour into vacuum containers.

Annie Emchil, New Castle, Ind.

MELON SHAKE

1 serving

1/2 cup watermelon, cantaloupe or honeydew melon balls
2 large scoops vanilla ice cream (about 1 cup)
1/4 cup milk

Place melon balls in blender. Add ice cream and milk. Cover and blend until smooth. Serve immediately.

Phyllis Beaty, Rossville, Ga.

LO-CALORIE BANANA MILK SHAKE

6 ounces skimmed milk
1/2 teaspoon vanilla
1 banana, sliced frozen
1/2 teaspoon Sprinkle Sweet or sweetener

Put milk in blender. Add vanilla and frozen banana, a little at a time. If a thicker shake is desired, add ice cubes until desired thickness.

Betty Klopfenstein, Waterman, IL

SPICY MILK TEA

Serves 4

6 whole cloves
4 thin slices fresh ginger or 1/2 teaspoon ground ginger
2 cinnamon sticks
4 cups water
4 teaspoons jasmine tea
1 cup milk or half-and-half
Honey
Cardamom, optional
Mint sprigs for garnish

Bring water to boil. Add cinnamon, cloves, and ginger. Cover; simmer 10 minutes. Add tea and steep for a few minutes. Add milk. Bring to boil again. Remove from heat. Strain into a teapot. Serve with a sprinkle of cardamom and a bit of honey. Garnish with mint.

For 1 serving:

Boil 1 cup water. Add 1/2 cinnamon stick, 3 cloves, 2 slices fresh ginger, and 1 teaspoon tea.

Arlene Ranney, Eureka, Calif.

Breads

TO MAKE

QUICK MIX (LIKE BISQUICK)
Makes 13 cups

8-1/2 cups all-purpose flour
3 tablespoons baking powder
1 tablespoon salt
2 teaspoons cream of tartar
1 teaspoon baking soda
1-1/2 cups instant nonfat dry milk
2-1/4 cups vegetable shortening

In a large bowl, sift together dry ingredients. Blend well. With pastry blender, cut in shortening until evenly distributed. Mixture will resemble cornmeal in texture. Put in a large airtight container. Label. Store in a cool, dry place. Use within 4 months.

This works with every Bisquick recipe I've ever tried — even when I used to live at a low altitude!

Michele Martindill, Calhan, Colo.

MUFFINS
Makes 1 dozen

1-1/2 cups biscuit mix
1/2 cup sugar
1 tablespoon poppy seeds
3/4 cup raisins, chopped
1 egg, beaten
3/4 cup sour cream
1 teaspoon vanilla

Combine biscuit mix, sugar, and poppy seeds; make a well in center of mixture. Add remaining ingredients. Stir until just moistened. Spoon into greased muffin pans, filling half full. Bake at 400 degrees for 20 minutes or until they test done.

Kit Rollins, Cedarburg, WI

INDIAN FRIED BISCUITS

2 cups flour
3 tablespoons baking powder
1/2 teaspoon salt
2 tablespoons sugar
2/3 or 3/4 cup milk

Mix dry ingredients; add milk and mix well. Pat out on floured flat surface to 1/4-inch thickness. Slice into 2x3-inch *or* 3x4-inch pieces. Fry in 1/2 inch hot oil, browning each side. Serve warm.

Edna Askins, Greenville, Texas

BRAN APPLESAUCE MUFFINS

1-1/4 cups whole-wheat flour
3/4 cup 100% bran cereal
1/2 cup sugar
1 teaspoon baking soda
1 teaspoon cinnamon
1/2 teaspoon salt
1/2 teaspoon nutmeg
1 cup applesauce
1/2 cup oil
1 teaspoon vanilla
2 eggs

Topping:
1 tablespoon sugar
1/2 teaspoon cinnamon

Heat oven to 400 degrees. Grease 12 muffin cups. Lightly spoon flour into measuring cup; level off. In large bowl, combine all muffin ingredients, stirring just until dry ingredients are moistened. Fill muffin cups two-thirds full. Combine topping ingredients; sprinkle over top of each muffin. Bake at 400 degrees for 15-20 minutes or until toothpick inserted comes out clean. Remove from pan immediately. Serve warm.

Cheryl Santefort, South Holland, Ill.

CRANBERRY BANANA BREAD

2 cups fresh cranberries
1 cup sugar
1 cup water
⅓ cup shortening
⅔ cup sugar
2 eggs
1¾ cups all-purpose flour
2 teaspoons baking powder
½ teaspoon salt
¼ teaspoon baking soda
1 cup mashed banana
½ cup coarsely chopped walnuts

Combine cranberries, 1 cup sugar and water; cook over medium heat about 5 minutes, or until cranberries begin to pop. Drain and set aside. Cream shortening; gradually add ⅔ cup sugar, beating until light and fluffy. Add eggs, 1 at a time, beating well after each. Combine dry ingredients; add to creamed mixture alternately with banana, mixing well after each addition. Fold in cranberries and walnuts. Line a greased 9 x 5 x 3-inch loaf pan. Spoon batter into pan. Bake at 350 degrees for 60 minutes, or until bread tests done. Cool 10 minutes in pan; remove from pan.

Mrs. Albert H. Foley, Lemoyne, Pa.

CHEDDAR SCONES
Makes 6

1½ cups all-purpose flour, unsifted
¼ cup chilled unsalted butter *or* vegetable shortening
2 cups (6 ounces) coarsely shredded sharp cheddar cheese
⅛ teaspoon salt
½ cup milk

Preheat oven to 450 degrees. Sift flour into shallow bowl. Cut in shortening until mixture resembles coarse meal. Mix in cheese and salt. Gradually stir in just enough milk to form stiff dough. Turn dough onto well-floured work surface. Roll out to ⅝-inch thickness. Cut into rounds using lightly floured, scalloped (3-inch) round cookie cutter. Arrange 1 inch apart on ungreased baking sheet. Reroll any remaining scraps and cut out additional rounds. Bake about 15 minutes, or until puffed and light brown. Serve hot.

SIX-WEEK BRAN MUFFINS
Makes 5-1/2 dozen

1 cup shortening
2-1/2 cups sugar
4 eggs
5 cups all-purpose flour
5 teaspoons baking soda
1/2 teaspoon salt
1 quart buttermilk
6 cups bran cereal, such as Kellogg's All-Bran®, not bran flakes
2 cups boiling water

Cream sugar and shortening together. Add eggs and mix, 1 at a time. Sift dry ingredients together and add alternately with buttermilk to shortening mixture. Add cereal and boiling water until blended. Fill muffin tins three-fourths full and bake at 400 degrees for 20–25 minutes. Batter can be stored in tightly covered bowl in refrigerator for 6–10 weeks.

Great to have on hand for busy morning breakfasts.

Marsha Miller, Hilliard, Ohio

RYE BREAD

2 packages yeast
1 cup lukewarm water
1/2 cup brown sugar
1 cup flour
3/4 cup molasses
Grated rind of 1 orange (optional)
1 tablespoon anise seed
1 tablespoon salt
3 or 4 tablespoons melted butter
2 cups rye flour
4 cups white flour

Dissolve yeast in warm water. Add brown sugar and 1 cup flour; mix and let rise. Heat 2 cups milk until lukewarm. Add remaining ingredients.

Mix with spoon and let rise in large mixing bowl. Stir down and add enough flour to make a soft dough. Turn onto floured surface and knead. Divide into 4 parts and knead each. Shape into loaves and put in greased bread pans. Let rise until even with pan tops. Bake at 400 degrees for 10 minutes; reduce to 325 degrees and bake 45 minutes. Turn out onto racks; butter crusts.

Marcella Swigert, Monroe City, Mo.

BUBBLE BREAD

3 loaves frozen bread dough
1 package butterscotch pudding (not instant)
1/2 cup butter over 2 bundt pans
1 cup pecans
1/4 cup cinnamon-sugar
1/4 cup Karo syrup
1 cup brown sugar

Thaw and shape dough into 1-inch balls. Sprinkle pudding mix, pecans, cinnamon-sugar, and brown sugar evenly over bottoms of the two bundt pans. Drizzle butter and Karo over mixture, and top with dough balls.

Let rise over night at room temperature. Bake at 350 degrees for 30-35 minutes. This is a wonderful bread for breakfast guests, as it can be prepared the evening before and popped into the oven to serve piping hot for breakfast.

Karen Pfeifer, Flagstaff, Ariz.

CARROT BREAD

2 eggs
1 cup sugar
⅔ cup oil
1½ cups flour
¾ teaspoon soda
1 teaspoon cinnamon
1 teaspoon nutmeg
½ teaspoon salt
1½ cups raw carrots, grated
1 cup walnuts
¾ cup raisins

Beat eggs; add sugar and oil. Sift together flour, soda, cinnamon, nutmeg and salt; add to egg mixture. Beat well. Add carrots, nuts and raisins. Grease 5 soup cans or 1 (9 x 5-inch) loaf pan. Fill cans half full. Bake at 350 degrees for 45–50 minutes for soup cans, or 1 hour for loaf pan.

Shari Crider, Stoughton, Wis.

SPOON BREAD

1 package yeast
1/4 cup water
1/4 cup sugar
1/3 cup shortening
1/2 cup cold water
1 egg, slightly beaten
1 teaspoon salt
Pinch alum
3/4 cup scalded milk
3-1/2 cups flour

Dissolve yeast in warm water. Set aside. Combine sugar, salt, alum and shortening in scalded milk. Stir until shortening is melted. Cool with 1/2 cup water. Pour this and egg into yeast; add flour and mix. Cover, let rise 45 to 60 minutes. Spoon down. Let rise again 45 minutes. Spoon into greased muffin pans. Let rise. Bake at 400 degrees 15 to 20 minutes.

Betty Ireton, Kingston, OH

BUTTERHORNS
Makes 3 dozen

1 cup milk
1/2 cup margarine
1/2 cup sugar
1/2 teaspoon salt
1 package yeast
3 eggs, beaten
4 1/2 cups flour
Melted butter

Heat milk to scalding; add margarine, sugar and salt. Cool to lukewarm. Add yeast; stir until dissolved. Add eggs, then flour; mix to a smooth, soft dough. Knead lightly on floured surface. Place dough in a greased bowl; cover. Let rise in warm place until doubled in bulk. Divide dough into thirds. Roll each third on lightly floured surface to size of 9-inch pie pan. Cut each round in 12 wedges; roll each triangle, starting with wide end and rolling to center. Arrange on greased baking sheet; brush lightly with melted butter. Cover; let rise until light. Bake in 350-degree oven for 15 minutes.

Very tender and good!

Mrs. George Franks, Millerton, Pa.

PECAN LOAF

2 cups flour
4 teaspoons baking powder
1 teaspoon salt
3 tablespoons margarine
2 tablespoons butter *or* other
    shortening
1 egg, plus 1 egg yolk
1 cup milk
1/2 cup pecans, chopped

Mix and sift flour, baking powder and salt. Cut in margarine and other shortening. Add beaten egg, egg yolk and milk, then pecans. Sugar may be added, as desired, if a sweeter bread is preferred (2 teaspoons). Turn into a buttered 10-inch loaf pan. Let stand 20 minutes. Then bake in 350-degree oven for 50 minutes.

This is really an unusual and delicious recipe!

Suzan L. Wiener, Spring Hill, Fla.

DATE NUT BREAD

1-3/4 cups milk, scalded
1/4 cup warm water
1 cake compressed yeast
1 cup brown sugar
1 cup chopped dates (or chopped
    raw prunes)
2 teaspoons salt
1/2 cup melted shortening
1/2 cup chopped walnuts
2 eggs, well-beaten
6 cups flour

Sift flour and measure. Soften yeast in warm water. Combine milk, salt, sugar, and shortening. Cool to lukewarm. Add yeast, nuts, eggs, dates, and flour. Mix thoroughly. Turn onto lightly floured board. Knead until smooth. Cover with warm damp cloth. Let rise until double in bulk. Form in loaves. Place in well-greased loaf pans. Cover with warm damp cloth. Let stand 30 minutes. Bake in moderate oven of 350 degrees for 50 minutes.

Mrs. E. O'Brien, Richmond, Va.

QUICK BUTTERMILK BREAD STICKS
Makes 8

These taste so good and freeze well, so I usually double the recipe (To double buttermilk use ¾ cup.)

1 cup flour, spooned
    lightly into cup
¼ teaspoon salt
½ teaspoon soda
2½ tablespoons butter *or*
    margarine
6 tablespoons buttermilk
    (I use ⅓ cup plus 1
    tablespoon)
Milk for glaze
Sesame *or* poppy
    seeds, if desired

Preheat oven to 450 degrees. Lightly grease a baking sheet.

Into a medium bowl measure flour, salt and soda; mix with pastry blender. Cut in butter until like fine crumbs.

Add buttermilk; mix gently until combined. On a lightly floured surface (I use a pastry cloth on the counter) knead until a smooth ball—less than 1 minute. Cut into 8 parts; roll each into a 6-inch bread stick. To simplify glazing, place bread sticks close together on baking sheet; rub tops with milk; sprinkle with seeds, if using, then rearrange so they are at least 1 inch apart. Bake until beginning to brown, about 12 minutes. Serve warm with butter. Freeze leftovers.

COCONUT MUFFINS

2 cups flour
1/2 teaspoon salt
4 teaspoons baking powder
1/4 cup sugar
3 tablespoons margarine, melted
1 egg, beaten
1 cup milk
1 cup coconut

Sift dry ingredients together. Combine milk, egg and melted margarine; add to dry ingredients. Add coconut and mix gently. Fill paper-lined muffin cups two-thirds full and bake at 450 degrees for 15 minutes.

Jodie McCoy, Tulsa, Okla.

STRAWBERRY BREAD

1-1/2 cups sifted flour
1/2 teaspoon baking soda
1/2 teaspoon salt
1 cup sugar
1 teaspoon orange extract
1 (10-ounce) package frozen
    strawberries, thawed
2 eggs, beaten
2/3 cup oil *or* melted butter
1/2 cup chopped walnuts

Sift dry ingredients into large bowl. Make a well in the center. Mix rest of ingredients and pour into the dry well. Stir just until blended. Pour into a 9x5-inch greased and lightly floured loaf pan and bake at 350 degrees for 1 hour. Can be served warm or cold.

Agnes Ward, Erie, Pa.

BANANA NUT BREAD

An old-time favorite, this is also an economical bread to bake. You can usually pick up overripe bananas in the store for a substantial savings. This bread can be spread with cream-cheese fillings, peanut butter (a favorite of children), or many other spreads.

1/2 cup shortening
1-1/3 cups sugar
2 large, ripe mashed bananas
2 tablespoons milk
2 eggs
1-3/4 cups flour
1/2 teaspoon soda
1-1/2 teaspoons baking powder
1 teaspoon salt
1 teaspoon nutmeg
1 cup chopped nuts

Cream together shortening and sugar; add mashed bananas and milk, and mix well. Add eggs and blend well. Mix together flour, soda, baking powder, salt and nutmeg, and add to mixture. Fold in nuts and bake at 350 degrees for 45 minutes, or until tested done. Cool on racks.

ORANGE MUFFINS
Makes 6

1 cup all-purpose flour
2 teaspoons baking powder
1/8 teaspoon salt
1-1/2 tablespoons melted butter or margarine
1 egg, beaten
1/2 cup milk
1/3 cup firmly packed brown sugar
Grated rind and juice of 1 orange

Combine flour, baking powder and salt. Add butter, egg, milk and sugar, stirring until just moistened. Blend in orange juice and rind.

Spoon batter into muffin cups in pans, filling two-thirds full. Bake at 400 degrees for 17–20 minutes, or until brown and tested done.

BUTTER CRUMB DUMPLINGS
Serves 8

2 cups sifted flour
4 teaspoons baking powder
1 tablespoon poppy seeds
1 teaspoon celery salt
1 teaspoon poultry seasoning
2 teaspoons dried onion flakes
1/4 cup oil
3/4 cup plus 2 tablespoons milk
1/4 cup melted butter or margarine
2 cups soft bread crumbs

Mix first six ingredients together. Mix and blend in oil and milk. Stir butter into crumbs. Drop dough by tablespoonfuls in 12 equal portions into buttered crumbs and roll to cover with crumbs. Place on top of hot meatballs and gravy.

Bake, uncovered, at 400 degrees for 20-25 minutes, until dumplings are golden. If extra sauce is desired, simmer 1 can cream of chicken soup with 1/4 teaspoon poultry seasoning and 1 teaspoon onion flakes. Stir in 1/2 cup sour cream and reheat.

Ann Gumperz, Santa Rosa, Calif.

FRESH FRUIT OAT MUFFINS
Makes 20

2 cups whole-wheat flour
1 cup rolled oats
1/2 cup unprocessed wheat bran
1/2 cup brown sugar (packed)
1-1/2 teaspoons baking soda
1 teaspoon salt
2 eggs
1-1/2 cups buttermilk
1/4 cup vegetable oil
3 cups finely chopped peaches (or 2 cups fresh Bartlett pears, nectarines or plums)
3 teaspoons orange juice
1-1/2 teaspoons cinnamon

Combine all ingredients in bowl. Blend. Spoon batter into 2-1/2-inch non-stick muffin cups. Bake in 400-degree oven for 20 minutes, or until pick inserted in center comes out dry. Serve warm. Muffins can be frozen.

Kit Rollins, Cedarburg, Wis.

GLAZED LEMON BREAD

1/3 cup melted butter or margarine
1 cup sugar
2 eggs
1/4 teaspoon almond extract
1 1/2 cups sifted all-purpose flour
1 teaspoon salt
1 teaspoon baking powder
1/2 cup milk
1 tablespoon lemon peel
1/2 cup chopped nuts

Blend together well the butter and 1 cup sugar. Beat in eggs; add extract. Sift dry ingredients; add to egg mixture alternately with milk. Blend just to mix. Fold in peel and nuts; turn into a greased (8 1/2)x(4 1/2)x(2 3/4)-inch glass loaf pan. Bake 70 minutes at 325 degrees. If you use a metal pan, bake at 350 degrees. I have also used 2 mini-loaf pans, and baked until loaves tested done in center.

Glazed Topping:
Mix 1/4 cup sugar (not powdered) with 3 tablespoons fresh lemon juice. Spoon over bread immediately, as it comes from oven.

Hazel Hullinger, Decatur, Ill.

SHORTBREAD

1/2 pound (2 sticks) butter
1/4 pound (1/2 cup) shortening
1 cup sugar
1 teaspoon nutmeg
1 egg
6 cups flour
3/4 teaspoon soda
1/2 teaspoon cream of tartar

Mix butter and shortening until soft. Mix with sugar and egg. Beat well. Mix flour, soda, cream of tartar, and nutmeg. Combine mixtures. Sprinkle sugar on pastry board and rolling pin. Toss dough onto board. Roll thin and cut in shapes. Bake on greased baking sheets. Bake in moderate 350-degree oven for 10 minutes.

Suzan L. Wiener, Spring Hill, Fla.

COTTAGE CHEESE BREAD

1 cup cottage cheese
2 eggs, beaten
1 cup sugar
3/4 cup milk
1 teaspoon vanilla
2-3/4 cups flour
2-1/2 teaspoons baking powder
1/2 cup raisins
1/2 cup walnuts
10 chopped cherries

Mix first 7 ingredients in order given; add raisins and walnuts. Pour into greased loaf pan. Decorate top with chopped cherries and sprinkle with sugar. Bake at 350 degrees for about 1 hour.

Sheila Symonowicz, Loganville, Pa.

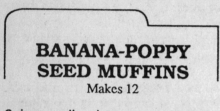

BANANA-POPPY SEED MUFFINS
Makes 12

2 ripe, medium bananas *or* 1 cup
1 egg
3/4 cup sugar
1/4 cup vegetable oil
2 teaspoons grated orange peel
2 cups flour
1-1/2 tablespoons poppy seeds
2 teaspoons baking powder
1/2 teaspoon salt
Citrus Glaze (recipe follows)

Purée bananas in blender. In a bowl mix bananas, egg, sugar, oil and orange peel until blended. Combine flour, poppy seeds, baking powder and salt. Stir banana mixture into dry mixture until moistened. Spoon batter into 12 greased muffin cups.

Bake at 375 degrees for 20 minutes. Remove from pan; cool. Top with glaze.

Citrus Glaze:
1-1/4 cups confectioners' sugar
1/4 cup orange juice
1 teaspoon grated orange peel
1 teaspoon vanilla

Combine ingredients and mix until smooth. Top each muffin with glaze.

Vickie Vogt, Kewaskum, Wis.

BROWN BREAD

1-1/2 cups all-purpose flour
1-1/2 cups rye flour
1 cup yellow cornmeal
1 teaspoon baking soda
1 teaspoon salt
1/2 cup raisins
1/2 cup walnuts
2 cups buttermilk
1/2 cup dark molasses

Mix flours, cornmeal, baking soda and salt together. Add raisins and nuts. Slowly add buttermilk and molasses alternately to dry ingredients; beat after each addition.

Pour into buttered 9-inch loaf pan. Bake at 375 degrees for 50 minutes, or until tested done.

Let stand in pan on wire rack for 5 minutes. Loosen sides with knife and turn out on rack.

Brush with butter while still warm. Coll before slicing.

CHEESE QUICK BREAD

2 cups all-purpose flour
4 teaspoons baking powder
1/4 teaspoon salt
1/4 cup butter
1 cup grated cheddar cheese
2 eggs
1/4 cup white sugar
1 cup milk

In a large bowl, sift together flour, baking powder, and salt; cut in the butter until particles are the size of small peas. Stir in the cheese. In small bowl beat eggs until foamy; beat in sugar, then milk. Pour egg mixture into flour mixture; stir only until evenly moistened. Transfer dough to a greased 9x5-inch loaf pan. Bake in a 350-degree oven for 50 minutes, or until toothpick inserted in center comes out clean. Remove from pan and serve hot or cold. This is a moist, tasty bread and makes great ham sandwiches.

Lillian Smith, Montreal, Quebec, Canada

PEPPERONI 'N CHEESE CRESCENTS
Serves 8

1 (8-ounce) can Pillsbury Crescent dinner rolls
24 slices pepperoni
2 slices mozzarella cheese
1 egg white

Separate dough into 8 triangles. Place 3 slices of pepperoni, slightly overlapping, on each triangle. Top each with 1/4 slice cheese. Roll up, starting at shortest side of triangle and roll to opposite point. Place point-side down on ungreased cookie sheet. Curve into crescent shape. Brush with egg white. Bake at 375 degrees for 10-15 minutes or until golden brown.

Helen Harlos, Ethel, Miss.

CINNAMON SWEET ROLLS
Makes 2 dozen

1 yellow cake mix
2 packages dry yeast
5 cups flour
2-1/2 cups *hot* water
4 tablespoons butter
Brown sugar
Cinnamon
Nuts (optional)

Topping:
1 stick margarine, melted
4 tablespoons brown sugar
3 tablespoons light corn syrup

Mix first 3 ingredients thoroughly. Add hot water and mix well. Let rise to double in size. Cut in half; roll to rectangular shape. Melt butter and spread over rolled dough. Sprinkle with brown sugar, cinnamon, and nuts. Roll like a jelly roll; cut in 1-1/2-inch pieces. Place on greased cookie sheet. Repeat with remaining dough. Cover and let rise to double in size.

Mix together topping ingredients and spread over top of rolls, just prior to baking. Bake at 375 degrees for 25 minutes. Be sure cookie sheet has sides.

Harold L. Bird, Muskegon, Mich.

FEATHER DUMPLINGS

2 cups flour
1 teaspoon salt
4 teaspoons baking powder
1/4 teaspoon salt
Mix and add:
1 egg, beaten
2 tablespoons butter, melted
2/3 cup milk

Mix well (stiff dough). Drop by teaspoonfuls into boiling, salted water or broth. Cover and simmer for 18-20 minutes. Dumplings are light as air; handle with care.

Ann Sterzer, Lincoln, Neb.

PUMPKIN-PECAN–RAISIN BREAD

3 cups flour
2 teaspoons baking powder
1¼ teaspoons salt
1 teaspoon baking soda
1 teaspoon cinnamon
½ teaspoon nutmeg
2 eggs
1 (16-ounce) can pumpkin
1 cup packed light brown sugar
½ cup maple syrup
¼ cup Crisco oil
½ cup raisins
½ cup chopped pecans

In large bowl mix the first 6 ingredients. In another bowl combine the next 5 ingredients. Grease a 9 x 5-inch loaf pan. Stir liquid ingredients into dry ingredients and stir until moistened. Add raisins and nuts, then spoon into loaf pan.

Bake for 1¼ hours in a 350-degree oven. Cool bread on a wire rack in the pan for 10 minutes. Then remove and let completely cool on rack.

This is a most delicious bread for the holidays and is also a tradition in my family.

Esther M. Garback, Gloversville, N.Y.

BUTTERHORN ROLLS

5 cups flour
2 packages yeast
1 cup warm tap water
2 tablespoons sugar
3 eggs, beaten
1/2 cup margarine or butter
1 teaspoon salt
1/2 cup sugar

Dissolve yeast and 2 tablespoons sugar in warm tap water. Cream 1/2 cup sugar and 1/2 cup butter or margarine with 3 well-beaten eggs. (I use the mixer.) Add yeast mixture and 1/2 cup flour and salt. Beat until smooth. Add rest of flour and mix by spoon. Place in greased bowl and cover. Set in refrigerator overnight.

Next day, divide in 4 parts. Roll each portion to about 1/4-inch thickness, like a pie in a circle. Brush top with Crisco oil and cut into pie-shaped wedges, about 8 or 9 pieces. Roll up beginning with wide end to form crescent roll. Let rise on greased cookie sheet for 3 to 4 hours. Bake at 400 degrees for about 5 to 7 minutes, until golden brown.

Eula Wilson, Bethel, Ohio

PUMPKIN BANANA NUT BREAD
Makes 2 loaves

1 cup solid-pack pumpkin
½ cup (1 medium) ripe banana, mashed
1 cup brown sugar, firmly packed
½ cup vegetable oil
2 eggs
2¼ cups all-purpose flour
1 teaspoon baking powder
½ teaspoon baking soda
1 teaspoon ground cinnamon
½ teaspoon ground ginger
¼ teaspoon salt
1½ cups nuts, chopped

In large mixer bowl, combine pumpkin, banana, sugar and oil; mix

well. Beat in eggs, 1 at a time. In medium bowl, combine flour, baking powder, baking soda, cinnamon, ginger and salt; beat into pumpkin mixture. Stir in nuts. Pour into 2 greased 7½ x 3½ x 2½-inch loaf pans. Bake in preheated 450-degree oven for 50–60 minutes, or until toothpick inserted in center comes out clean. Cool 5 minutes in pans. Remove and cool completely before slicing.

Note: Bread may be frozen.

Diane Votaw, Decatur, Ind.

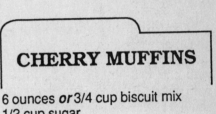

CHERRY MUFFINS

6 ounces *or* 3/4 cup biscuit mix
1/2 cup sugar
3/4 cup whole milk
2 tablespoons margarine
1 egg
1/2 cup cottage cheese
1 cup tart cherries, water-packed

Blend milk, margarine and egg, and stir into combined dry ingredients. Fold in cherries and cottage cheese. Spoon into 12 medium-size muffin tins until two-thirds full. Bake at 425 degrees for 20–25 minutes.

These muffins are really unusual and very delicious.

Suzan L. Wiener, Spring Hill, Fla.

COUNTRY HAM MUFFINS
Makes 12

1 (12-ounce) package corn muffin mix
4 ounces cooked ham, cut into ½-inch cubes
¼ teaspoon maple extract

Heat oven to 400 degrees. Grease 12 (2½-inch) muffin-pan cups. Prepare muffin mix according to package directions, adding the ham with dry ingredients and the maple extract with liquid ingredients. Spoon batter into prepared muffin-pan cups. Bake 15 minutes, or until golden brown. Serve warm.

MINCEMEAT MUFFINS
Makes 12

- 2 cups all-purpose flour
- 1 cup chopped pecans, toasted
- 1/3 cup granulated sugar
- 2 teaspoons baking powder
- 1 teaspoon grated orange peel
- 1/2 teaspoon salt
- 1/4 teaspoon freshly grated nutmeg
- 1/3 cup milk
- 2 large eggs
- 1 1/4 cups prepared mincemeat

Heat oven to 400 degrees. Grease 12 (2½-inch) muffin-pan cups. In large bowl stir flour, pecans, sugar, baking powder, orange peel, salt and nutmeg to mix well. In small bowl, using wire whisk or fork, thoroughly beat milk and eggs; add to flour mixture along with mincemeat, stirring until just blended. Spoon batter into prepared muffin-pan cups; bake 15 minutes until golden.

Marcella Swigert, Monroe City, Mo.

PUMPKIN ROLLS
Makes 15 rolls

- 1 (16-ounce) package hot roll mix
- 1/3 cup warm water (105–115 degrees)
- 1 cup canned *or* cooked, mashed pumpkin
- 1 egg
- 2 tablespoons sugar

Filling:
- 2 tablespoons butter *or* margarine, melted
- 1/2 cup sugar
- 1½ teaspoons pumpkin pie spice
- 1/3 cup raisins

Glaze:
- 1 cup sifted confectioners' sugar
- 1 tablespoon plus 1 teaspoon milk
- 1/4 teaspoon vanilla extract

Dissolve yeast packet from hot roll mix package in warm water; let stand 5 minutes. Combine pumpkin, egg and 2 tablespoons sugar; mix well. Add yeast; stir in flour packet from hot roll mix package to make a stiff dough. Place dough in a well-greased bowl, turning to grease top. Cover; let rise in a warm place (85 degrees) 45 minutes, or until doubled in bulk. Turn dough out onto a floured surface; knead 12 times. Roll dough into a 15 x 12-inch rectangle. Spread with melted butter. Combine ½ cup sugar and pumpkin pie spice; sprinkle over butter. Top with raisins. Beginning at long side, roll up jelly-roll fashion; press edges and ends together securely. Cut into 1-inch slices; place rolls, cut side down, in a greased 13 x 9 x 2-inch baking pan. Cover; let rise in a warm place (85 degrees) free from drafts, about 30 minutes, or until doubled in bulk. Bake at 375 degrees for 20 minutes, or until golden. Combine glaze ingredients until smooth; drizzle over warm rolls.

Helen P. Webb, Hillsborough County, Fla.

MONKEY BREAD

- 2 (10-ounce) packages canned biscuits
- 1/2 cup sugar
- 2 teaspoons cinnamon
- 3/4 cup brown sugar
- 1 stick margarine
- 1/2-3/4 cup chopped nuts

Mix sugar and cinnamon together. Cut each biscuit into fourths and roll each small piece in cinnamon-sugar mixture. Place in greased bundt pan. Sprinkle in nuts as you add the biscuit pieces. Combine brown sugar and margarine; heat until margarine is melted and sugar is dissolved. Pour over top of biscuit pieces. Bake in 325-degree oven for 30 minutes or until done. Cool slightly and invert on plate. So easy to make and enjoyed by all ages.

Mary M. West, Columbia, Ind.

LOW-CHOLESTEROL COTTAGE CHEESE BREAD

- 1 cup cottage cheese
- 2 eggs, beaten
- 1 cup sugar
- 3/4 cup milk
- 1 teaspoon vanilla
- 2-3/4 cups flour
- 2-1/2 cups baking powder
- 1/2 cup raisins
- 1/2 cup nuts, chopped

Mix in order given; add raisins and chopped nuts. Pour into greased loaf pan. Bake at 350 degrees for 60 minutes. Decorate top of loaf with chopped cherries and sprinkle with sugar before baking.

Sheila Symonowicz, Loganville, Pa.

BUTTERNUT-NUT RAISIN BREAD
Makes 3 loaves

- 3 1/2 cups unbleached flour
- 2 teaspoons soda
- 1 cup raisins
- 1 cup vegetable oil
- 2 cups sugar
- 4 eggs
- 1 1/2 cups cooked butternut squash, mashed
- 1/2 cup honey
- 1 cup water
- 1 1/2 teaspoons ground nutmeg
- 1 1/2 teaspoons ground cinnamon
- 1 teaspoon ground mace
- 1 1/2 teaspoons salt

Combine flour, soda and raisins; stir well and set aside. Combine oil, sugar and eggs in large mixing bowl; beat well. Stir in squash, honey, water, spices and salt. Add flour mixture; stir just until all ingredients are moistened. Pour batter into 3 greased 9 x 5 x 3-inch loaf pans. Bake at 350 degrees for 1 hour. Cool.

Note: Batter may be baked in 3 greased 1-pound coffee cans. Bake at 350 degrees for 1 hour and 20 minutes.

Sandra Russell, Gainesville, Fla.

RAISIN BREAD

2 cups flour
4 teaspoons baking powder
2 tablespoons shortening
1/2 cup sugar
1/4 cup raisins
1/2 cup currants
Dash of nutmeg
1 egg
1/2 cup milk

Mix dry ingredients; cut in the shortening. Add raisins and currants. Beat whole egg and add milk to it. Combine the 2 mixtures as in baking powder biscuits; put in a greased pan and bake in a moderate 350-degree oven for 40-45 minutes.

Lucy Dowd, Sequim, Wash.

DILLY BREAD

Wonderful with pork or beef slices, or a tuna-salad mixture.

1 package dry yeast
1/4 cup warm water
1 cup creamed cottage cheese
1 tablespoon butter or margarine
2 tablespoons sugar
1 tablespoon minced onion
2 teaspoons dill seed
1 teaspoon salt
1/4 teaspoon soda
1 egg
2–2-1/2 cups all-purpose flour

Dissolve yeast in warm water; set aside. Heat cottage cheese and margarine to lukewarm. Combine yeast and cottage cheese mixtures in bowl, and add sugar, onion, dill seed, salt, soda, and egg. Add flour until stiff dough forms. Cover; let rise until double. Turn into greased 1-1/2-quart casserole or 8-inch cake pan. Let rise in pan 30–40 minutes, or until light.

Bake at 350 degrees approximately 50 minutes. Brush with butter. Cool completely before slicing.

Brown breads long ago were steamed and served only with baked beans. This bread is also delicious when sliced for sandwiches.

GINGER MUFFINS

1 cup shortening
1 cup sugar
1 cup waffle syrup (may use part molasses)
3 eggs
1 cup buttermilk
1-3/4 teaspoons soda
3 teaspoons ginger
2 teaspoons cinnamon
1 teaspoon nutmeg
1/2 teaspoon salt
3 cups flour

Cream shortening and sugar. Add eggs, one at a time. Add syrup, then milk with soda dissolved in it. Then add flour and spices. Bake at 375 degrees for 10–12 minutes.

Diantha Susan Hibbard, Rochester, N.Y.

YAM DINNER ROLLS

⅔ cup warm water
1 package yeast
1½ tablespoons sugar
1½ teaspoons salt
1 tablespoon shortening, softened
1 (No. 2) can yams, drained and mashed
3½ cups all-purpose flour, sifted
¾ cup raisins (optional)

Measure water into large mixing bowl. Stir in sugar and salt. Add yeast and dissolve. Add shortening and yams; mix until thoroughly blended. Combine flour and raisins; add to yeast mixture in 2 additions, mixing until blended after each addition. Turn onto floured surface and knead until dough is smooth and elastic. Place in greased bowl; cover and let rise in warm place until double in bulk. Punch down and let rise a second time. Roll out to ¼-inch thickness and cut with floured 2-inch round cutter or shape into rolls. Place on greased baking sheets. Cover and let rise. Bake in hot oven of 425 degrees for 12 minutes.

Fay Duman, Eugene, Ore.

CORN BREAD LOAF

1 cup flour
3/4 cup yellow cornmeal
1/4 cup white sugar
1/2 teaspoon salt
4 teaspoons baking powder
2 eggs
1-1/4 cups milk
1/4 cup melted butter or shortening

In mixing bowl, mix together all dry ingredients. In a small bowl, beat eggs; add milk and melted butter. Add liquid to dry ingredients, mixing just until blended. Pour into a greased 8-1/2x4-1/2x2-1/2-inch loaf pan. Bake in 350-degree oven for 40 to 45 minutes or until golden brown and tester inserted in the center comes out clean. Cool for 5 minutes in the pan, then turn out onto rack. Serve warm with butter. This is a moist even-textured corn bread, and it is an "easy-to-slice" loaf.

Lillian Smith, Montreal, Quebec Canada

NO-KNEAD POTATO ROLLS
Makes 2 dozen

1 cup scalded milk
3 tablespoons shortening
1 tablespoon sugar
2 teaspoons salt
1 package compressed or granular yeast
2 eggs
1 cup leftover mashed potatoes
4 cups enriched flour

Combine scalded milk, shortening, sugar, and salt. Cool to lukewarm, adding yeast that has been dissolved according to package directions. Stir in eggs and mashed potatoes; blend well. Add flour, a cup at a time. Cover and let stand 15 minutes. Shape dough into walnut-size balls, and place them on a greased baking sheet. In a warm place, allow rolls to rise, about an hour, until double in size. Bake in 400-degree oven for 15-20 minutes.

Mae Gianocca, Half Moon Bay, Calif.

SWEDISH RYE BREAD
Makes 2 loaves

3 cups milk, scalded
1 package dry yeast
1/2 cup granulated sugar
3 tablespoons brown sugar
3/4 cup dark corn syrup
2 cups rye flour
3-1/2 cups all-purpose flour, or
   enough to make a stiff dough

Dissolve yeast in 1/4 cup milk. Add yeast, brown and white sugars, corn syrup, and rye flour to the scalded milk; beat well. Add white flour; mix well; cover, and let rise overnight.

Shape into 2 loaves and place on a buttered cookie sheet. Cover with towel; let rise until double in bulk. Preheat oven to 350 degrees and bake bread 1 hour, or until loaf sounds hollow when tapped with finger.

Agnes Ward, Erie, PA

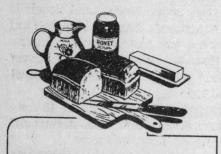

HEALTH BREAD

3 packages dry yeast
2 cups warm water
1/2 cup sugar

Dissolve yeast in warm water; add sugar and set aside.

Mix together:
2 cups hot water
1 cup shortening
1 cup molasses
2 cups All Bran
2 cups oatmeal
2 cups rye or cracked wheat flour
2-1/2 teaspoons salt
1/2 cup wheat germ

When cool, add yeast mixture and stir well. Add enough white flour to handle dough easily. Knead; let double in bulk. Put into bread pans; let rise again. Bake at 350 degrees for 1 hour.

VITAMIN-RICH BREAD
Makes 1 loaf

1 cup seedless raisins
1/2 cup white raisins
2 teaspoons baking soda
1 tablespoon melted butter or
   margarine
1-1/2 cups orange juice or apple
   juice (heated)
2 eggs
1 cup sugar
1-1/4 cups sifted flour
1/4 teaspoon salt
2 cups bran flakes

Combine raisins, white raisins, baking soda, butter, and heated orange or apple juice in a bowl. Let stand for 10 minutes. Beat eggs and sugar together well. Stir in flour and salt. Combine with raisin mixture and bran flakes; beat only until well-blended. Turn into greased 9-inch loaf pan and bake at 350 degrees for about 1 hour. Cool 5 minutes in pan before turning out onto rack. Store 24 hours for easier slicing.

Agnes Ward, Erie, Pa.

THRIFTY THREE-GRAIN BREAD
Serves 12

1 cup cornmeal, yellow or white
1 cup rye flour
1 cup graham flour
2 teaspoons baking soda
1 teaspoon salt
1/4 teaspoon allspice
1/8 teaspoon ginger
3/4 cup molasses
1-3/4 cups sour milk
1/4 cup light cream

Place dry ingredients in a large mixing bowl; mix well. In separate bowl stir together molasses, sour milk, and cream. Pour liquid into dry mixture; stir only until well moistened. Pour batter into greased 9-inch loaf pan; bake at 350 degrees for 1 hour and 15 minutes. Cool thoroughly before slicing.

Gwen Campbell, Sterling, Va.

IRISH SODA BREAD

4 cups flour
1 teaspoon salt
1 teaspoon baking soda
4 tablespoons caraway seeds
2 cups buttermilk
2 cups raisins

Mix dry ingredients and seeds; add liquid and stir to blend, just until all ingredients are moistened. Add more buttermilk, if needed. Mix in raisins. Place dough in greased 9 x 5 x 3 inch loaf pan. Bake at 425 degrees for approximately 45 minutes, until toothpick inserted in center comes out clean. If loaf is browning too fast, place sheet of aluminum foil on top. Remove from pan and cool on a wire rack.

Note: This bread has a hard crust, but a moist interior.

Carme Venella, Laurel Springs, Nj.

PEANUT BUTTER BREAD

3/4 cup sugar
1/2 cup peanut butter
1 teaspoon vanilla
1-3/4 cups milk
2-1/4 cups flour
4 teaspoons baking powder
1/2 teaspoon salt

Cream together sugar, peanut butter, and vanilla. Add milk and mix well. Combine flour, baking powder, and salt . Add to creamed mixture and beat well. Place in a greased loaf pan and bake at 350 degrees for 45-50 minutes, or until golden brown. Allow to cool for 10 minutes before removing from pan. This is a very moist loaf with a rich peanut taste.

Lillian Smith, Quebec, Canada

CALIFORNIA PRUNE-NUT BREAD

1 cup chopped dried prunes
2 teaspoons shredded orange peel
1 cup orange juice
2 cups sifted flour
3/4 cup sugar
3 teaspoons baking powder
1/2 teaspoon salt
1/2 teaspoon cinnamon
2 beaten eggs
2 tablespoons salad oil
1/2 cup chopped walnuts

Combine prunes, orange peel and juice; let stand 30 minutes. Sift together dry ingredients. Combine eggs, oil and prune mixture; add to dry ingredients, mix well. Add nuts; turn into greased 9 x 5 x 3-inch loaf pan. Bake in 350 degree oven for 50 to 60 minutes. Remove from pan and cool.

Judie Betz, Lomita, CA

CHOCOLATE NUTBREAD

6 cups sifted flour
1 teaspoon salt
2 cups sugar
6 teaspoons baking powder
1/2 cup cocoa
2 eggs
2 cups rich milk
1 tablespoon butter, melted and cooled
1 cup chopped pecans
1 cup ground pecans

Combine flour, salt, sugar, baking powder, and cocoa; sift together into mixing bowl. Beat eggs with milk. Add liquid to the dry ingredients and blend. Add butter, chopped nuts, and ground nuts; mix thoroughly. Divide dough evenly between 2 greased loaf pans. Let stand in a warm place for 30 minutes. Bake in a 325 degree oven for 1 to 1-1/4 hours or until tested done. Turn out on a rack to cool. Let stand for 24 hours before slicing.

CHERRY NUT BREAD

2-1/2 cups flour
1 cup sugar
2 teaspoons baking powder
1/2 teaspoon salt
1/2 cup shortening
12-14 chopped maraschino cherries
3/4 cup chopped nuts
2 eggs beaten
1/2 cup milk
1/4 cup maraschino cherry juice

Sift dry ingredients together. Cut in shortening, then add cherries and nuts. Combine liquid ingredients; add liquid to dry ingredients. Stir only until flour is moistened. Pour into greased 9x5x3 inch loaf pan. Bake at 350 degrees 50-60 minutes.

Dorothy Pelster, Hastings, Neb.

MAPLE-NUT BREAD

2 cups sifted flour
3 teaspoons baking powder
1 teaspoon salt
1/2 cup brown sugar
1/4 cup shortening
2 eggs
1/2 cup milk
1/4 cup maple flavored syrup
1/2 teaspoon maple extract
3/4 cup chopped nuts

Sift together flour, baking powder and salt. Add sugar, shortening, eggs, milk, syrup and maple extract. Stir until blended; beat 2 minutes on low speed of mixer. Stir in nuts; pour into a well greased 8-1/2 x 4-1/2-inch loaf pan. Bake 1 hour at 350 degrees.

Mrs. Betty Slavin, Omaha, NE

POLISH DARK RYE BREAD WITH CARAWAY

2 cups scalded milk
2 tablespoons sugar
1 package dry yeast
4 cups rye flour
2 tablespoons caraway seeds (optional)
2 tablespoons butter
1 teaspoon salt
1/2 cup lukewarm water
2-1/2 cups whole wheat flour

Pour scalded milk over butter, sugar, and salt in large bowl. Stir and cool. Dissolve yeast in lukewarm water. Add softened yeast, 3 cups rye flour to milk; mix and beat well. Beat in remaining rye flour. Cover and let rise in warm place until double. Turn out onto well-floured board and knead in whole wheat flour and caraway seeds. Knead until dough is smooth and elastic. Divide in half and shape into round or oblong loaves. Place in well-greased pans. Cover and let rise in warm place until double.

Bake at 450 degrees for 15 minutes. Reduce heat to 350 degrees and bake 35-40 minutes more.

Marie Micco, Somerville, MA

ALL AMERICAN CORNBREAD
Serves 12

2 cups biscuit mix
1 cup butter
1 cup half and half
1 cup yellow cornmeal
1/2 teaspoon baking soda
1/2 teaspoon salt
3/4 cup sugar
2 eggs, slightly beaten

Scald half and half with butter; add to thoroughly mixed dry ingredients. Mix in eggs. Pour into greased and floured 13x9x2-inch pan. Bake at 350 degrees for 30 minutes. Allow to stand for several minutes before cutting.

Marcella Swigert, Monroe City, Mo.

Brunch BUFFET

SCRAPPLE

1½ pounds pork sausage
4 cups water
1 teaspoon salt
2 teaspoons sage
1 cup yellow cornmeal
1 cup cold water

In a large saucepan, break sausage into small pieces. Add 4 cups water, stirring to separate meat. Bring to a boil. Reduce heat; simmer 20 minutes. Drain meat, reserving 3 cups broth. Add salt and sage. Bring again to a boil. Combine cornmeal and 1 cup cold water; gradually add to broth, stirring constantly. Cover and cook over low heat for 10 minutes. Stir occasionally. Add sausage. Pour into 1¼ x 5 x 3-inch loaf pan. Refrigerate overnight. Slice and fry. Very good served with eggs.

Helen Harlos, Ethel, Miss.

THE CALCIUM CRUNCH BREAKFAST TREAT
Serves 4

2 cups plain, non-fat yogurt
3 cups melon, cut in cubes
3 cups berries
1/2 cup Grapenuts cereal

Place 1/2 cup of yogurt in a cereal bowl. Sprinkle 2 tablespoons of grapenuts on top of yogurt. Top with 1-1/2 cups of fruit. (175 calories per serving)

HAM WAFFLES
Serves 6

1 cup 100% Bran cereal
2 cups milk
2 cups sifted flour
1 tablespoon baking powder
¾ teaspoon salt
½ cup shortening
2 eggs, separated
1 cup diced ham

Soak cereal in milk for 5 minutes. Sift together flour, baking powder, and salt. Cut in shortening until it is as fine as meal. Add to soaked cereal along with beaten egg yolks and diced ham. Blend thoroughly. Beat egg whites until stiff and fold them into the cereal batter. Bake in a hot waffle iron until golden brown.

Mrs. Robert T. Shaffer, Middleburg, Pa.

COUNTRY SAUSAGE QUICHE
Serves 8–10

Ready-made crust for 12-inch quiche pan
1 egg, separated
1¼ pounds pork sausage, cooked and crumbled
2 Golden Delicious apples, peeled and thinly sliced
¼ cup walnuts, chopped
2 cups cheddar cheese, shredded
3 eggs
¼ teaspoon coriander
¼ teaspoon dry mustard
¼ teaspoon salt
2 cups milk

Fit pastry into dish; crimp dough edges; brush with white of the separated egg. Spread sausage over crust; arrange apples in a single layer over sausage. Sprinkle with walnuts; add cheese; spread evenly. Beat egg yolk with whole eggs, coriander, dry mustard and salt; add milk. Pour over cheese/apple mixture; bake at 375 degrees for 45–50 minutes until custard is set.

Gwen Campbell, Sterling, Va.

BELGIAN DESSERT WAFFLES
Makes 6 waffles

1 package Pillsbury yellow cake mix
1-1/2 cups milk or light cream
4 eggs
1/2 teaspoon salt

Preheat waffle iron at medium heat. Lightly oil the waffle grid surface to prevent sticking. In large mixing bowl, combine cake mix, milk, eggs, and salt. Blend and beat as directed on package. Batter will be thick. Pour about 1 cup batter for a 9-inch waffle in preheated waffle iron. Bake until waffle is golden brown, about 2-4 minutes. Waffles will become more crisp upon cooling. Cool waffles on a wire rack. Stack sections of waffles with whipped cream and fresh, canned, or frozen fruit. Drain liquid from fruit, if necessary.

Annie Cmehil, New Castle, Ind.

SAUSAGE NOODLE BAKE

1 (10-1/2-ounce) can cream of chicken soup
1/2 cup milk
1-1/2 cups shredded cheddar cheese
1 pound pork sausage, cooked and crumbled
1 (12-ounce) package wide noodles
1 medium green pepper, chopped
1 medium onion, chopped
Buttered cracker crumbs

Preheat oven to 350 degrees. Generously butter a 2-quart casserole dish. Combine soup and milk, blending well. Heat over medium heat stirring occasionally. Add 1 cup of the cheddar cheese and stir until melted. Cook noodles according to directions. Add cooked sausage, drained noodles, green pepper, and onions to cooked noodles. Mix well. Pour soup/milk/cheese sauce over all and mix well. Pour into buttered casserole dish. Top with cracker crumbs and remaining 1/2 cup cheese. Cover and bake for 20 minutes. Uncover and bake for an additional 15 minutes until top is golden and bubbly.

Serve this delicious casserole with a crisp green salad. I guarantee your family will love it and it will quickly become a family favorite.

Phyliss Dixon, Fairbanks, Alaska

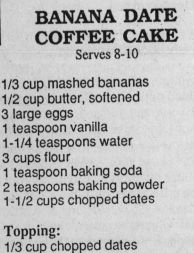

BANANA DATE COFFEE CAKE
Serves 8-10

1/3 cup mashed bananas
1/2 cup butter, softened
3 large eggs
1 teaspoon vanilla
1-1/4 teaspoons water
3 cups flour
1 teaspoon baking soda
2 teaspoons baking powder
1-1/2 cups chopped dates

Topping:
1/3 cup chopped dates
1/3 cup chopped nuts
1/3 cup flaked coconut

Beat together mashed bananas and butter until creamy. Add eggs, vanilla, and water; beat well. Blend in flour, baking soda, and baking powder, and beat well; stir in 1-1/2 cups chopped dates. Spoon batter into a greased and floured 9x13-inch baking pan. Combine topping ingredients and sprinkle over batter. Bake in a 350-degree oven for 20-25 minutes, or until knife inserted comes out clean. Cool on rack.

Mrs. D. Garms, Anaheim, Calif.

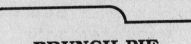

BRUNCH PIE
Serves 6

3 tablespoons margarine
2 (15-ounce) cans corned beef hash
3 eggs
1/2 cup chopped onion
1 cup grated cheddar cheese
1 (16-ounce) can mixed vegetables, drained
1/2 cup evaporated milk
1 tablespoon flour
1/2 teaspoon dry mustard
Dash garlic powder

Coat a 9-inch pie pan with margarine. Mix hash and 1 beaten egg; press into plate to form crust. Bake at 375 degrees for 10 minutes. Sauté onion in 3 tablespoons margarine. Layer cheese, sautéed onion, and vegetables all into crust. Beat together remaining eggs, evaporated milk, flour, mustard, and garlic powder. Pour over mixture in crust. Bake at 350 degrees for 30-40 minutes, until filling is set. Let stand 10 minutes before cutting.

Mrs. Albert H. Foley, Lemoyne, Pa.

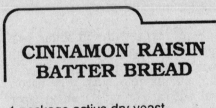

CINNAMON RAISIN BATTER BREAD

1 package active dry yeast
1-1/2 cups warm water (105-115 degrees)
2 tablespoons honey
2 tablespoons butter
1 teaspoon salt
3 cups flour, divided
1 tablespoon cinnamon
1 cup raisins

In a large bowl, dissolve yeast in warm water. Stir in honey. Add butter, salt, and 2 cups of the flour. Beat with electric mixer on low speed until blended. Beat 1 minute on high speed. Stir in remaining flour with a wooden spoon. Cover and let rise in a warm place until doubled in size. Punch down by stirring with a heavy spoon. Add cinnamon and raisins. Spoon batter into a loaf pan. Let rise again until batter reaches the top of the pan (not over!). Bake in preheated 350-degree oven for about 40 minutes or until loaf sounds hollow when lightly tapped. Cool on wire rack.

This batter bread is a wonderful treat for breakfast or in the "munchkin's" lunch sack as a peanut-butter-and-jelly sandwich.

Phyliss Dixon, Fairbanks, Alaska

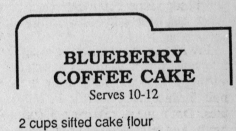

BLUEBERRY COFFEE CAKE
Serves 10-12

2 cups sifted cake flour
1 teaspoon baking powder
1 teaspoon baking soda
1 cup sugar
2 sticks (1/2 pound) margarine
2 eggs
1 cup cultured sour cream
1 teaspoon vanilla
1 can blueberry pie filling

Preheat oven to 375 degrees. Sift flour, baking powder, soda, and sugar together into a large bowl. Cut in margarine as you would for pie crust. Beat together eggs, sour cream, vanilla, and combine with flour mixture, blending well. Spread half the batter in a greased 13x9x2-inch baking pan. Spoon pie filling over batter and spread evenly. Spread remaining batter over blueberry filling. Sprinkle with the following topping:

Blend together as for pie crust 1/4 cup cake flour, 3 tablespoons margarine, and 1/4 cup sugar. Sprinkle over top of batter in pan. Bake in a moderately hot oven of 375 degrees for 40 minutes, or until lightly browned. Serve warm or cold.

Trenda Leigh, Richmond, Va.

OMELET SUPREME
Serves 3

3 slices bacon, cut into small pieces
2 small potatoes, peeled and sliced
8 fresh spinach leaves, stems removed, sliced into 1/4 inch slices
6 eggs, lightly beaten with fork
1/2 cup yogurt
Salt and pepper to taste

In skillet, heat bacon; add potatoes; fry until bacon is crisp, and potatoes lightly browned. Add spinach; remove mixture to bowl. In shallow bowl, mix eggs, yogurt, salt, and pepper; pour into skillet. Distribute potato mixture evenly over eggs; cook over low heat without stirring. As eggs set on bottom, lift edges; let uncooked mixture run underneath. When omelet is set, fold with fork. Serve immediately.

June Harding, Ferndale, Mich.

OLD FASHIONED BREAD OMELET

Combine and soak for 10 minutes:
2 cups bread cubes
1 cup milk

Preheat oven to 325 degrees.
Combine in bowl:
5 eggs, beaten
1/2 cup grated cheese
1 cup alfalfa sprouts, chopped
1 small onion, finely chopped
1 tablespoon parsley flakes
1 teaspoon garlic powder
Salt and pepper to taste
Bread and milk mixture

Heat in skillet:
1/4-1/2 cup bacon pieces until done

Pour in egg mixture and cook over medium heat without stirring, about 5 minutes. When browned underneath, place pan in oven for 10 minutes to finish cooking the top. Turn out onto hot platter. Omelet can be folded in half.

Christine Nofziger, Elmworth, Alberta, Canada

BROCCOLI OVEN OMELET
Serves 6

9 eggs
1 (10 ounce) package frozen chopped broccoli, thawed and drained
1/3 cup finely chopped onion
1/4 cup grated Parmesan cheese
2 tablespoons milk
1/2 teaspoon salt
1/2 teaspoon dried basil
1/4 teaspoon garlic powder
1 medium tomato, cut into 6 slices
1/4 cup grated Parmesan cheese

Beat eggs with whisk in bowl until light and fluffy. Stir in broccoli, onion, 1/4 cup Parmesan cheese, milk, salt, basil, and garlic powder. Pour into ungreased 11x7x2 inch baking dish. Arrange tomato slices on top. Sprinkle with 1/4 cup Parmesan cheese. Bake uncovered in 325 degree oven until set, 25-30 minutes.

Great for holiday brunch, also as vegetable side dish.

Cheryl Santefort, Thornton, Ill.

QUICHE LORRAINE

1 (9-inch) pie crust
1 tablespoon soft butter
12 bacon slices
4 eggs
2 cups whipping cream
3/4 teaspoon salt
1/8 teaspoon nutmeg
1/4 pound natural Swiss cheese, shredded (1 cup)

Spread crust with soft butter; beat eggs, cream, salt, and nutmeg with wire whisk; stir in cheese and pour egg mixture into crust. Fry bacon until crisp and brown. Drain on paper towels and crumble; sprinkle in pie crust. Bake 15 minutes at 400 degrees; turn oven to 325 degrees and bake 35 minutes. Quiche is done when knife inserted in center comes out clean. Let stand 10 minutes before serving.

1933 Queen Dorothy Edwards Conlon

GARDEN MEDLEY
Serves 6

1/4 cup butter or margarine
2 cups cauliflower
1/4 cup chopped onion
2 cups sliced zucchini
1/2 cup halved cherry tomatoes
1/4 teaspoon salt
1/4 teaspoon thyme leaves, crushed
2 tablespoons grated Parmesan cheese, if desired

In large skillet, melt butter. Add cauliflower and onion; sauté 2-3 minutes. Add zucchini; cover and cook over medium heat, stirring occasionally, 3-5 minutes, or until vegetables are crisp-tender. Stir in tomatoes, salt, and thyme; cook 1-2 minutes until thoroughly heated. Spoon into serving dish; sprinkle with Parmesan cheese. (100 calories per serving)

Mrs. Sherwin Dick, Inman, Neb.

QUICK AND EASY BUCKWHEAT PANCAKES

1/2 cup bread crumbs
2-1/2 cups scalded milk
2 cups buckwheat flour
1/2 teaspoon salt
1/2 yeast cake
2 tablespoons molasses
1/4 teaspoon baking soda

Add bread crumbs and salt to scalded milk. Cool. When lukewarm add yeast and stir until yeast is dissolved. Add buckwheat flour and stir until smooth. Put in warm place overnight. In the morning add molasses and soda mixed with a little lukewarm water. Beat smooth. Bake on hot griddle.

These pancakes are delicious and more healthful than the regular kind. Your family will love them!

Suzan L. Wiener, Spring Hill, Fla.

CHOCOLATE-ALMOND ZUCCHINI BREAD

Makes 2 loaves

3 eggs
2 cups sugar
1 cup vegetable oil
2 squares (2 ounces) unsweetened chocolate
1 teaspoon vanilla
2 cups finely grated zucchini
3 cups flour
1 teaspoon salt
1 teaspoon cinnamon
1/4 teaspoon baking powder
1 teaspoon baking soda
1 cup coarsely chopped almonds

Preheat oven to 350 degrees. In small bowl, beat eggs until lemon colored; beat in sugar and oil. Melt chocolate over hot water. In large bowl, add egg mixture, vanilla, and zucchini to chocolate.

Sift together flour, salt, cinnamon, baking powder, and baking soda. Stir into zucchini mixture. Mix in nuts. Pour batter into 2 well-greased 9x5x3 inch loaf pans. Bake 1 hour and 20 minutes or until done. Cool in pans 15-20 minutes. Turn out onto rack. Cool thoroughly before serving.
Agnes Ward, Erie, Pa.

JIFFY RAISIN LOAF

Makes 1 loaf

3/4 cup golden seedless raisins
Hot water
2 cups prepared biscuit mix
3/4 cup sugar
1 teaspoon cinnamon
1/3 cup chopped nuts
1 egg
3/4 cup milk

Rinse raisins in hot water. Drain. Combine with biscuit mix, sugar, cinnamon, and nuts. Beat egg slightly. Add to milk. Stir into dry ingredients. Pour batter into greased 8-1/2x4-1/4x2-1/2 inch loaf pan. Bake at 350 degrees for 50-60 minutes. Cool on wire rack.
Mrs. R. S. Lewis, Dubuque, Iowa

GRANOLA

4 cups uncooked oatmeal
1-1/2 cups wheat germ (raw or toasted)
1 cup grated coconut
1/4 cup powdered milk
1/2 tablespoon cinnamon
1 tablespoon brown sugar
1/3 cup vegetable oil
1/2 cup honey
1 tablespoon vanilla
1/2 cup sesame seeds (optional)
1/2 cup raw nuts, seeds, or raisins, etc. (optional)

In a large bowl, mix dry ingredients. In a saucepan, combine oil, honey, and vanilla; warm. Add these to the dry ingredients; stir until all the particles are coated. Hand mixing works well here. Spread this mixture out in a long, low pan or rimmed baking sheets that have been well greased; bake at either 250 degrees for 1 hour or 300 degrees for 30 minutes. Turn mixture with spatula from time to time. When finished toasting, add dried fruits, such as raisins. Cool and store in an airtight container.

Marcella Swigert, Monroe City, Mo.

LUSCIOUS BANANA-APRICOT BREAD

Makes 2 loaves

2 cups white flour
1-1/2 cups whole wheat flour
2 teaspoons baking powder
1 teaspoon baking soda
1 teaspoon salt
4 eggs
1 cup sugar
2/3 cup shortening
1/2 cup sour milk
6-7 bananas, mashed
1/4 cup wheat germ
1 cup chopped dried apricots
3 teaspoons black walnut flavoring (or 3 cups chopped nuts)

Mix first 5 ingredients by sifting into bowl. Blend in eggs, sugar, shortening, and sour milk, beating well into dry ingredients. Add bananas, flavoring or nuts, apricots, and wheat germ. Stir well. Bake in greased and floured loaf pans at 350 degrees for 50 minutes.
Mary Rahorn, Orangeville, Ill.

HAM 'N EGG CREPES

(Serves 4-6)

1 (10-1/2 ounce) can condensed cream of chicken soup
1 cup dairy sour cream
1 cup finely chopped cooked ham
6 hard cooked eggs, chopped
1 tablespoon chives, chopped
1/4 teaspoon dry mustard
1/4 cup milk
1/4 cup grated Parmesan cheese
1 recipe for basic crepes

Mix 1/2 can of soup, sour cream, ham, eggs, chives, and mustard; set aside. Combine remaining soup, milk, and half the cheese; set aside. Put about 1/4 cup ham-egg filling on each crepe and roll up. Arrange filled crepes in greased 13x9x2-inch baking dish. Pour sauce over top and sprinkle with remaining cheese. Bake in preheated 350 degree oven for 30 minutes, or until hot and bubbly.
Diantha Susan Hibbard, Rochester N.Y.

MEAT BALL PANCAKES

3 egg yolks, lightly beaten
1/2 pound ground beef, browned
1/4 teaspoon baking powder
1/2 teaspoon salt
Dash of pepper
1 tablespoon grated onion
1 teaspoon lemon juice
1 tablespoon parsley
3 egg whites, stiffly beaten

Mix all ingredients, *excluding* egg whites. Blend well. Fold in egg whites. Drop by spoonfuls onto greased hot griddle. When puffed and browned, turn and brown other side. Serve at once, with a mushroom sauce or a creamed vegetable.
Laura Hicks, Troy, Mont.

Candies

& CONFECTIONS

MARSHMALLOW WALNUT FUDGE
Makes 64 1-inch squares

1/2 pound (2 sticks) butter
8 squares (8 ounces) unsweetened chocolate
1 cup coarsely chopped walnuts
1 pound sifted confectioners' sugar
1 teaspoon vanilla extract
32 marshmallows

Combine butter and chocolate in saucepan. Melt over low heat. Pour into a large bowl and add nuts, sugar and vanilla. Knead until blended well, then pat into a greased 8-inch square pan. Cut marshmallows in half crosswise. Place marshmallows cut side down at 1-inch intervals so marshmallow will be in the center of each piece. Cut between the marshmallows into 1-inch squares.

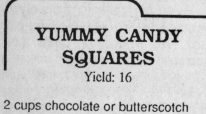

YUMMY CANDY SQUARES
Yield: 16

2 cups chocolate or butterscotch chips
2/3 cup sweetened condensed milk
1 teaspoon vanilla
1/8 teaspoon salt
3/4 cup oatmeal
1/3 cup chopped nuts
1/4 cup flaked or shredded coconut

Melt chocolate or butterscotch chips over hot water; blend in remaining ingredients. Mix thoroughly. Spread into an 8-inch square pan. Chill until firm. Cut into squares.

Agnes Ward, Erie, Pa.

PEANUT CLUSTERS

2 cups chocolate chips
1 cup peanut butter
2 cups Spanish peanuts

Melt chocolate chips and peanut butter in top of double boiler. Add peanuts; stir and drop by teaspoons on waxed paper.

These are very good, and so simple and easy to make.

Elaine Dodd, Pasco, Wash.

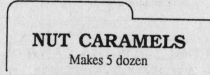

NUT CARAMELS
Makes 5 dozen

1/4 cup butter or margarine
1 cup evaporated milk
1 cup sugar
1 cup dark corn syrup
Dash salt
1/4 teaspoon vanilla
1 cup pecans, coarsely broken

Heat butter and evaporated milk in small saucepan, cook sugar, corn syrup and salt over medium heat until it reaches firm-ball stage, 244 degrees on candy thermometer, stirring often. Slowly stir in milk so sugar mixture does not stop boiling. Cook, stirring constantly, until mixture reaches firm-ball stage again. Remove pan from heat and stir in vanilla and pecans. Mix well. Pour into well-buttered 8-inch square pan. When firm, turn out onto cutting board or wax paper. Cut into 1-inch squares and wrap each in plastic wrap.

Leona Teodori, Warren, Mich.

PECAN PRALINES
Makes 36

1 cup sugar
1 cup firmly packed brown sugar
1/3 cup evaporated milk
1/2 stick butter or margarine, softened
1-1/2 cups pecans or small can coconut

Combine sugars and evaporated milk in heavy saucepan; cook over medium heat. Stir in butter and pecans; cook until candy reaches soft-ball stage. Cool for 2 minutes. Beat until thick, but glossy. Drop by tablespoons onto waxed paper. Cool thoroughly.

Marcella Swigert, Monroe City, Mo.

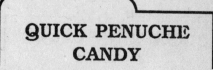

QUICK PENUCHE CANDY

1/2 cup margarine
1/4 cup milk
1 cup packed brown sugar
1-3/4 to 2 cups sifted powdered sugar
1 cup chopped pecans

Melt margarine, add brown sugar and cook over low heat 2 minutes. Add milk and continue cooking until mixture boils. Remove from heat and let cool at room temperature. Gradually add powdered sugar until like a fudge consistency. Add nuts and spread in buttered 8-inch square pan. Cool.

Jodie McCoy, Tulsa, Okla.

PEANUT BUTTER BALLS

1/2 cup honey
1 cup peanut butter
1 cup powdered sugar
Corn flakes, crushed

Blend honey, peanut butter and powdered sugar until smooth. Roll into small balls, roll in crushed corn flakes. Refrigerate one hour or until cold.

Agnes Russell, Concord, N.H.

DOUBLE PEANUT CLUSTERS

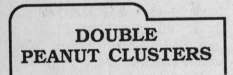

1/2 cup peanut butter, smooth or crunchy
12-ounce package chocolate chips
2 cups dry-roasted peanuts, coarsely chopped.

Melt chocolate chips and peanut butter in top of double boiler or in saucepan over low heat or hot water. Stir in peanuts. Drop by teaspoonsful into foil baking cups or onto foil or waxed paper. Chill and store clusters in refrigerator.

Rich and delicious!

Cynthia Cardwell, Sterling, Ill.

EASY MARSHMALLOW FUDGE

2/3 cup evaporated milk
1 1/2 cups sugar
1/2 teaspoon salt
32 marshmallows (1/2 pound)
12-ounce package semisweet chocolate chips
1 teaspoon vanilla extract
1/2 teaspoon peppermint extract

Combine evaporated milk, sugar, salt and marshmallows in a saucepan. Cook over low heat, stirring constantly, until marshmallows melt. Blend in chocolate chips; stir until smooth. Add both extracts. Pour into a buttered 8-inch square pan. Chill. Cut into squares.

Patty Ross, Trenton, Ohio

WHITE FUDGE
Makes 1-1/2 pounds

2 cups granulated sugar
1/2 cup sour cream
1/3 cup white corn syrup
2 tablespoons butter
1/4 teaspoon salt
2 tablespoons vanilla, rum or brandy flavoring
1/4 cup quartered candied red cherries
1 cup chopped walnuts

In heavy 2-quart saucepan, combine sugar, sour cream, syrup, butter and salt. Bring to boil slowly, stirring until sugar dissolves. Boil, without stirring, over medium heat to 236 degrees, or until a little mixture dropped in cold water forms a soft ball.

Remove from heat and let stand 15 minutes. Do not stir. Add flavoring and beat until mixture starts to lose its gloss, about 8 minutes. Stir in cherries and nuts quickly. Pour into greased 8x8-inch pan. Cool and cut into squares.

Betty Burt, Winnemucca, Nev.

CHOCOLATE CARAMEL LOLLIPOPS
Makes 20

100	small chocolate caramels
16	cups rice cereal, toasted in oven
¾	cup water
20	wooden lollipop sticks
20	(5-ounce) paper cups

In double boiler top, combine caramels with water. Cook over hot water, stirring occasionally, until caramels melt. In a bowl combine caramel mixture and cereal. Using a wooden spoon, stir until cereal is well-coated. Spoon mixture into paper cups. Insert 1 lollipop stick into center of each cup. Refrigerate for 30 minutes to an hour. Remove lollipops from paper cups before serving.

Shari Crider, Stoughton, Wis.

CINNAMON FILBERTS

2 cups (1/2 pound) shelled filberts
1 egg white
1/2 cup sugar
1 teaspoon ground cinnamon
1/4 cup (1/2 stick) butter or margarine

Put nuts on shallow baking pan and toast in preheated slow oven (325 degrees) for 10 minutes. Beat egg whites until foamy; add sugar and cinnamon gradually and beat until stiff. Add nuts and mix well. Melt butter in same baking pan you used for toasting nuts and spread nut mixture over butter. Bake for 30 minutes, stirring every 10 minutes. Store in airtight container.

OLD-FASHIONED TAFFY PULL
Makes 1½ pounds

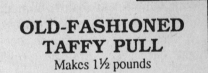

2	cups light molasses
1	cup dark brown sugar firmly packed
2	tablespoons butter
⅓	cup water
1	tablespoon apple cider vinegar
	Pinch of baking soda

Cook all ingredients together in a heavy saucepan over medium heat. Stir constantly until sugar is dissolved, until mixture reaches the hard-ball stage (260 degrees on candy thermometer) and a small bit makes a hard ball when dropped into cold water. Pour onto a buttered cookie sheet. Cool. When cool enough to handle, rub butter on your hands and pull the candy, small portions at a time, until it is light golden in color and candy has a satiny finish. Pull into long strips ¾ inch in diameter and cut into 1-inch pieces with scissors. When cooled, wrap each piece in waxed paper.

You may add lemon, maple, almond or vanilla extract for variety, or divide the recipe and flavor each section with a different extract.

Diantha Susan Hibbard, Rochester, N.Y.

OLD-FASHIONED PEANUT BRITTLE
Serves 24

Quick-cooking in microwave in 9 minutes.

1 cup raw peanuts
1 cup sugar
½ cup light corn syrup
⅛ teaspoon salt
1 teaspoon baking soda
1 teaspoon vanilla
1 teaspoon butter

In a 1½-quart casserole, stir together peanuts, sugar, syrup and salt. Cook 8 minutes on HIGH, stirring well after 4 minutes. Add butter and vanilla. Cook 1 minute longer on HIGH. Add baking soda and quickly stir until light and foamy. Immediately pour onto lightly buttered baking sheet. Spread out thin. When cool, break into pieces. Store in airtight container.

Katherine W. Frierson, Deland, Fla.

CHOCOLATE MARSHMALLOW FUDGE

4-1/2 cups sugar
2 tablespoons butter
1 (1-2/3 cups) tall can evaporated milk
Pinch of salt
12 ounces semi-sweet chocolate chips
12 ounces German Sweet Chocolate
1 pint marshmallow creme
2 cups pecans or walnuts

Heat first 4 ingredients to a rolling boil. Place remaining 4 ingredients in large bowl. Pour boiling syrup over ingredients in bowl, stir until chocolate is all melted and pour into 9x13-inch pan.

It is easier to remove from pan if pan is buttered and lined with foil first. Let stand few hours before cutting. Where German Sweet Chocolate is not available, 3 to 4 squares of unsweetened chocolate may be used.

Katherine Frierson, Deland, Fla.

COCONUT TREATS

1 cup sugar
1/2 cup water
1 1/2 cups corn syrup
1 14-ounce package shredded coconut
1/2 teaspoon vanilla
Melted chocolate

Combine sugar with water and syrup; stir over heat to dissolve sugar. Cook without stirring to 236 degrees (soft-ball stage) on candy thermometer. Remove from heat; add coconut and vanilla. Cool. With teaspoon, shape into small balls and dip in melted chocolate.

PEANUT BUTTER CUPS

1/2 cup butter or margarine
1 pound powdered sugar
2 cups creamy peanut butter
3 cups Rice Krispies, crushed
2 cups (12 ounces) chocolate chips
4 tablespoons shortening

Mix butter, powdered sugar, peanut butter and Rice Krispies together well, (may need to use hands). Melt chips with shortening. Roll candy into small balls and dip in chocolate. Chill until chocolate hardens.

Judy Haffner, Auke Bay, Alaska

LOLLIPOPS

Combine over low heat:
2 cups sugar
2/3 cup light corn syrup
1/2 cup water

Cook without stirring to just past the crack stage (to 310 degrees on thermometer). Remove syrup from heat. Stir in a few drops of food coloring, all one color, or many if you want to divide candy into small pans. Flavor with 1 teaspoon vanilla or fruit flavors, peppermint, etc. Pour syrup by the tablespoonfuls onto a greased sheet. Press stick into each one.

Karin Shea Fedders, Dameron, Md.

MRS. MARTIN'S QUICK PEANUT CANDY
Makes 1 1/4 pounds

1/2 cup light corn syrup
1/2 cup sugar
1/2 cup peanut butter
4 cups crispy rice cereal
1 cup peanuts

Grease a large baking sheet. In a 3-quart saucepan, mix syrup and sugar. Stirring constantly, bring to a boil over medium heat; boil 1 minute. Remove from heat. Stir in peanut butter. Add cereal and peanuts. Quickly stir until well-coated. Spoon onto greased baking sheet. With greased hands, pat evenly to 1/2-inch thickness. Cool and then break into pieces.

Agnes Ward, Erie, Penn.

CANDIED CHERRY-PECAN SLICES
Makes 144

1 cup butter *or* margarine, softened
1 cup confectioners' sugar
1 egg
1½ teaspoons vanilla
2¼ cups flour
Dash of salt
2 cups candied cherries, halved
1 cup pecans

In small mixer bowl, cream butter until fluffy. Gradually add sugar, beating until light. Beat in egg and vanilla. Stir in flour and salt; mix well. Stir in cherries and pecans. Cover airtight and chill 1 hour. Divide dough into thirds. On lightly floured pastry cloth or other surface, with floured hands, shape each piece of dough into 12-inch roll. Wrap each roll in waxed paper; chill at least 3 hours, or until firm. Cut in ¼-inch slices (serrated knife). Place slices about 1 inch apart on ungreased cookie sheets. Bake in preheated 350-degree oven for 12–15 minutes, or until light brown at edges. Cool on racks. Store airtight in cool, dry place.

Diantha Susan Hibbard, Rochester, N.Y.

CLASSIC CHRISTMAS CANDY CANES

1 cup water
3 cups sugar
1-1/2 tablespoons heavy cream
1-1/2 teaspoons white vinegar
1/4 teaspoon salt
2 tablespoons butter or margarine
4-5 drops peppermint extract
3-4 drops red food coloring

Combine sugar, cream, vinegar, salt and butter in mixing bowl; cream as for a cake. Boil water; remove from heat; stir creamed mixture into hot water. Clip on candy thermometer; boil to crack stage (258 degrees). Remove from heat; pour mixture onto lightly-buttered baking sheet placed over cooling rack. Cool; add flavoring; work candy with spatula. Divide mixture into portions; leave one portion white; tint the second with red food coloring. Pull each portion separately into a rope 1/2 inch in diameter; twist the two together to form one rope. Cut into 4 to 5-inch lengths; curl one end over to form the candy cane shape.

Mrs. Gwen Campbell, Sterling, Va.

SOUR CREAM FUDGE

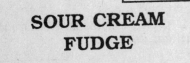

2 cups sugar
2 tablespoons white corn syrup
2 tablespoons butter
3/4 - 1 cup sour cream (depending upon consistency, thin dairy sour cream with milk until consistency of thick whipping cream).
1 teaspoon vanilla
1/2 cup walnuts

Mix sugar, corn syrup, butter and sour cream well. Cook over medium heat until soft ball stage. Cool. Add vanilla. Cool to room temperature. Beat until thick. Add nuts. Pour at once into buttered platter. Do not spread. Top will be glossy and uneven. Cut into 3/4-inch squares when firm.

Phyllis Lien, Stoughton, Wis.

HELEN'S SUNFLOWER BRITTLE

2 cups sugar
1 cup light corn syrup
1/2 cup water
Pinch of salt
1 cup raw sunflower seeds
1 tablespoon butter
1 teaspoon vanilla
1 teaspoon baking soda

Butter two cookie sheets well.

Mix sugar, corn syrup, water and salt in saucepan and bring to boil at 212 degrees F. on a candy thermometer. Add sunflower seeds; cook to 275 degrees F. Stir in butter and cook to 300 degrees F.

Remove from heat; add vanilla and mix well; add baking soda. Stir well. Pour onto buttered cookie sheets and spread into thin, even layer. Let cool, then break into pieces.

Mrs. Helen Beebe, St. Charles, Ill.

MOM'S CREAM CHEESE MINTS

Makes 7 dozen

4 ounces cream cheese, softened
2 cups confectioners' sugar
Peppermint extract, about 1/4 teaspoon or to taste
Wintergreen extract, about 1/4 teaspoon or to taste
Red food coloring
Green food coloring
Granulated sugar

Mix cream cheese and confectioners' sugar by hand until smooth and doughy. Divide mixture in half; add a few drops of peppermint extract to one half and a few drops of wintergreen extract to other half. Taste and adjust flavor. Blend green food coloring (several drops at a time) into peppermint mixture until soft green; blend red food coloring (several drops at a time) into wintergreen mixture until pastel pink. Pinch off small pieces of dough; roll into balls and dip into granulated sugar. Refrigerate, covered.

Marcella Swigert, Monroe City, Mo.

CATHEDRAL WINDOW CANDY

2 tablespoons butter
1 cup chocolate chips
1 beaten egg
1 cup confectioners' sugar
3 cups colored miniature marshmallows

Place butter and chocolate chips in medium, heat-resistant bowl. Heat, uncovered, in microwave oven for 4 minutes, or until melted. Combine egg and sugar; add slowly to chocolate mixture. Stir in marshmallows to coat well. Pour onto waxed paper. Shape into 18-inch log. Refrigerate. Slice before serving.

Sue Hammer

MILLION-DOLLAR FUDGE

Makes 2½ pounds

2 cups granulated sugar
Pinch of salt
1 tablespoon butter
1 (5½-ounce) can evaporated milk, undiluted
1 (6-ounce) package semisweet chocolate bits
6 ounces sweet baking chocolate, cut into small pieces
1 (8-ounce) jar marshmallow creme
1 cup coarsely broken walnuts *or* pecans

Butter an 8-inch square pan; set aside.

Into a 2-quart heavy saucepan place sugar, salt, butter and evaporated milk. Stirring constantly, cook over medium-high heat until mixture comes to a full boil. Boil 5 minutes, stirring constantly.

Remove from heat. Add chocolate and marshmallow creme; stir vigorously and speedily until chocolate is melted and mixture is uniform in color. At once, stir in the nuts and pour into prepared pan. When cool, cut into desired size squares. Store in airtight container.

Nora Leigh, Richmond, Va.

PEANUT BUTTER BONBONS

Makes about 100

2 cups peanut butter
1/2 cup butter or margarine
1 pound sifted confectioners' sugar
3 cups crisp rice cereal
2 (6 ounce) packages butterscotch pieces (2 cups)
2 (6 ounce) packages semi-sweet chocolate pieces (2 cups)

In saucepan, melt peanut butter and butter. In large bowl, combine sugar and cereal. Pour peanut butter mixture over cereal mixture. Blend together with hands. Form into 1/2-inch balls. Chill until firm. Melt butterscotch pieces and chocolate pieces in separate double boilers. Dip half the candies in each coating. Swirl tops with back of teaspoon. Place on waxed paper-lined baking sheet. Chill.

Bea Comas, Portland, Maine

PECAN PRALINES

Makes 1½ dozen

1   (3½-ounce) package butterscotch pudding and pie filling mix
1   cup sugar
½   cup firmly packed brown sugar
½   cup evaporated milk
1   tablespoon margarine *or* butter
1½ cups pecan halves

In a large saucepan combine pudding mix, sugar, brown sugar, milk and margarine or butter. Cook over low heat, stirring constantly, until sugar dissolves and mixture comes to a boil. Continue cooking and stirring until mixture reaches the soft-ball stage (235 degrees) on candy thermometer, or until a small amount dropped into cold water forms a soft ball. Remove from heat; add nuts. Beat until mixture begins to thicken. Drop by tablespoonfuls onto waxed paper, making each praline about 3 inches in diameter. Cool until firm.

Leota Baxter, Ingalls, Kan.

OLD-FASHIONED TAFFY

Makes about 40 1-inch pieces

2 1/2 cups sugar
1/2 cup water
1/4 cup vinegar
1/8 teaspoon salt
1 tablespoon butter
1 teaspoon vanilla

Combine sugar, water, vinegar, salt and butter in a small Dutch oven. Cook without stirring over medium heat until mixture reaches 270 degrees (soft crack stage). Remove from heat at once and add vanilla.

Pour onto a greased 15x10x1-inch pan. Cool until it can be handled; then butter hands and pull candy until it is light in color and difficult to pull. Divide candy in half and pull each half into a rope 1 inch in diameter. Cut into 1-inch pieces; wrap each piece individually in waxed paper.

MYSTERY DROPS

Makes 30 candies

2 cups granulated sugar
2/3 cup milk
3/4 cup finely-ground soda crackers (30 crackers)
1/2 cup finely-chopped pecans
1 teaspoon vanilla
7 tablespoons peanut butter, smooth or crunchy

Combine sugar and milk in 2-quart heavy saucepan. Bring to boil, stirring until sugar is dissolved. Boil 3 minutes. Remove from heat. Add remaining ingredients, mixing quickly. Beat until mixture is thick enough to drop from teaspoon onto waxed paper.

Mrs. W. T. Gore, Aztec, N.M.

GLAZED NUTS

1 cup brown sugar
1-1/2 cups white sugar
1/2 cup sour cream
1 teaspoon vanilla

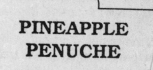

2 cups whole pecan halves *or* walnut halves

Combine both sugars and sour cream. Cook over medium heat until sugar is dissolved. While stirring cook to 238 degrees exactly on a candy thermometer. Remove from heat. Add vanilla and nuts. Turn onto waxed paper; separate with fork. Allow to dry before serving.

Brenda Peery, Tannersville, Va.

PINEAPPLE PENUCHE

1 cup white sugar
1/2 cup light brown sugar
1/4 cup heavy cream
1/2 cup well-drained crushed pineapple
1 tablespoon butter (no substitutes)
1 teaspoon vanilla
1/2 cup chopped pecans

Place butter, sugars, cream and pineapple in large stainless steel or enamel kettle. Bring to a boil over medium heat, stirring constantly. Boil to soft ball stage. Remove from heat and beat hard with wooden spoon. Add vanilla and nuts and beat well, until mixture is getting quite thick. Pour out onto buttered platter, spreading if needed, to edges. Allow to cool. Cut with sharp knife into bite-sized pieces.

Pearle Goodwin, South Ryegate, Vt.

FESTIVE MINTS

Makes about 9 dozen

1 1-pound package confectioners' sugar
1/2 cup (1 stick) margarine, softened
2 tablespoons evaporated milk
4-5 drops peppermint extract
Few drops food coloring

Combine all ingredients in a large bowl; beat at high speed until well-blended. Knead until smooth. Shape the mints in rubber candy molds. Place on cookie sheets which have been covered with paper towels and cover mints with additional layer of paper towels. Leave overnight to harden.

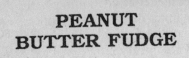

PEANUT BUTTER FUDGE

3 cups granulated or brown sugar
1/2 cup milk
2 tablespoons margarine
3 tablespoons marshmallow fluff
3 tablespoons peanut butter
1 teaspoon vanilla

Bring sugar, milk, and margarine to a boil; let boil for 3 minutes. Then take off stove; add marshmallow fluff, peanut butter, and vanilla. Beat with spoon for a few minutes. Poor into greased pan. Let set; cut into squares.

Zenana Warren, Bloomville, Ohio

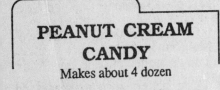

PEANUT CREAM CANDY

Makes about 4 dozen

1 cup firmly-packed brown sugar
1 cup granulated sugar
1 cup dairy sour cream
Dash salt
1 cup creamy peanut butter
1 teaspoon vanilla

Combine sugars, sour cream and salt in saucepan and mix well. Cook over medium heat, stirring until mixture reaches soft ball stage (236 degrees) or until small amount forms a soft ball when dropped in cold water. Cool to lukewarm. Stir in peanut butter and vanilla. Mix well. Drop by teaspoonfuls onto greased baking sheets. Cool.

Judy Haffner, Auke Bay, Alaska

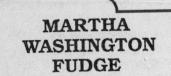

MARTHA WASHINGTON FUDGE

1 cup butter, softened
2 pounds confectioners' sugar
1 (14-ounce) can sweetened
   condensed milk
1 (7-ounce) can flaked coconut
2 cups chopped nuts
1 pound semisweet chocolate bits
4 ounces melted paraffin
1 teaspoon vanilla extract

Beat butter until creamy. Gradually mix in sugar, then blend in milk. Stir in coconut and nuts. Let stand for a while and then shape into balls. Melt chocolate and paraffin in top of double boiler over simmering water, just until smooth. Stir in vanilla. Keep warm. One by one, spear coconut balls on a toothpick and dip into chocolate mixture. Place on waxed-paper-covered baking sheet until coating hardens.

Store in airtight container.

Mrs. J.B. Blass, Richmond, Va.

PEANUT BUTTER BARK CLUSTERS

1-1/2 pounds almond bark
1-1/2 cups peanut butter
1-1/2 cups mini marshmallows
2 cups Rice Krispies
1-1/2 cups peanuts

Melt bark and add peanut butter; stir and set aside. Mix marshmallows, cereal and nuts and pour bark mixture over, stirring until well coated. Drop by teaspoons on waxed paper and cool.

A. M. Everett, Stoughton, Wis.

FIESTA FUDGE

Yield: 3 pounds

2-1/2 cups sugar
3/4 cup margarine
2/3 cup evaporated milk
1/2 teaspoon salt
1-1/2 cups peanut butter
1 jar (7 ounces) marshmallow
   creme
1 teaspoon vanilla
1-1/2 cups plain M & M candies

Combine sugar, margarine, milk, and salt in saucepan. Bring to full rolling boil over high heat, stirring constantly. Continue boiling over medium heat for 5 minutes, stirring constantly.

Remove from heat. Stir in peanut butter until melted. Stir in marshmallow creme and vanilla until well blended. Fold in candies and immediately spread in 13x9-inch pan. Cool at room temperature.

Melba Bellefeuille, Libertyville, Ill.

HOMEMADE CHOCOLATES

1 cup sweetened condensed milk
1/4 pound soft margarine
2-1/2 pounds powdered sugar
Flavoring to taste (such as: vanilla, rum, lemon, etc.)
12 ounces semi-sweet chocolate bits
4 ounces sweet or unsweetened chocolate
1/2 block paraffin wax
Toothpicks

Blend well sweetened condensed milk, margarine, sugar and flavoring. Shape into tiny balls; chill or freeze.

In double boiler, blend semi-sweet chocolate, sweet or unsweetened chocolate and wax. Blend well.

Impale each candy with a toothpick and dip quickly into chocolate, push from toothpick onto waxed paper and dribble a bit of chocolate over hole.

Agnes Russell, Concord, N.H.

BROWN SUGAR CANDY

Makes 1½ pounds

2	cups pecans (small or broken pieces)
½	cup butter
⅔	cup firmly packed brown sugar
1	(14-ounce) can sweetened condensed milk
1	teaspoon vanilla

Place pecans on large glass plate and microwave on HIGH (100 percent) power for 8 minutes, stirring every 2 minutes. Set aside. In an 8-cup measure, microwave butter on HIGH for 1 minute. Stir in brown sugar and milk until blended. Microwave on HIGH 7 minutes, stirring every 2 minutes. Beat with wooden spoon until stiff, about 5 minutes. Stir in vanilla and roasted pecans. Spread in lightly buttered 8-inch square glass dish. Chill until firm. Cut into squares.

Jen Lien, Stoughton, Wis.

WHITE CHOCOLATE CREAM FUDGE

Makes 6 dozen pieces

3 cups sugar
1 cup evaporated milk
¾ stick butter
1 (1-pint) jar marshmallow creme
12 ounces white chocolate, cut in small pieces
1 cup chopped pecans
1 (4-ounce) jar candied cherries

Bring sugar, milk and butter to a boil over low heat, stirring constantly. Cook to 237 degrees. Remove from heat; add marshmallow creme, white chocolate, nuts and cherries. Stir until marshmallow creme and chocolate are melted. Pour into a 13 x 9 x 2-inch buttered baking dish. Cool before cutting.

Joy B. Shamway, Freeport, Ill.

ORANGE PUFFS

Makes 4 dozen candies

2 3/4 cups sugar
1/2 cup orange juice
1/2 cup water
1 tablespoon grated orange rind
1/2 teaspoon grated lemon rind
2 egg whites, stiffly beaten
1/8 teaspoon salt

Combine sugar, orange juice, water, orange and lemon rinds. Stir over low heat until sugar dissolves. Cook to light crack stage (260 degrees on a candy thermometer). Gradually pour syrup over egg whites, beating constantly until mixture holds shape. Add salt. Drop from teaspoon onto waxed paper.

Blanche Towner

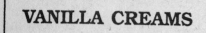

VANILLA CREAMS

2 cups white sugar
2 tablespoons butter
1/4 teaspoon cream of tartar
1 cup undiluted canned milk
1-1/2 teaspoons vanilla
1 cup finely chopped walnuts

Combine sugar and cream of tartar and stir until no lumps remain. Add butter and milk and place in large enamel kettle. Bring to boil, stirring enough to keep mixture from sticking to kettle. Using candy thermometer, cook to medium soft ball stage. Remove from heat and beat in vanilla. Beat vigorously until quite thick. Fold in nuts. Drop by teaspoonfuls onto buttered cookie sheet. Let harden.

Pearle Goodwin, South Ryegate, Vt.

PROFESSIONAL PEANUT BRITTLE

1-1/2 cups white sugar
1/2 cup light brown sugar
1 cup light Karo syrup
3 cups raw Spanish peanuts
1/2 teaspoon soda
Dash salt
1 teaspoon vanilla

Blend together in saucepan sugar, brown sugar and light syrup. Boil to 236 degrees, using candy thermometer. Add peanuts and cook to 300 degrees. Remove from heat. Mix soda, salt and vanilla together, add to mixture and stir well. Pour out onto marble slab, stretch out into thin sheet or use two lightly buttered cookie sheets. When cold, break into pieces and store in tight container.

This is a perfect peanut brittle and you'll never have a failure. Keeps for a long period with no quality loss.

Fay Duman, Eugene, Ore.

QUICK FUDGE SQUARES

2 squares (2 ounces) unsweetened chocolate
1/3 cup butter
2/3 cup sugar
1/4 cup light corn syrup
1/2 teaspoon salt
1 1/2 teaspoons vanilla extract
1/2 cup chopped nuts
2 cups uncooked oats

Melt chocolate and butter in top of double boiler over boiling water. Add remaining ingredients, except nuts and blend thoroughly.

Pack firmly into a greased 8-inch square pan. Sprinkle chopped nuts on top. Bake at 425 degrees for 12 minutes. When cool, turn out of pan and cut into small squares.

Lou Roehr, Hammond, Ind.

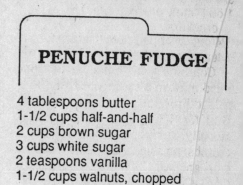

PENUCHE FUDGE

4 tablespoons butter
1-1/2 cups half-and-half
2 cups brown sugar
3 cups white sugar
2 teaspoons vanilla
1-1/2 cups walnuts, chopped

Melt butter, making sure it coats bottom and sides of saucepan. Pour half-and-half into pan; bring to boil. Add brown and white sugar and stir until dissolved. Stirring constantly, cook until mixture reaches soft ball stage. Remove from heat. Place pan in two inches of cold water. Add vanilla and walnuts. Beat with wooden spoon until thick. Pour into buttered fudge pan. Score while warm. Cut into squares when fully cooled.

Agnes Russell, Concord, N.H.

PECAN CANDY CLUSTERS

Makes about 24

1/2 cup sugar
1/2 cup evaporated milk
1 tablespoon corn syrup
1 cup semisweet chocolate chips
1 cup diced pecans
1/2 teaspoon vanilla

Put sugar, milk and syrup in a 2-quart pot. Stir over medium heat until bubbly all over top. Boil and stir 2 minutes more. Remove from heat. Stir in chocolate chips and vanilla, until chips are melted. Add nuts. Mix well. Drop by teaspoonsful onto waxed paper. Chill to set.

Kathrine Van Boxtel, Downey, Calif.

FUDGE NOUGATS
Makes 40 pieces

2 cups sugar
1/2 cup butter
1 cup evaporated milk
1 cup semisweet chocolate chips
3/4 cup all-purpose flour
1 cup finely crushed graham
 crackers
3/4 cup chopped nuts
1 teaspoon vanilla

Combine sugar, butter, and evaporated milk in a saucepan. Bring to a full rolling boil, stirring constantly. Boil for 10 minutes, stirring occasionally. Stir in chocolate chips, flour, crumbs, nuts and vanilla. Spread in a well-greased 12x8- or 12x9-inch pan. Cool. Cut into squares.

Mrs. Dorothy Trunnels
Angels Camp, Calif.

SEA FOAM CANDY

2 cups sugar
2 cups water
1/8 teaspoon salt
1/4 teaspoon cream of
 tartar
2 egg whites, stiffly
 beaten
1 teaspoon vanilla
 Food coloring (optional)

Combine first 4 ingredients. Cover and boil for 5 minutes. Uncover and boil, without stirring, to soft-ball stage. Pour slowly over 2 stiffly beaten egg whites, mixing as you pour. (You may need help with this.)

Add 1 teaspoon vanilla and beat until it holds shape when dropped from a spoon. Add food coloring, if you like. Drop by tablespoon onto waxed paper placed on a cookie sheet.

Jean Baker, Chula Vista, Calif.

BABY RUTH SQUARES

1 cup corn syrup

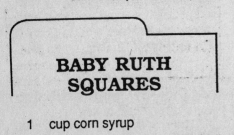

1 cup sugar
1½ cups salted peanuts
6 cups Rice Krispies
1 heaping cup peanut
 butter

Topping:
1 cup sugar
¼ cup milk
1 cup chocolate chips
2 tablespoons butter

Cook corn syrup and sugar until it boils. Remove from heat and stir in peanut butter, peanuts and cereal. Press into 9 x 13-inch pan. Cook topping ingredients, except chocolate chips, to full boil. Remove from heat and stir in chips. Spread on top of cereal mixture. Cut into small squares.

Cheryl Santefort, Thornton, Ill.

BEST PEANUT BUTTER BALLS
Makes 3 dozen

1 cup peanut butter
¼ cup margarine
2¼ cups sifted confectioners' sugar
1½ cups rice cereal
6 ounces semisweet
 chocolate bits
2 tablespoons butter

Melt peanut butter and margarine over low heat, stirring to prevent scorching. Mix together sugar and cereal in a large bowl. Add peanut butter mixture and mix well. Form into small balls with a teaspoon or fingers. Place in freezer. Melt chocolate with butter in a double boiler. Dip frozen balls into chocolate to cover and place on waxed paper. Store in refrigerator.

Lucy Dowd, Sequim, Wash.

CHOCOLATE-DIPPED APRICOTS

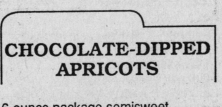

6-ounce package semisweet
 chocolate chips
2 tablespoons shortening
8 ounces dried apricots, halved

In top of double boiler over hot water, stir chocolate and shortening until melted and smooth. Keep warm.

Insert toothpicks into apricot halves; dip in chocolate. Allow excess to drip off back into pot. Place on waxed paper and remove toothpicks.

Let dry at room temperature for about 30 minutes or until chocolate is firm. Store in refrigerator or in a cool, dry place, packed loosely between sheets of waxed paper.

MINCEMEAT CANDIES
Makes 6 dozen

1 (9 ounce) package condensed
 mincemeat, finely crumbled
1/4 cup orange juice
1/4 cup light corn syrup
1/4 cup butter or margarine, melted
1/2 cup corn flake crumbs
1/2 cup chopped walnuts
1/2 cup finely-chopped dried apricots
1 cup finely-chopped walnuts for
 coating

In large bowl, mix all ingredients except walnuts for coating until well blended. Chill thoroughly. Shape into 1-inch balls, roll in remaining nuts. Place on wax paper-lined baking sheet. Refrigerate until firm. Store in tight container.

Melba Bellefeuille, Libertyville, Ill.

APRICOT CANDIES

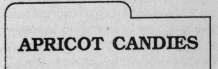

3/4 cup dried apricots
1/2 cup nut meats
3/4 cup fresh coconut, grated
1 tablespoon lemon juice
1/4 teaspoon salt
1 teaspoon vanilla
1 teaspoon lemon rind, grated
1 teaspoon orange rind, grated

Wash apricots and put them in food chopper with nut meats. Add coconut, lemon juice, grated orange and lemon rind. Mix and knead well. Roll out onto sugared board to about 1/4 inch thickness. Cut in squares and roll in confectioners' sugar.

Susan Wiener, Spring Hill, Fla.

BUTTER MINTS

3 cups sugar
1/4 pound (1 stick) butter
1 cup hot water
Dash of salt
Few drops of mint flavoring
Few drops of food coloring

Stir sugar with butter and hot water; add salt; bring to a boil in saucepan. Cover and wait for 3 minutes. Remove lid and wash down sides of pan with a brush dipped in water. Cook without stirring to 248 degrees.

Pour candy onto a buttered slab and allow to cool. Add a few drops of flavoring and food coloring. Pull candy until it loses its gloss. Stretch into a rope and cut into pieces. Wrap individual pieces in waxed paper or plastic wrap so they do not stick together.

Store candy in an airtight can.

HOLIDAY MINTS

3 egg whites
6 cups confectioners' sugar
Red and green food coloring
1/2 teaspoon peppermint extract
1/2 teaspoon spearmint extract

Beat egg whites until stiff, adding sugar gradually. Divide candy into 2 portions. Tint half green and half red. Add peppermint extract to red mixture and spearmint extract to green mixture. Roll candy between 2 pieces of waxed paper. Cut with small round cookie cutter. Let dry overnight.

Barbara Beauregard - Smith, Northfield, S. A., Australia

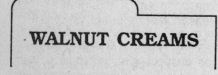

WALNUT CREAMS

1-1/2 cups granulated sugar
1-1/2 cups light brown sugar
1 cup milk
1/8 teaspoon salt
1 cup walnuts, chopped
1/2 teaspoon almond extract

Put sugar and milk into large saucepan; stir until sugar is dissolved. Boil until soft ball is formed when mixture is tested in cold water. Let stand until lukewarm. Beat vigorously. When it begins to get creamy, add nuts and extract. Pour into buttered pan. When hard, cut into squares with a knife which has been dipped in boiling water.

Susan Wiener, Spring Hill, Fla.

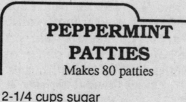

PEPPERMINT PATTIES
Makes 80 patties

2-1/4 cups sugar
1/2 cup water
1/4 cup light corn syrup
1 egg white, stiffly beaten
4 drops peppermint oil
1 (12-ounce) package chocolate chips, melted

Combine sugar, water, and corn syrup in small saucepan; bring to gentle boil and cook, covered, for 6 minutes. Uncover and boil to 225-238 degrees on candy thermometer, without stirring. Cool until just warm, then beat with wooden spoon until mixture gets cloudy. Add beaten egg white, a little at a time. Add oil of peppermint and beat until milky white. Cool, then shape into 1-1/2-inch patties and dip in melted chocolate.

Agnes Ward, Erie, Pa.

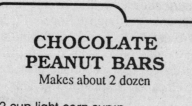

CHOCOLATE PEANUT BARS
Makes about 2 dozen

1/2 cup light corn syrup
1/4 cup brown sugar
Dash of salt
1 cup peanut butter
1 teaspoon vanilla
2 cups crispy rice cereal
1 cup cornflakes, slightly crushed
1 6-ounce package chocolate chips

Combine corn syrup, sugar and salt in a saucepan; bring to a full boil and then stir in peanut butter. Remove from heat and stir in remaining ingredients. Press into a greased 9-inch square pan. Chill for 1 hour. Cut in squares. Store in the refrigerator.

Amelia M. Brown, Pittsburgh, Penn.

TOASTED ALMOND BALLS
About 6-1/2 dozen

1 cup semi-sweet chocolate chips
1 cup butterscotch chips
3/4 cup powdered sugar
1/2 cup cultured sour cream
1-1/2 teaspoons grated orange rind
1/4 teaspoon salt
2 cups vanilla wafer crumbs
3/4 cup finely-chopped toasted almonds

Melt chocolate and butterscotch chips at low heat. Mix in sugar, sour cream, orange rind, salt and crumbs; chill. Shape into 3/4-inch balls; roll in almonds.

Barbara Beauregard - Smith, Northfield, S. A., Australia

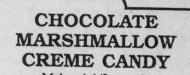

CHOCOLATE MARSHMALLOW CREME CANDY
Makes 4-1/2 pounds

3-1/2 sticks margarine
1 (15-ounce) can evaporated milk
5 cups granulated sugar
1-pound package Hershey's kisses
1 regular-size jar marshmallow creme
1 pound pecans (optional)

Melt margarine, add sugar and milk; bring to a boil. Boil for 5 minutes. Take off heat and add Hershey's kisses, marshmallow creme, and pecans. Spread waxed paper on cookie sheets and drop mixture by teaspoonfuls onto paper.

Stacie Adamson, Gallatin, Tenn.

Celebration CAKES

SELF-FILLED CUPCAKES

1 package Deluxe Devil's Food
   cake mix
1 (8-ounce) package cream cheese
1 egg
1/2 teaspoon salt
1/3 cup sugar
2 (8-ounce) package semisweet
   chocolate chips

Mix cake according to package directions. Place individual baking liners in muffin pan. Fill cup two-thirds full. Cream the cheese with the sugar. Beat in egg and salt; stir in chocolate chips. Drop rounded tea-spoonfuls of mixture in cake batter. Bake as cake directs.

Dovie Lucy, McLoud, Okla.

FRUIT UPSIDE-DOWN CAKE

(Electric Fry Pan)

1/2 cup butter
1/2 cup packed brown sugar
1 (20-ounce) can sliced pineapple,
   drained
1 (25-ounce) jar pitted prunes,
   drained
1 (15-ounce) can apricot halves,
   drained
12 pecan halves
1 (18-1/2-ounce) package yellow
   cake mix
2 eggs
1 cup water
2 teaspoons grated lemon rind
Pecan halves

In preheated 12-inch electric skillet, melt butter; coat pan with melted butter by rotating pan to cover sides and bottom. Sprinkle in brown sugar to cover bottom evenly. Arrange the fruit over brown sugar. Prepare cake according to directions *but* use 2 eggs, 1 cup water, and lemon rind; beat smoothly. Spoon batter over fruit, spreading carefully to edges. Cover tightly and set temperature at 300 degrees. Cook, covered, for 40 minutes; do not remove lid until finished. Loosen cake with sharp knife and unmold while hot onto serving dish. Serve warm with whipped cream.

Agnes Ward, Erie, Pa.

PRINCESS CAKE

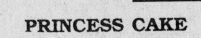

Cake:
1 (16-ounce) package white cake
   mix
1 (3-3/4-ounce) package strawberry
   pudding mix
3 eggs
1 cup water
1 cup vegetable oil
1/2 cup sour cream
1/2 cup chopped nuts

Frosting:
2-1/4 cups cold milk
2 (1-1/2-ounce) packages powdered
   whipped topping
1-1/2 (3-3/4-ounce) packages
   strawberry pudding mix

Preheat oven to 350 degrees. Grease and flour a 10-inch tube pan. Blend all cake ingredients, except nuts, in a large bowl; beat 2 minutes at medium speed. Stir in nuts. Turn batter into prepared pan and bake 40-50 minutes, or until tested done. Cool 15 minutes in pan, then remove to rack to finish cooling. Split cooled cake crosswise into 2 layers. Whip all frosting ingredients until mixture thickens (about 5 minutes)). Spread frosting between cake layers as well as on the top and sides. Decorate the cake lavishly with 3-4 cups sliced strawberries.

Agnes Ward, Erie, Pa.

OLD FASHIONED FUDGE CAKE

1 cup white sugar
1 egg
1-1/2 cups white flour
1 teaspoon baking soda
1/4 teaspoon baking powder
1/4 teaspoon salt
1 cup sour milk (to sour, add 1
   teaspoon vinegar)
3 tablespoons butter
4 level tablespoons cocoa
1 teaspoon vanilla

Melt butter and cocoa together over low heat, beat until smooth. In large mixer bowl, beat together sugar, egg and vanilla. Sift dry ingredients and add alternately with milk. Beat smooth. Add warm cocoa mix slowly to batter as you mix on low speed. Beat until smooth and creamy. Pour into prepared 9-inch layer cake pans or 9x13-inch pan. Bake in preheated 350 degree oven for 25 minutes for layers, or 30 minutes for flat cake. Test middle with toothpick for doneness. Cool on rack. Ice with favorite frosting.

Pearle M. Goodwin, South Ryegate, Vt.

PINEAPPLE UPSIDE-DOWN CAKE
Serves 6-8

1/4 cup butter
2/3 cup light brown sugar, packed
6-7 pineapples slices, drained
6-7 maraschino cherries, drained
2 eggs, separated
3/4 cup granulated sugar
1/4 cup boiling pineapple juice
3/4 cup sifted cake flour
1/2 teaspoon baking powder
1/8 teaspoon salt
1/2 teaspoon vanilla

Melt butter in a 10-1/2-inch oven-proof skillet. Remove from heat. Sprinkle brown sugar over melted butter. Arrange pineapple over this mixture with a cherry in each pineapple center. Beat egg yolks until light, adding granulated sugar gradually. Stir in hot juice. Sift in dry ingredients; mix well. Add vanilla. Fold in stiffly beaten egg whites. Pour cake batter over pineapple mixture. Bake in 325-degree oven for 30 to 35 minutes. Let cool 3 to 5 minutes before inverting on cake plate. Serve warm or cold, with or without whipped cream or whipped topping.

Mrs. E. O'Brien, Richmond, Va.

LOVELY LUAU CAKE

3/4 cup butter or margarine
1-1/2 cups sugar
1 teaspoon lemon extract
1-1/4 teaspoons vanilla extract
3 cups cake flour, sifted
1/4 teaspoon salt
4 teaspoons baking powder
1/4 cup flaked coconut, toasted
1 cup unsweetened pineapple juice
5 large egg whites, stiffly beaten
Luau Whipped Cream Icing (recipe
    follows)

Cream butter; gradually add sugar; cream until light and fluffy. Add extracts. Sift together flour, salt, and baking powder; add toasted coconut. Add to creamed mixture alternately with pineapple juice. Fold in stiffly beaten egg whites. Turn into 3 greased and floured 9-inch cake pans. Bake at

350 degrees for 25-30 minutes. When cool, frost.

Luau Whipped Cream Icing:
1 teaspoon unflavored gelatin
2 tablespoons cold water
3 tablespoons sugar
1 teaspoon vanilla extract
1 pint whipping cream

Soften gelatin in cold water for 5 minutes; dissolve over hot water. Whip cream until stiff; beat in sugar and vanilla. Add cooled gelatin; beat mixture until it forms peaks. Spread between layers and on cake.

Gwen Campbell, Sterling, Va.

LEMON SURPRISE CAKE

1 box Duncan Hines Butter Cake Mix
1 (6-ounce) box lemon gelatin (dry)
2 cups hot water
1 (4-ounce) box French vanilla instant pudding; dry
1 (12-ounce) container Cool Whip
1 large (15-ounce) can crushed pineapple, drained

Bake cake mix according to directions. While still warm, mix gelatin with hot water; cool gelatin liquid until lukewarm. Punch holes into cake with fork, and pour gelatin over top of cake. Let cool completely.

Drain pineapple (save juice) and mix with instant pudding. Add Cool Whip and mix well. If too stiff, add a little pineapple juice. Nuts can be added. Spread on cooled cake. Refrigerate.

Leota L. Arnold, Vincennes, Ind.

CHOCOLATE PEANUT BUTTER CAKE

2-1/4 cups flour
1 cup peanut butter
1/2 cup butter or margarine, softened
2 cups brown sugar, packed
1 cup milk

3 eggs
1 teaspoon baking powder
1/2 teaspoon baking soda
1 teaspoon vanilla
1 (6-ounce) package chocolate chips

In large mixing bowl, combine flour, peanut butter, margarine and brown sugar until crumbly, using mixer's low speed. Measure 1 cup crumbs for topping. To remaining crumbs, add milk, eggs, baking powder, baking soda, and vanilla. Blend until moistened. Beat 3 minutes on medium speed, scraping bowl often.

Generously grease and flour 9x13-inch pan. Pour batter into pan and sprinkle with reserved crumbs. Sprinkle with chocolate chips. Bake at 350 degrees for 35-40 minutes.

This is my grandchildren's *favorite* cake!!

Dorothy Sorensen, Muskego, Wis.

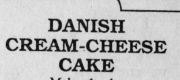

DANISH CREAM-CHEESE CAKE
Makes 1 cake

1 package (8-roll size) crescent roll dough
1 large package (8 ounces) cream cheese, softened
1 egg beaten
1 1/2 tablespoons flour
1/2 cup sugar
1 teaspoon vanilla
1/2 cup chopped nuts
1/2 cup sugar
1 teaspoon cinnamon
Additional nuts for garnish
Confectioners' sugar

Unroll crescent roll dough onto a greased cookie sheet. Pinch perforations between individual rolls to seal dough. Combine cream cheese, egg, flour, sugar and vanilla, and beat until fluffy. Spread filling over dough. Combine 1/2 cup nuts, the sugar and cinnamon, and sprinkle over cheese mixture. Fold dough around filling. Sprinkle with additional nuts.

Bake in a preheated 350-degree oven for 30 minutes, or until browned. Cool. Sprinkle with confectioners' sugar.

This is easy and quick, and delicious with morning coffee.

Mrs. Doris Szabo, Fonda, N.Y.

CRANBERRY SWIRL CAKE

Makes one 10-inch tube or bundt cake

1/4 cup butter
1 cup sugar
2 eggs
2 cups flour
1 teaspoon baking powder
1 teaspoon baking soda
1/2 teaspoon salt
1 cup sour cream
1 teaspoon vanilla
1 cup whole-berry cranberry sauce
1/3 cup chopped nuts
Glaze:3/4 cup confectioners' sugar
1/2 teaspoon vanilla
Warm water

Cream butter and sugar until fluffy. Add eggs and blend well. Sift dry ingredients together and add to creamed mixture alternately with sour cream which has been mixed with vanilla. Mix well.

Pour half the batter into a greased 10-inch tube or bundt pan. Top with 1/2 cup cranberry sauce, and pour remaining batter over sauce. Top with remaining cranberry sauce, and swirl through batter with a knife. Sprinkle nuts on top.

Bake in preheated 350-degree oven for about 50 minutes, or until done. Cool cake.

Make *Glaze* by mixing sugar and vanilla with enough warm water to make a glaze consistency. Top cooled cake with *Glaze*.

Judy Haffner, Auke Bay, Alaska

BLACK BOTTOM CUPCAKES

Part 1:
8 ounces cream cheese, softened
1 egg
1/3 cup granulated sugar
1/8 teaspoon salt
Large handful of chocolate chips

Part 2:
1-1/2 cups plus 1 tablespoon all-purpose flour
1 cup granulated sugar
1/4 cup cocoa powder
1/2 teaspoon salt
1 cup warm water

1 teaspoon soda mixed with 1 tablespoon white vinegar
1/2 cup salad oil
1 teaspoon vanilla

Mix Part 1 ingredients together, adding chocolate chips last; set aside. Mix Part 2 ingredients together. Fill paper-lined muffin cups half-full of Part 2 and top each with 1 tablespoon of Part 1. Bake at 350 degrees for 20-25 minutes, until toothpick comes out clean.

These cupcakes are wonderful treats for all ages!

Sandra J. Stevenson, Matthews, N.C.

PUMPKIN FRUIT CAKE

1 package (15 ounces) seedless raisins
1/2 cup self-rising flour*
1-1/2 pounds mixed candied fruit
2 cups chopped walnuts
2 teaspoons cinnamon
2 teaspoons nutmeg
1 teaspoon ginger
1 cup melted margarine
3 cups mashed, cooked pumpkin
3 eggs, well beaten
3/4 cup sugar

Preheat oven to 325 degrees. Combine first four ingredients in a bowl. Combine remaining ingredients and mix well. Add fruit mixture and mix until well blended. Spoon into greased 10-inch tube pan or two 9-inch bread pans. Bake for 2-1/2 hours, or until done.

*Can use 1/2 cup all-purpose flour, adding 1/4 teaspoon salt, 1 teaspoon baking powder, and 1/2 teaspoon soda.

Judy Haffner, Auke Bay, Alaska

BROWNIES IN A CONE

Makes 12

12 flat-bottom ice-cream cones
1 (21- or 23-ounce) box brownie mix
1 (6-ounce) package chocolate chips
3/4 stick butter (or 6 tablespoons)
Candy sprinkles

Preheat oven to 350 degrees. Place cones in muffin tins or on baking sheet. Prepare brownie mix according to package directions. Spoon batter into cones, three-fourths full. Bake for 30-35 minutes, or until tops are cracked and have risen above the rims of the cones. Remove the cones from oven and cool to room temperature.

Frosting:

Melt chips and butter. Stir until smooth. Dip tops of brownies into chocolate. If not well-covered, dip again. Stand the cones upright and sprinkle tops with candy sprinkles. Let cones stand at room temperature until the chocolate hardens.

Vickie Vogt, Kewaskum, Wis.

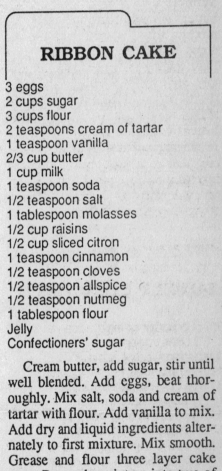

RIBBON CAKE

3 eggs
2 cups sugar
3 cups flour
2 teaspoons cream of tartar
1 teaspoon vanilla
2/3 cup butter
1 cup milk
1 teaspoon soda
1/2 teaspoon salt
1 tablespoon molasses
1/2 cup raisins
1/2 cup sliced citron
1 teaspoon cinnamon
1/2 teaspoon cloves
1/2 teaspoon allspice
1/2 teaspoon nutmeg
1 tablespoon flour
Jelly
Confectioners' sugar

Cream butter, add sugar, stir until well blended. Add eggs, beat thoroughly. Mix salt, soda and cream of tartar with flour. Add vanilla to mix. Add dry and liquid ingredients alternately to first mixture. Mix smooth. Grease and flour three layer cake pans. Pour cake mixture into two of them. To remaining cake mixture add molasses, raisins, sliced citron, cinnamon, cloves, allspice, nutmeg, and flour; mix well. Pour into third cake pan. Bake 25 minutes in moderate 350 degree oven. Turn out of pans and cool. Put layers together with jelly. Dust top layer with confectioners' sugar.

Susan Wiener, Spring Hill, Fla.

CARDAMOM POUND CAKE

1 pound butter
1 pound brown sugar
6 eggs
2 teaspoons vanilla
4 cups sifted all-purpose flour
1 teaspoon baking powder
1-1/2 teaspoons ground cardamom
2 cups cut dates
2 cups diced candied cherries
Powdered sugar

Have ingredients at room temperature. Cream butter; add sugar gradually; beat in eggs one at a time; mix well. Add vanilla. Blend in sifted dry ingredients. Stir in dates and cherries. Pour into greased and floured 10-inch tube pan. Bake at 300 degrees about 1 hour and 45 minutes. Cool in pan 10 minutes before removing. Cool completely, wrap and store in refrigerator at least a week before serving. Sprinkle with powdered sugar before serving.   **Kit Rollins, Cedarburg, Wisc.**

PUMPKIN SPICE CAKE
Serves 16

2¼ cups cake flour, sifted
1½ teaspoons ground cinnamon
¾ teaspoon ground nutmeg
1 cup pumpkin
Non-calorie liquid sweetener equal to ½ cup sugar
1 (1¼-ounce) envelope low-calorie dessert topping mix, whipped
1 tablespoon baking powder
¾ teaspoon ground cloves
7 eggs, separated
½ cup cooking oil
½ teaspoon finely shredded orange peel
½ teaspoon cream of tartar

Sift together flour, baking powder, spices and ¼ teaspoon salt. Combine egg yolks, pumpkin, cooking oil, sweetener and orange peel; beat until

smooth. Wash beaters; beat egg whites and cream of tartar to stiff peaks. Fold pumpkin mixture into whites. Sprinkle ¼ dry ingredients atop. Fold in dry ingredients, adding ¼ at a time. Turn into an ungreased 9-inch tube pan. Bake in 325-degree oven for 45 minutes. Invert in pan; cool. Remove from pan; serve with topping.
Diane Votaw, Decatur, Ind.

SWEET APPLE CIDER CAKE

4 cups all-purpose flour
3 teaspoons baking soda
¼ teaspoon salt
1 teaspoon cinnamon
¼ teaspoon allspice
⅛ teaspoon cloves
1 cup currants
½ cup vegetable shortening
½ cup brown sugar, firmly packed
½ cup granulated sugar
4 eggs, separated
2 cups sweet apple cider

Mix and sift dry ingredients; add currants. Cream shortening and sugars. Add egg yolks; beat thoroughly. Add flour mixture alternately with cider; fold in stiffly beaten egg whites. Turn into greased loaf pan; bake at 350 degrees for 1 hour. Dust top with confectioners' sugar.
Gwen Campbell, Sterling, Va.

SOUR CREAM TOPPED CHOCOLATE TORTE

1 package fudge brownie mix
2 teaspoons vanilla extract
1/3 cup chopped cashew nuts
2 tablespoons chopped walnuts
Raspberry jam
Coconut for garnish
Chocolate frosting (recipe follows)

Prepare the package of fudge brownie mix according to box directions. Add vanilla extract, walnuts and cashews; mix well. Spread in

well-greased 15x10x1-inch baking pan. Bake in preheated hot 400 degree oven 10-12 minutes. Cool; cut crosswise into 3 equal parts. Put layers together with a thin layer of raspberry jam and chocolate frosting. Spread remaining frosting on top. Sprinkle with coconut for garnish.

Chocolate Frosting:
1 (4 ounce) package sweet cooking chocolate
1/2 cup sour cream

Melt cooking chocolate over hot water. Add sour cream and blend well. Use immediately.
Marie Fusaro, Manasquan, N.J.

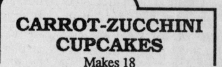

CARROT-ZUCCHINI CUPCAKES
Makes 18

1 1/2 cups all-purpose flour, unsifted
1 cup sugar
1 teaspoon baking powder
1 teaspoon ground cinnamon
1/2 teaspoon salt
1/2 teaspoon baking soda
3/4 cup vegetable oil
2 large eggs
1 teaspoon vanilla extract
1 cup coarsely shredded carrots
1 cup coarsely shredded zucchini
1/2 cup golden raisins
Cream Cheese Frosting (recipe follows)

Preheat oven to 350 degrees. Line 18 muffin-pan cups with fluted paper liners. In large bowl, combine flour, sugar, baking powder, cinnamon, salt and baking soda.

In cup or small bowl, beat together oil, eggs and vanilla. Stir oil mixture into flour mixture just until mixed. Fold in carrots, zucchini and raisins. Spoon into cups. Bake for 20–25 minutes. Cool cupcakes on wire rack. Prepare Cream Cheese Frosting. Frost cupcakes and sprinkle with nuts.

Cream Cheese Frosting:
In a small bowl, using electric mixer, cream 3 ounces cream cheese, softened, with 1 1/2 cups sifted confectioners' sugar and 1 teaspoon vanilla extract; beat until fluffy.
Mrs. K.W. Kenney, Richmond, Va.

PEANUT BUTTER CAKE

1 package butter cake mix
1/2 cup smooth peanut butter
1 stick soft butter or margarine
2/3 cup water
4 eggs

Mix as directed on cake mix package, adding peanut butter to water. Bake according to directions on package. When cool frost with Peanut Butter Frosting (recipe follows).

Peanut Butter Frosting:
1 box confectioners' sugar
1 cup peanut butter
1/2 cup butter
1/4–1/3 cup cream *or* milk

Mix all ingredients until smooth and fluffy. If frosting is too thin, add additional confectioners' sugar.

Leota Baxter, Ingalls, Kan.

GAIL'S RICH CHOCOLATE CAKE

4 (1-ounce) squares unsweetened chocolate, melted
3/4 cup butter or margarine, melted
2 cups sugar
4 eggs, beaten
2 cups sifted flour
1 teaspoon vanilla
1/2 teaspoon baking powder
1 cup buttermilk

Grease and flour 2 (9-inch) layer cake pans. Preheat oven to 350 degrees. Mix chocolate and butter (or melt together). Gradually add sugar to eggs; beat well. Blend in chocolate mixture and vanilla. Stir in blended dry ingredients, alternately with buttermilk. Bake at 350 degrees, for 30-35 minutes or until cake tests done.

Chocolate Cream Cheese Frosting:
1 (3-ounce) package cream cheese, softened
1-1/2 teaspoons milk
1/4 cup unsweetened cocoa
2-1/2 cups sifted confectioners'
sugar
1 teaspoon vanilla

Blend cream cheese and milk. Add combined confectioners' sugar and cocoa to make a frosting of spreading consistency. Add more milk, if needed. Add vanilla. This cake freezes very well, even frosted.

Gail Scharenbroch, Charlevoix, Mich.

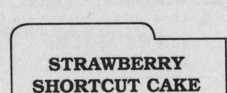

STRAWBERRY SHORTCUT CAKE

1-1/2 cups miniature marshmallows
2 cups **or** 2 (10-ounce) packages frozen sliced strawberries (completely thawed and drained), reserve syrup
1 (3-ounce) package strawberry gelatin
2-1/4 cups all-purpose flour
1-1/2 cups sugar
1/2 cup solid shortening **or** margarine
3 teaspoons baking powder
1/2 teaspoon salt
1 cup milk
1 teaspoon vanilla
3 eggs

Generously grease bottom only of 9x13-inch baking pan. Sprinkle marshmallows evenly over bottom of pan. Combine thawed berries, gelatin, and syrup from berries; stir thoroughly. Set aside.

Combine rest of ingredients, beating about 3 minutes until thoroughly mixed. Pour batter evenly over marshmallows in prepared pan. Spoon strawberry mixture over batter.

Bake at 350 degrees for 45-50 minutes. Serve with whipped cream.

Dorothy Sorensen, Muskego, Wis.

CHOCOLATE-CHERRY UPSIDE-DOWN CAKE

1   (21-ounce) can cherry pie filling
2¼ cups all-purpose flour
1½ cups sugar
¾   cup unsweetened cocoa powder
1½ teaspoons baking soda
¾   teaspoon salt
1½ cups water
¼   cup cooking oil
¼   cup vinegar
1½ teaspoons vanilla

Spread cherry pie filling evenly over bottom of greased 13 x 9 x 2-inch pan. In large bowl, stir flour with sugar, cocoa, soda and salt.

In another bowl, combine water, oil, vinegar and vanilla. Add liquid to dry mixture, all at once. Stir just to moisten. Pour batter evenly in pan over cherry filling.

Bake in preheated 350-degree oven for 30–35 minutes. Cool 10 minutes in pan; invert onto plate and cool.

Corena J. Bennington, Whitestown, Ind.

CHOCOLATE DREAMS
Makes 24

1 package (18.5 ounce) chocolate cake mix
1 cup water
1/3 cup buttermilk
1/2 teaspoon vanilla
2 eggs
1 package (8 ounce) cream cheese, softened
1/2 cup sugar
1 egg
1/2 teaspoon salt
1 package (6 ounce) semi-sweet chocolate pieces
1/2 cup chopped pecans

Preheat oven to 350 degrees. In large bowl, combine cake mix, water, buttermilk and vanilla. Mix until well blended. Add 2 eggs, one at a time, beating after each addition until well blended and smooth. Spoon mixture into greased paper lined muffin tins, filling each cup half full.

In medium bowl, beat together cream cheese and sugar until light and fluffy; beat in 1 egg and salt. Stir in chocolate pieces. Drop 1 tablespoon cheese mixture on each cupcake; sprinkle with nuts. Bake 25-30 minutes or until done.

Bobbie Mae Cooley, Bowen, Ill.

APPLESAUCE CUPCAKES

Makes 1 dozen

1/2 cup shortening
1 egg
1/3 cup sugar
1-3/4 cups sifted cake flour
1 teaspoon baking soda
1/4 teaspoon salt
1 teaspoon cinnamon
1/4 teaspoon cloves
1/4 teaspoon allspice
1/4 teaspoon ginger
1 cup unsweetened applesauce
1/2 teaspoon lemon juice
1 teaspoon vanilla
1/3 cup raisins

Preheat oven to 375 degrees. Cream shortening until fluffy. Beat egg and sugar until lemon-colored. Add to shortening and blend well. Sift together all dry ingredients; add to shortening mixture, alternately with applesauce, blending well after each addition. Stir in lemon juice, vanilla, and raisins. Line 2 small cupcake pans with paper baking cups. Pour batter into paper liners. Fill liners two-thirds full and bake 15 to 20 minutes. If paper cups are not used, grease the cupcake pans very lightly.

Suzan L. Wiener, Spring Hill, Fla.

CRANBERRY-PECAN UPSIDE-DOWN CAKE

1½ cups cranberries
½ cup chopped pecans
½ cup butterscotch topping
⅓ cup margarine
⅔ cup sugar
1 egg
½ teaspoon vanilla
1 cup flour
1½ teaspoons baking powder
½ teaspoon salt
½ cup milk

Arrange cranberries and nuts in the bottom of a greased 8-inch square

pan. Pour topping over. Cream margarine and sugar until light and fluffy. Blend in egg and vanilla. Add combined dry ingredients to creamed mixture alternately with milk, mixing well after each addition. Pour batter over topping mixture. Bake at 350 degrees for 45 minutes, or until toothpick inserted comes out clean. Immediately invert onto serving platter. Serve warm, topped with whipped cream or ice cream.

Shari Crider, Stoughton, Wis.

DOUBLE CHOCOLATE SNACK CAKES

1 2/3 cups all-purpose flour
1 cup packed brown sugar
1/4 cup Hershey's cocoa
1 teaspoon baking soda
1/2 teaspoon salt
1 cup water
1/3 cup vegetable oil
1 teaspoon vinegar
3/4 teaspoon vanilla
1/2 cup Hershey chocolate chips

Heat oven to 350 degrees. Grease and flour 8x8x2-inch square pan *or* 12-cup muffin pan. Combine dry ingredients. Add water, oil, vinegar and vanilla. Beat until smooth. Pour into pan or muffin tin. Sprinkle chocolate chips on top. Bake 35–40 minutes for cake *or* bake 25–30 minutes for cupcakes.

Delicious, easy and economical!
Carol Johnson, Mableton, Ga.

DATE NUT CAKE WITH WHIPPED CREAM

Serves 6

2 large eggs
3/4 cup sugar
1/4 cup evaporated milk
1 (8-ounce) package dates, pitted
1 cup coarsely chopped nuts
3 tablespoons flour
1 teaspoon baking powder
1/2 teaspoon salt

1 cup heavy cream
Maraschino cherries for garnish

In medium bowl of electric mixer, combine eggs, sugar, and evaporated milk; beat well. Fold in dates and nuts until well-combined. Mix together flour, baking powder, and salt; mix into date batter thoroughly. Pour into well-greased 8x12-inch baking pan. Bake at 325 degrees for 20 to 25 minutes, until puffed and slightly browned on top. Remove and cool completely on wire rack. Cake will fall slightly. Just before serving time, whip cream until stiff peaks form. Cut cake into bite-size pieces and layer in serving dish with whipped cream. Garnish with maraschino cherries.

Leona Teodori, Warren, Mich.

APPLE WALNUT CAKE

Serves 12–15

1 (21-ounce) can apple pie filling
1 cup sugar
2 cups flour
1 teaspoon salt
1½ teaspoons soda
2 eggs, beaten
1 teaspoon vanilla
⅔ cup cooking oil
¾ cup chopped walnuts

Topping:
½ cup sour cream
1 cup sugar
½ teaspoon salt

Preheat oven to 350 degrees. Spread pie filling in bottom of 9 x 13-inch pan. Combine sugar, flour, salt and soda. Sprinkle sugar mixture over pie filling. In bowl combine eggs, vanilla and oil. Mix well. Add ½ cup nuts. Pour over ingredients in pan. Bake at 350 degrees for 40–50 minutes until cake springs back from light touch. Cool on rack for about 20 minutes. Pierce warm cake with a fork.

Combine topping ingredients and stir over medium heat until boiling. Pour over cake and sprinkle with remaining nuts.

Leota Baxter, Ingalls, Kan.

PRUNE SPICE CAKE

1½ cups flour
1 teaspoon baking powder
½ teaspoon soda
½ teaspoon cinnamon
¼ teaspoon ginger
¼ teaspoon salt
¾ cup sugar
¼ cup brown sugar
½ cup oil
1 egg
1 small jar baby prunes
1 teaspoon vanilla
½ cup cold water
½ cup raisins
½ cup nuts, chopped

Sift together the flour, baking powder, soda, cinnamon, salt and ginger. Set aside. Mix together the sugars, oil, egg, prunes and vanilla. Add mixture to dry ingredients. Stir in the cold water and beat 1 minute at medium speed. Stir in the raisins and nuts. Pour into loaf pan which has been greased and floured. Bake 30 minutes at 350 degrees. Let cool in pan. Remove from pan and glaze with ½ cup confectioners' sugar, 1 tablespoon cream and ¼ teaspoon vanilla.

Margaret Hamfeldt, Louisville, Ky.

JAVA SPICE CAKE

2 cups hot, strong coffee
1 cup finely chopped prunes
¾ cup raisins
1 cup finely chopped pecans
2¾ cups cake flour
1 tablespoon baking powder
½ teaspoon baking soda
½ teaspoon ground allspice
½ teaspoon ground pepper
6 tablespoons butter, room temperature
1½ cups sugar
3 eggs
Coffee Frosting (recipe follows)

Coffee Frosting:
½ cup butter, room temperature
6 ounces cream cheese, room temperature
3 tablespoons instant coffee powder, dissolved in 6 tablespoons hot coffee
7–8 cups sifted confectioners' sugar
3–4 drops angostura bitters

Preheat oven to 350 degrees. Grease 3 (9-inch) round cake pans. Dust with flour. In small bowl, pour hot coffee over prunes and raisins. In another bowl, mix pecans with ¼ cup flour. Sift together remaining flour, baking powder, baking soda, allspice and pepper. In a large bowl, cream butter with sugar. Add eggs. Beat until light and fluffy. Add flour mixture alternately with prune-coffee mixture, stirring well after each addition. Fold in flour-coated pecans. Pour into prepared pans. Bake 30–40 minutes, or until top springs back when touched lightly. Turn out onto rack. Cool completely. Prepare Coffee Frosting. Put layers together with about half the frosting. Cover sides and top with remaining frosting. Garnish with pecan halves.

Frosting:
Cream butter and cream cheese until smooth. Add dissolved coffee. Beat until blended. Add confectioners' sugar. Continue to beat until light and fluffy. Stir in bitters. If needed, add more confectioners' sugar to bring to spreading consistency.

Laura Hicks, Troy, Mont.

MOM'S APPLE CAKE

2 cups sugar
4 eggs
1 cup salad oil
3 cups flour
1 teaspoon baking soda
½ teaspoon salt
1 teaspoon ground cinnamon
1 teaspoon vanilla extract
2 cups diced apples

1 cup dark, seedless raisins
1 cup nuts (optional)
Apple Glaze (recipe follows)

Preheat oven to 350 degrees. With mixer beat sugar and eggs for 5 minutes. Slowly beat in salad oil. Beat in flour, soda, salt, cinnamon and extract. With spoon stir in apples, raisins and nuts. Bake 1 hour and 10 minutes, or until done. Remove cake from pan.

Apple Glaze:
1⅓ cups confectioners' sugar
2 tablespoons apple juice
Nuts

Mix well; sprinkle with nuts and spoon over cake, letting some run down the sides.

APRICOT-APPLE-SAUCE CAKE

Serves 12-15

1 cup all-purpose flour
3/4 cup whole-wheat flour
2 teaspoons ground allspice
1 teaspoon baking soda
1/2 cup sugar
1/2 cup shortening
1 cup applesauce
2 eggs
3/4 cup diced, dried apricots
1/2 cup chopped nuts (pecans, walnuts, or almonds)
Confectioners' sugar

Preheat oven to 350 degrees. Grease a 12-cup bundt pan or tube pan. Combine flours, allspice, and baking soda; set aside. In a large bowl, with mixer at low speed, cream sugar and shortening; beat in applesauce and eggs until fluffy. Add flour mixture; beat at medium speed for 2 minutes, scraping bowl occasionally. Stir in apricots and nuts. Pour batter into pan and bake 30-40 minutes until top springs back when lightly touched with finger. Cool cake in pan 10 minutes; invert onto serving platter and dust lightly with confectioners' sugar.

Leota Baxter, Ingalls, Kan.

JELLY BEAN CONFETTI CAKE

2 cups all-purpose flour
3/4 cup miniature jelly beans, cut in half (not licorice)
1 cup sugar
1 cup butter or margarine, softened
1 (8-ounce) package cream cheese, softened
1 teaspoon vanilla
3 eggs
1-1/2 teaspoons baking powder
1/4 teaspoon salt
Confectioners' sugar

Heat oven to 325 degrees. Generously grease and flour 12-cup fluted tube pan or angel-cake pan. Lightly spoon flour into measuring cup. Level off. In small bowl, toss jelly beans with 2 tablespoons of the flour. Set aside.

In large bowl, beat sugar, butter, cream cheese, and vanilla until well blended. Add eggs one at a time, beating well after each addition. Add remaining flour, baking powder, and salt. Blend well. Spoon 1 cup of batter evenly over bottom of prepared pan. Stir jelly beans into remaining batter; spoon into baking pan. Bake in a 325 degree oven for 50 to 60 minutes, or until toothpick inserted in center of cake comes out clean. Cool upright in pan 10 minutes. Invert on serving plate. Cool completely. Sprinkle with confectioners' sugar.

MOCK CRAB CAKES

2 cups zucchini squash, peeled and grated
1 cup seasoned bread crumbs
1 teaspoon Old Bay seasoning
1 egg, well beaten
1 tablespoon mayonnaise
Butter flavored Crisco

Mix all ingredients together. Form mixture into individual serving patties, then roll in bread crumbs. Fry patties in butter flavored Crisco until crispy and golden brown.
Peggy Fowler Revels, Woodruff, S.C.

APPLE CAKE WITH NUT TOPPING

3/4 cup cooking oil
2 cups sugar
2 eggs beaten
3 cups flour
1-1/2 teaspoons soda
1 teaspoon salt
1 teaspoon vanilla
1 cup chopped walnuts
3 cups chopped apples (with peelings)

Mix oil, sugar, and eggs and blend well. Add dry ingredients and vanilla by hand. Blend in nuts and apples. Spoon batter into a well-greased tube or bundt pan. Bake at 350 degrees for 1 hour. Remove from oven and pour topping over cake. Return cake to oven and bake 15 minutes more. Cool on wire rack. Slide knife around cake to loosen.

Topping:
1 cup light brown sugar
1 stick butter or margarine
1/4 cup orange juice
Cook over low heat for 3 minutes after the mixture starts boiling. Pour over cake and continue as directed.
Mrs. P. B. Brothers, Richmond, Va.

SOUR CREAM DEVILS FOOD CAKE

2 cups sour cream
2 teaspoons soda
4 eggs
1 teaspoon vanilla
2 cups sugar
2 cups flour
6 tablespoons cocoa

Beat sour cream, soda, eggs, and vanilla until foamy; add sugar, flour, and cocoa that has been sifted together. Pour into a greased and floured pan. Bake at 350 degrees for 30 minutes. Frost with your favorite frosting.
Mildred Sherrer, Bay City, Texas

CREAM CHEESE POUND CAKE

3/4 cup butter or margarine
1 (8-ounce) package cream cheese, room temperature
1-1/2 cups sugar
1-1/2 teaspoons vanilla
4 eggs
1-3/4 cups flour
1-1/2 teaspoons baking powder

Cream butter and cream cheese until light; add sugar gradually, beating constantly. Add vanilla. Beat in eggs, one at a time. Combine flour and baking powder; add to creamed mixture, beating well. Pour into greased 9x5-inch loaf pan. Bake at 350 degrees for 1 hour and 15 minutes or until wooden pick inserted in center comes out clean. Cool in pan 10 minutes. Turn onto a cake rack to cool completely
Suzanne Dawson, Cypress, Tex.

RHUBARB CAKE

1-1/2 cups brown sugar
1/2 cup shortening
1 egg
1 teaspoon vanilla
2 cups flour
1 teaspoon soda
1/2 teaspoon salt
1 cup buttermilk or sour cream
1-3/4 cups chopped rhubarb, may use frozen
1/2 cup chocolate chips

Topping:
1/2 cup brown sugar
1 teaspoon cinnamon
1/2 cup chopped nuts
1/2 cup chocolate chips

Cream 1-1/2 cups brown sugar, 1/2 cup shortening; add egg and vanilla. Combine flour, soda, and salt together. Add flour mixture, alternating with buttermilk, beating after each addition. Stir in rhubarb and chocolate chips. Pour into greased 9x13-inch pan. Combine topping and sprinkle over cake mixture. Bake at 350 degrees for 45 minutes.

This is a delicious cake. Serve with ice cream, whipped cream, or just plain. You will get raving reviews.
Roselyn Finan, Fort Wayne, Ind.

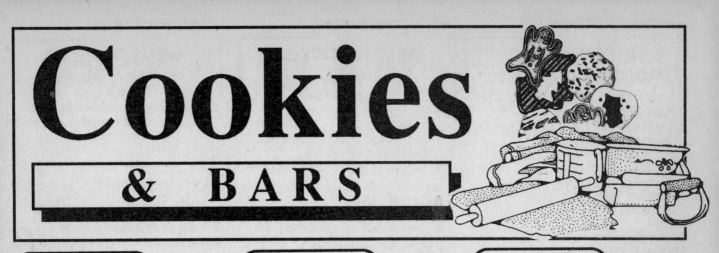

Cookies
& BARS

ENERGY COOKIES

1/2 cup (1 stick) butter, softened
1 egg
1 teaspoon vanilla
1 cup oatmeal
1/2 cup flour
1 1/4 cups big raisins
1/2 cup walnuts or almonds
2 tablespoons Bran Buds®
1/2 cup chocolate chips

Preheat oven to 350 degrees. Grease an 8-inch square pan.

In large bowl, combine butter, egg and vanilla; beat until well-blended. Add oats and flour, stirring to mix well. Stir in raisins and walnuts. Spread batter evenly over bottom of pan. Sprinkle with bran. Bake for 25 minutes at 350 degrees. Cool in pan. Cut into squares.

Lucy Dowd, Sequim, Wash.

PECAN BUTTERY COOKIES

1 stick butter (1/2 cup)
1/2 stick margarine
1 package butter pecan instant pudding mix
1-1/4 cups all-purpose flour
1 teaspoon vanilla extract
1/4 teaspoon almond extract

Cream together first 3 ingredients. Add flour and extracts; mix well; chill. Shape into 1-inch balls; press down with fork to make an attractive design. Bake at 350 degrees for 10–12 minutes.

Gwen Campbell, Sterling, Va.

PISTACHIO PUDDING COOKIES
Makes 7 dozen

2¼ cups unsifted all-purpose flour
1 teaspoon baking soda
1 cup margarine, well-softened
¼ cup granulated white sugar
¾ cup brownulated light brown sugar
½ teaspoon vanilla
½ teaspoon almond extract
1 (4-ounce) package pistachio instant pudding (used dry)
2 eggs
1 (12-ounce) package butterscotch morsels
1 cup chopped walnuts
Few drops green food coloring, if desired

Mix flour and baking soda in medium bowl. Combine margarine, both sugars, both extracts and instant pudding powder in large mixing bowl. Beat until smooth. Beat in eggs, 1 at a time. Gradually stir in flour mixture. Stir in morsels and nuts. Batter will be very stiff; mix well with floured hands. Cover bowl; chill several hours or overnight for easier shaping. Form into smooth balls by teaspoonfuls. Place 2 inches apart on ungreased cookie sheets. Bake at 375 degrees for 8–10 minutes. Do not overbake. If desired, drizzle with confectioners' sugar icing mixed with a few drops of green food coloring.

These are absolutely delicious. Don't wait for St. Patrick's Day to enjoy them. Have them anytime during the year when you feel like a special cookie treat!!

Hyacinth Rizzo, Snyder, N.Y.

LEMON DROPS
Makes 4 dozen

3 eggs, separated
1 teaspoon grated lemon rind
½ teaspoon lemon extract
½ cup confectioners' sugar
⅓ cup sifted flour

Beat egg yolks until thick and lemon-colored. Stir in rind and extract. Beat egg whites until stiff but not dry. Gradually add confectioners' sugar and beat until stiff. Fold in egg yolk mixture. Gently fold in flour. Drop by teaspoon onto paper-lined baking sheets. Bake in moderate 350-degree oven about 12 minutes, or until golden brown.

Agnes Ward, Erie, Pa.

BASIC BUTTER COOKIES
Makes 30 cookies

1 cup all-purpose flour
1/2 cup cornstarch
1/2 cup powdered sugar
3/4 cup (1-1/2 sticks) real butter, room temperature
1/2 cup coarsely-chopped walnuts

Preheat oven to 300 degrees. Sift first 3 ingredients into large bowl. Add butter and mix well. Stir in walnuts. Drop by teaspoons onto baking sheets. Bake until cookies are lightly golden, about 20-25 minutes.

NOTE: Real butter is the secret of these buttery-tasting cookies.

Agnes Ward, Erie, Pa.

SPRITZ

Makes 7–8 dozen

- 1 cup (2 sticks) butter
- ½ cup sugar
- 1 egg
- ½ teaspoon almond extract
- 2¼ cups all-purpose flour
  Food coloring
  Decorative candies

Preheat oven to 350 degrees. Cream butter. Gradually add sugar and continue beating until blended. Beat in egg and almond extract. Gradually blend in flour. Add food coloring, if desired. Fill cookie press. Using star attachment, form circles on unbuttered cookie sheets ... or use other press designs. Decorate with sugar crystals, other candies or nuts. Bake 8–10 minutes. Remove to wire rack to cool.

MISSISSIPPI MUD BARS

- 2 cups sugar
- 1 cup margarine
- 3 tablespoons cocoa
- 4 eggs
- 1½ cups flour
- 1¼ cups coconut
- 1½ cups chopped nuts
- 1 (7-ounce) jar marshmallow creme

Cream together sugar, margarine and cocoa. Add eggs and mix well. Add flour, coconut and nuts. Blend thoroughly.

Bake in greased 12 x 15-inch cookie sheet at 350 degrees for 25–30 minutes. Remove from oven and spread with marshmallow creme.

Frosting:
- 1 pound confectioners' sugar
- ½ cup evaporated milk
- ½ cup cocoa
- ½ cup soft margarine
- 1 teaspoon vanilla

Cream together frosting ingredients, blending well. When bars are cool, frost.

Mrs. L. Mayer, Richmond, Va.

APPLE-BUTTER BARS

Makes 3 dozen

- 1½ cups flour
- 1 teaspoon baking soda
- 1 teaspoon salt
- 1½ cups quick-cooking oats, uncooked
- 1½ cups sugar
- 1 cup butter *or* margarine, melted
- 1½ cups apple butter
- 1 cup chopped pecans *or* walnuts

Combine flour, baking soda and salt in a large mixing bowl. Mix in oats and sugar. Pour in melted butter and mix well.

Press half of this mixture into a greased 13 x 9 x 2-inch baking pan. Mix apple butter and nuts together; spread over mixture in pan. Sprinkle with remaining crumbly mixture.

Bake at 350 degrees for 50–60 minutes, or until brown. Cool before cutting into bars.

Mary Williams, Columbus, Ohio

HERMITS

Makes 4 dozen

- 1 cup light brown sugar
- ¼ cup margarine, softened
- ¼ cup shortening
- ¼ cup cold coffee
- 1 egg
- 1 teaspoon ground cinnamon
- ½ teaspoon ground nutmeg
- 1¾ cups all-purpose flour
- ½ teaspoon baking soda
- 1¼ cups seedless raisins
- ¾ cup chopped walnuts

In large bowl, mix together brown sugar, margarine, shortening, coffee, egg, cinnamon and nutmeg. Stir in remaining ingredients. Drop dough by rounded teaspoonfuls, 2 inches apart, onto ungreased cookie sheet.

Bake in preheated 375-degree oven for 10 minutes. Immediately remove from cookie sheet.

June Harding, Royal Oak, Mich.

STIR 'N DROP COOKIES

Makes 5 dozen
(A new version of old-fashioned sugar cookies)

- 2 eggs
- 2/3 cup cooking oil
- 2 teaspoons vanilla
- 1 teaspoon grated lemon peel
- 3/4 cup sugar
- 2 cups sifted all-purpose flour
- 2 teaspoons baking powder
- 1/2 teaspoon salt

Heat oven to 400 degrees. Beat eggs with fork. Stir in oil, vanilla, lemon peel. Blend in sugar (reserve 1 tablespoonful).

Sift together flour, baking powder, salt; add to egg mixture. Drop by teaspoonfuls about 2 inches apart onto ungreased cookie sheets. Stamp each cookie flat with bottom of glass dipped in sugar. (Lightly oil glass, then dip in reserved sugar — continue dipping sugar). Bake 8 to 10 minutes. Remove at once from cookie sheet. If you bake the cookies one sheet at a time, stir the mixture between each batch. (50 calories per cookie)

Note: When dipping glass in sugar, cookies can be decorated with colored candy bits (not counted in calories). Cookies bake in perfect rounds; come out shiny with sugar and fragrant with homemade flavor!

Claire Marie J. Heroux, Linwood, Mass.

BANANA COOKIES (DIABETIC)

Makes 2 dozen

- 3 medium bananas, mashed
- ⅓ cup oil
- 1 teaspoon vanilla extract
- 2 cups old-fashioned rolled oats
- 1¼ cups chopped walnuts
- ¼ cup raisins

Combine bananas, oil and vanilla. Stir in oats, walnuts and raisins. Drop by tablespoonfuls onto greased cookie sheets. Press down lightly with fork. Preheat oven to 350 degrees. Bake 10–12 minutes until golden brown.

Kit Rollins, Cedarburg, Wis.

MAPLE BARS

1 1/2 cups milk
1/2 cup shortening
4 tablespoons sugar
2 teaspoons salt
2 yeast cakes
4 tablespoons warm water
4 3/4 cups flour
3 eggs, beaten well
Frosting (recipe follows)

Bring milk to boiling point and pour over shortening, sugar and salt in a large bowl. Cool to lukewarm. Dissolve yeast in warm water, and add to lukewarm mixture in bowl along with flour and eggs. Mix well.

Grease bowl and add dough, turning to grease top. Cover and let rise in a warm place until doubled. Turn out onto a well-floured board, and roll 1/2 inch thick. Cut into 2x4-inch pieces. Let rise again in warm place until double.

Deep-fry in oil heated to 375 degrees in deep skillet or fryer until golden on all sides. Remove to paper towels to drain. Make *Frosting,* and frost bars while still warm.

Frosting:
1 1/2 cups confectioners' sugar
3 tablespoons butter
Milk
Maple syrup

Cream sugar and butter, adding a little milk and maple syrup to form an icing of spreading consistency.

Laura Kinzler, Camano Island, Wash.

HEAVENLY CRUNCH

1 package from a box of graham crackers
2 sticks margarine
½ cup sugar
⅔ cup chopped pecans

Spread crackers in large jelly roll pan. Chop pecans and sprinkle over crackers. Melt margarine in saucepan. Add sugar; boil 3 minutes. Pour over crackers. Bake in 350-degree oven for 10–15 minutes. Remove from pan before they cool completely. Break into sections. These are delicious!

Joni Bowen, Belen, Miss.

PRIDE OF OHIO COOKIES

1 cup brown sugar
1 cup white sugar
1 cup shortening
1 cup flour
2 eggs
1 cup coconut
1 cup nut meats, chopped
1 teaspoon vanilla
1 teaspoon soda
1 teaspoon baking powder
½ teaspoon salt
3 cups quick rolled oats

Beat eggs in mixing bowl; add sugars and softened shortening. Blend well. Stir in coconut, nuts and vanilla. Sift flour and measure, then add soda, baking powder and salt, then sift again. Combine with other mixture. Stir in rolled oats; mix thoroughly by hand. Roll in small balls the size of a walnut and place on ungreased cookie sheet. Bake at 375 degrees for about 9 minutes, or until nicely browned.

Marjorie Baxla, Greenfield, Ohio

CHOCOLATE FUDGE COOKIES

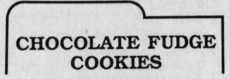

1¼ cups brown sugar
½ cup butter
1 egg
½ cup milk
2 teaspoons baking powder
2 cups flour
1 teaspoon vanilla
¼ teaspoon salt
2½ squares chocolate, melted

Cream butter and add sugar gradually. Add egg and beat. Mix baking powder with salt and flour, then add vanilla to milk. Add liquid and dry ingredients alternately to egg mixture. Add dry ingredients first and last. Add melted chocolate. Drop from teaspoon onto greased baking sheets and bake 10 minutes in a moderately hot 375-degree oven.

These cookies are delicious plain or iced with chocolate frosting!

Suzan L. Wiener, Spring Hill, Fla.

PEANUT JEWELS

1 cup creamy peanut butter
1 cup seedless raisins
½ cup honey
1 teaspoon vanilla
1 cup coconut, flaked or shredded

Mix peanut butter and honey; add raisins and vanilla. Spread coconut on waxed paper or cookie sheet. Drop mixture on coconut, in teaspoonfuls. Roll to coat. Chill.

Suzan L. Wiener, Spring Hill, Fla.

ICED MOLASSES BARS

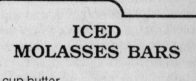

1 cup butter
1/2 cup sugar
1 cup light molasses
1 egg
3-1/2 cups cake flour, sifted
1 teaspoon soda
1 teaspoon ginger
1 teaspoon cinnamon
1 teaspoon salt
1/2 cup sour cream

Cream butter and sugar until light. Beat in molasses and egg. Add sifted flour, soda, seasonings, and sour cream. Beat until smooth. Spread in greased jelly roll pan. Bake in a moderate oven of 350 degrees for 30 minutes. Cool in pan.

Sour Cream Frosting:
1 cup sour cream
2 cups sugar
Dash of salt
1 teaspoon vanilla

Blend sour cream, sugar, and salt in heavy saucepan. Put over high heat and cook, stirring rapidly, for about 10 minutes, or until smooth and mixture forms a soft ball when tested in cold water. Add vanilla. Spread on top of baked layer and cut into bars. (If preferred, the molasses bars may be iced with your favorite chocolate frosting.)

Trenda Leigh, Richmond, Va.

SOFT GINGER COOKIES

1/2 cup shortening
1 cup sugar
1 egg
1/3 cup molasses
1 1/2 teaspoons cinnamon
1 1/2 teaspoons cloves
1 1/2 teaspoons nutmeg
1/4 teaspoon salt
1 teaspoon ginger
1/2 cup milk
2 1/2 cups flour
1 teaspoon baking powder
1 teaspoon baking soda

Cream together first four ingredients. Stir in spices, salt and milk. Add dry ingredients, and mix well. With teaspoon heap on dough and dip in sugar. Slide off onto cookie sheet. Bake in a 350-degree oven for 8-10 minutes.

These are soft cookies and very good.

Emma B. Walters, Dayton, Wyo.

CRUNCHY OATMEAL COOKIES
Makes 4 dozen

1 cup flour
2 teaspoons baking soda
1 teaspoon baking powder
½ teaspoon salt
1 cup shortening
2 cups cornflakes
1 cup sugar
1 cup brown sugar, packed
2 eggs
1 teaspoon vanilla extract
2 cups uncooked, quick-cooking oats

Combine flour, soda, baking powder and salt. Set aside. In large bowl, cream shortening and sugars; beat in eggs and vanilla. Add flour mixture, mixing well. Stir in oats and cornflakes. Drop by heaping tablespoonfuls onto lightly greased cookie sheets. Bake at 325 degrees for 12–14 minutes.

Cool for 2 minutes on cookie sheet; remove to wire racks and cool completely.

Fran Sievers, Atlanta, Ga.

FORGOTTEN COOKIES

1 large egg white
1/8 teaspoon salt
1/3 cup sugar
1/2 cup chopped pecans
1/2 cup miniature chocolate chips

Beat egg white and salt to soft peaks. Add sugar, 1 tablespoon at a time, beating until stiff and glossy. Stir in chips and nuts. Drop by teaspoon onto foil-covered cookie sheet. Preheat oven to 350 degrees. Place cookies in oven and then turn oven temperature dial off. Do not open the door; leave in oven overnight.

Sharon McClatchey, Muskogee, Okla.

LEMON SUGAR COOKIES
Makes 4 dozen

2¾ cups flour
2 teaspoons baking powder
¼ teaspoon salt
1 cup butter
2 cups sugar
2 eggs
2 teaspoons grated lemon rind
3 tablespoons lemon juice
1 cup quick oats

Sift together flour, baking powder and salt. In large bowl, cream butter and sugar. Add eggs, beating well. Beat in lemon rind and juice. Gradually add flour mixture, then stir in oats. Chill dough thoroughly (at least 2 hours). Roll level tablespoons dough into balls and place on greased cookie sheets, allowing room for cookies to spread. Using a flat-bottom glass or custard cup that has been greased and dipped in sugar, flatten each ball to ¼-inch thickness (dip glass in sugar each time). Bake at 375 degrees until lightly browned around edges, about 8–10 minutes. Cool for 1 minute, then carefully remove from cookie sheets; cool on racks. These cookies are delicate and delicious.

Barbara Beauregard-Smith, Northfield, South Australia

CRUNCHY PEANUT BUTTER COOKIES

Makes 3 - 3-1/2 dozen

1/2 cup margarine (softened)
1/2 cup brown sugar
1/2 cup granulated sugar
1/4 cup peanut butter
1 egg
1/2 teaspoon vanilla
1 cup flour
1/2 teaspoon baking powder
1/2 teaspoon soda
1/2 teaspoon salt
1 cup corn flakes
1 cup rolled oats

Preheat oven to 375 degrees. Cream margarine and both sugars. Beat in peanut butter, egg, and vanilla. Stir in remaining ingredients until well-blended. Drop by teaspoonfuls, 2 inches apart, on lightly greased cookie sheets. Bake 10-12 minutes, or until golden brown.

Jodie McCoy, Tulsa, Okla.

BUTTER CRISPS
Makes 7 dozen

1 cup (2 sticks) butter
1 (3-ounce) package cream cheese, softened
1 cup sugar
1 egg yolk
1 teaspoon vanilla extract
2 cups all-purpose flour
¼ teaspoon *each* salt, baking powder

Preheat oven to 350 degrees. Cream together butter and cream cheese. Gradually add sugar and continue beating until blended. Beat in egg yolk and vanilla. Combine flour, salt and baking powder; gradually add to creamed mixture. Fill cookie press. Use attachments to form cookie designs on unbuttered cookie sheets. Bake 12–15 minutes. Remove to wire rack to cool.

Note: Before baking, dough may be tinted, sprinkled with colored sugar or a cinnamon-sugar mixture, or decorate cookies with a tinted frosting after baking.

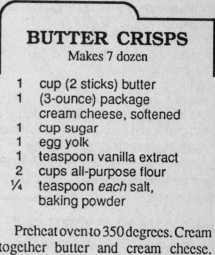

COWBOY COOKIES

Makes 6 dozen

1 1/2 cups sugar
1 1/2 cups brown sugar
3/4 cup shortening
3/4 cup margarine
3 eggs
1 teaspoon vanilla
3 cups flour
1 1/2 teaspoons baking soda
3/4 teaspoon baking powder
3/4 teaspoon salt
3 cups oatmeal
1 package (6 ounces) chocolate or
  butterscotch morsels

Cream shortening and margarine; add both sugars, eggs and vanilla. Mix in flour and other dry ingredients. Add chocolate chips.

Drop by well-rounded teaspoonsful onto ungreased cookie sheets. Bake at 350 degrees for 12-15 minutes.

Mrs. Cleo Brown, Shelby, Ohio

BUTTER PECAN TURTLE BARS

Makes 2 dozen

Crust:
  2 cups flour
  2 cups firmly packed brown
    sugar
  1/2 cup soft butter

Combine all ingredients. Mix at medium speed with mixer, 2–3 minutes, or until particles are fine. Pat into ungreased 9 x 12-inch pan.

Filling:
  1 cup pecan halves or hickory
    nuts
  2/3 cup butter
  1/2 cup firmly packed brown sugar
  1 cup milk chocolate chips

Spread nuts over crust. Cook, stirring constantly, the butter and brown sugar over medium heat until entire surface of mixture begins to boil, about 1 minute. Pour over pecans. Bake for 20 minutes at 350 degrees. Remove from oven; sprinkle with chocolate chips. Marble chips after they have melted.

Ida Bloedow, Madison, Wis.

OLD-FASHIONED SOFT MOLASSES COOKIES

Makes 2 dozen

2½ cups sifted all-purpose flour
  2 teaspoons soda
  1 teaspoon cinnamon
  1 teaspoon ginger
  1 egg, unbeaten
  ½ cup water
  ¼ teaspoon salt
  ½ cup shortening
  ½ cup sugar
  ½ cup molasses

Sift together flour, soda, cinnamon, ginger and salt. Cream shortening and sugar until light and fluffy. Add egg and molasses; mix well.

Add dry ingredients to the mixture alternately with water, beginning and ending with dry ingredients.

Drop heaping teaspoonfuls on ungreased baking sheet. Bake in moderate 350-degree oven for about 8 minutes.

Elinor Mesch, Collins, N.Y.

OATMEAL BARS

Makes 5 dozen

1 cup (2 sticks) butter
1-1/3 cups dark brown sugar, firmly
  packed
3/4 cup light corn syrup
5-1/3 cups quick-cooking oats
2 teaspoons vanilla extract

Glaze:
1 (12-ounce) package semisweet
  chocolate chips
1 cup peanut butter

Preheat oven to 350 degrees and position oven rack near the center of the oven. Coat 9x13-inch pan with butter or vegetable shortening. Cream butter and sugar. Mix in syrup, oats, and vanilla. Spread in pan and bake 16 minutes. Cool until lukewarm.

Glaze: Put chips and peanut butter in pan. Stir over low heat until mixture is smooth. Spread over warm bars. Cool and refrigerate. When cool cut into bars.

Kit Rollins, Cedarburg, Wis.

WHOLE-WHEAT GINGERSNAPS

3/4 cup brown sugar
3/4 cup margarine
1 egg
1-1/3 cups white flour
1-1/3 cups whole-wheat flour
2 teaspoons baking soda
1-1/4 teaspoons ground ginger
1 teaspoon cinnamon
1/2 teaspoon salt
1/2 teaspoon ground cloves

Cream brown sugar, margarine, and egg. Add remaining ingredients. Roll dough into walnut-size balls. Flatten these on ungreased baking sheet with a glass dipped in sugar. Bake for 8-10 minutes at 375 degrees.

Marcella Swigert, Monroe City, Mo.

PUMPKIN-FILLED COOKIES

Filling:
  1 cup pumpkin
  ½ cup sugar
  ½ teaspoon cinnamon
  ½ teaspoon ginger
  ¼ teaspoon nutmeg
  ¼ teaspoon salt

Blend ingredients together. Set aside.

Cookies:
  3 cups flour
  1 teaspoon salt
  ½ teaspoon baking soda
  ½ cup brown sugar
  ¾ cup soft shortening
  1 egg
  ¼ cup molasses
  1 cup rolled oats

Mix and sift together flour, salt and baking soda. Combine sugar, shortening, egg and molasses; mix well. Add dry ingredients to molasses mixture. Add oats. Chill 30 minutes. Roll out ⅛ inch thick; place 1 tablespoon filling on 1 cookie and cover with second cookie. Press together; slit top. Bake 375 degrees for 15 minutes.

Agnes Ward, Erie, Pa.

ANGEL COOKIES

1½ cups bread crumbs
½ cup chopped nuts
½ teaspoon vanilla or almond extract
⅔ cup sweetened condensed milk
3 drops red food coloring
30 nut halves (walnut or pecan)

Soak bread crumbs in condensed milk to which the extract and coloring have been added. Add chopped nuts. Drop by spoonfuls onto greased cookie sheets. Top each with a nut half; bake at 350 degrees for 12 minutes.

Fun for children to make!

Mrs. Don Shamway, Freeport, Ill.

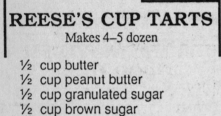

REESE'S CUP TARTS

Makes 4–5 dozen

½ cup butter
½ cup peanut butter
½ cup granulated sugar
½ cup brown sugar
1 egg
1 teaspoon vanilla
1½ cups all-purpose flour
1 teaspoon soda
½ teaspoon salt
Reese's miniature peanut-butter cups—foil removed

Cream butters and sugars thoroughly. Add egg and vanilla. Beat well. Combine flour, soda and salt. Add to creamed mixture. Take rounded teaspoons of dough and place in greased miniature muffin pans. Bake at 350 degrees for 8–10 minutes, or until cookie puffs up and is barely done. Remove from oven and immediately push a peanut-butter cup into each cookie-filled muffin cup. The cookies will deflate and form a tart shell around the peanut butter cup. Let cool in pan, then refrigerate until shine leaves the chocolate. Gently lift each tart out with tip of sharp knife.

These are easy to prepare and are very elegant. I make them for lots of school parties, showers and special occasions.

Brenda K. Peery, Tannersville, Va.

SHORTBREAD COOKIES

Makes 4 dozen

1 cup butter *or* margarine, softened
½ cup sugar
1 teaspoon vanilla
2¼ cups flour

Preheat oven to 325 degrees. Cream together the butter and sugar, then add vanilla and blend until light and fluffy. Stir in flour until well-mixed. Place dough on a floured surface and knead until smooth (do not overwork). Place dough in refrigerator until chilled.

Remove a small portion of dough at a time so the rest will remain chilled. Roll the dough to ¼-inch thickness and cut with cookie cutters. Place cookies on an ungreased cookie sheet and bake for 12–15 minutes, or until the cookies are light brown. Remove cookies to a flat surface to cool. Sprinkle cinnamon/sugar or colored sugars on top of cookies before baking, if desired.

Marg Hale, Tulsa, Okla.

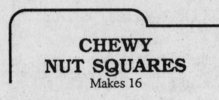

CHEWY NUT SQUARES

Makes 16

1 cup unsifted flour
1/2 cup firmly packed brown sugar
1/2 cup (1 stick) margarine
1/4 cup flour
1/2 cup brown sugar
2 eggs, slightly beaten
1/2 cup dark corn syrup
1 teaspoon vanilla
1/4 teaspoon salt
1/2 cup chopped pecans
1/2 cup flaked coconut

Combine 1 cup unsifted flour with 1/2 cup brown sugar; cut in margarine until fine crumbs form; pat into greased 8-inch square pan. Bake in preheated 325-degree oven for 20 minutes or until lightly browned. Remove from oven.

Mix remaining ingredients. Pour over crust; bake 30 more minutes, or until top is set. Cool. Cut into squares.

Mrs. Ben Winter, Altamont, Ill.

GRANOLA BARS

6 eggs
3 cups granola cereal
1 cup raisins, chopped
1/2 cup almonds, finely chopped
1/2 cup sesame seeds
1/4 cup sunflower seeds

Beat eggs in medium-size bowl. Add remaining ingredients; mix well with spoon. Batter will be thick. Let mixture stand 15 minutes. Pour mixture into well-oiled 9-inch square pan. Press mixture into pan and smooth top. Bake at 350 degrees for 25–30 minutes, until done (lightly browned and firm). Remove from oven and cut into 1x2-inch bars while still hot. Remove from pan by loosening edges gently with a spatula. Cool. Store in an airtight container.

Mrs. L. Mayer, Richmond, Va.

CHERRY POM PONS

Makes 4½ dozen

½ cup cooking oil
2 egg yolks, beaten
3 tablespoons milk
½ teaspoon almond extract
3 tablespoons cherry-flavored gelatin
1 small package instant vanilla pudding
1 cup sifted flour
½ teaspoon baking powder
¾ cup chopped pecans
⅔ cup flaked coconut
2 egg whites
1 teaspoon water
1 cup flaked coconut

Combine oil, egg yolks, milk, extract, gelatin, pudding, flour and baking powder in mixing bowl; mix well. Blend in pecans and ⅔ cup coconut. Shape a teaspoonful of dough into balls; dip into combined egg whites and water. Roll in remaining coconut. Place on an ungreased cookie sheet. Bake at 350 degrees for about 12 minutes.

Shari Crider, Stoughton, Wis.

BUTTERSCOTCH REFRIGERATOR COOKIES

Makes 5 dozen

- ½ cup soft butter or shortening
- 1 cup light brown sugar (firmly packed)
- 1 egg, well-beaten
- 1½ cups sifted flour
- 1½ teaspoons baking powder
- ¼ teaspoon salt
- ½ cup chopped nuts
- 1 teaspoon vanilla

Blend all ingredients in a mixing bowl until dough can be handled with your hands. Form into 1 longer or 2 shorter rolls; wrap in plastic wrap or aluminum foil. Chill several hours or overnight in refrigerator. Slice into ⅛-inch-thick slices. Place on lightly greased cookie sheet and bake in 375–400-degree oven for 8–10 minutes.

Marjorie Baxla, Greenfield, Ohio

ITALIAN BOW KNOT COOKIES

Makes 6 dozen medium cookies

- 4 cups flour
- 4 teaspoons baking powder
- 2 teaspoons salt
- 6 eggs, beaten
- 1 cup sugar
- ½ cup oil
- 1½ teaspoons lemon extract

Blend beaten eggs into dry ingredients, following with all other ingredients. Knead until smooth. Roll into pencil lengths and tie in bow knots. Bake on greased cookie sheets in a 400-degree oven for 15 minutes.

Lemon Icing:
- ¼ cup butter
- 1 pound confectioners' sugar
- Juice of 2 lemons

Cream butter; add remaining ingredients. Stir until well-blended. If too thin, add more sugar—too thick, add more lemon juice.

Mrs. Dan Crisla, Fennville, Mich.

SOUR CREAM NUTMEG COOKIES

Makes 3 dozen

- 2 cups sifted flour
- 1 teaspoon nutmeg
- ½ teaspoon baking soda
- 2 teaspoons baking powder
- ¼ teaspoon salt
- ½ cup shortening
- 1 cup sugar
- 1 egg
- ½ cup sour cream
- ½ cup chopped nuts

Sift flour, nutmeg, baking soda, baking powder and salt together. Cream shortening and sugar until light and fluffy. Add egg; beat well. Add sour cream and sifted dry ingredients alternately, beating well after each addition. Add nuts. Drop by teaspoonfuls 2 inches apart onto well-greased baking sheets.

Bake in moderate oven 375 degrees for 10–12 minutes.

Betty Slavin, Omaha, Neb.

SOUR CREAM COCONUT COOKIES

Makes 2½ dozen

- ½ cup shortening
- ½ cup dairy sour cream
- 1 cup sugar
- 1 egg
- 1 egg yolk
- 1 teaspoon vanilla
- 2¾ cups sifted flour
- ¾ teaspoon salt
- ½ teaspoon baking powder
- ½ teaspoon baking soda
- ½ cup flaked coconut

Cream shortening, sour cream and sugar well. Beat in egg, egg yolk and vanilla. Gradually blend in dry ingredients which have been sifted together; add coconut. Chill the dough. Roll to ⅛- to ¼-inch thickness on a lightly floured surface. Cut cookies with floured cookie cutters. Bake on ungreased cookie sheets at 375 degrees for 8–10 minutes. Frost, if desired.

Lisa Boryszewski, Middleport, N.Y.

SOFT CHOCOLATE CHIP COOKIES

- 2-1/4 cups flour
- 3/4 cup sugar
- 1 cup whipped margarine
- 2 eggs
- 1 teaspoon vanilla
- 2 cups chocolate chips
- 1 teaspoon salt
- 1 teaspoon baking soda
- 3/4 cup brown sugar, packed

Preheat oven to 375 degrees. Lightly grease cookie sheets. Mix dry ingredients together and set aside. In a larger bowl combine margarine and both sugars; beat well. Add eggs and vanilla; mix well. Gradually add flour mixture. Stir in chocolate chips. Mixture should be sticky, not stiff. Drop by spoonfuls onto cookie sheet. Bake 15 minutes at 375 degrees.

Juanita Tate, Bloomington, Ind.

WALNUT MERINGUE BARS

Makes 4 dozen

- 2½ cups all-purpose flour
- 5 eggs, separated
- 6 tablespoons sugar
- 1 cup sweet butter
- 2 teaspoons vanilla
- 2 cups apricot jam
- 1 cup sugar
- 3 cups ground walnuts
- Confectioners' sugar

In a bowl, combine flour, egg yolks, sugar, butter and vanilla. Blend with fork until dough comes away from sides of bowl. Press dough into an 11 x 16-inch pan. Spread with jam. Beat egg whites until stiff, gradually beating in 1 cup sugar. Fold in nuts. Spread over dough. Bake at 350 degrees for 40 minutes. Sprinkle with confectioners' sugar. Cool and cut into bars.

Any kind of jam can be substituted for the apricot. The cookie is very rich, so make the bars small.

Ella Evanisky, Fayetteville, Texas

ALMOND MACAROONS
Makes 1½ dozen

- 1 egg white
- ¼ teaspoon salt
- ¾ cup confectioners' sugar
- 1 cup finely minced almonds *or*
- 1 cup finely grated coconut
- ½ teaspoon almond extract

Lightly grease a cookie sheet. Preheat oven to 250 degrees. Beat egg white with salt until stiff. Gradually add ⅔ cup sugar, beating well. Fold in remaining sugar, nuts or coconut. Add flavoring, folding in. Beat well. Drop by teaspoonfuls on prepared sheet and bake for 25 minutes in 250-degree oven. Store in a covered container for 1 week to develop best flavor.

Agnes Ward, Erie, Pa.

BUTTERSCOTCH COCONUT COOKIES

- 2 cups flour
- ½ teaspoon soda
- ½ teaspoon salt
- ½ cup margarine, softened
- ½ cup granulated sugar
- ½ cup packed brown sugar
- 2 eggs
- 1 teaspoon vanilla
- 1 cup butterscotch chips
- ½ cup chopped pecans
- 2½ cups coconut
  Pecan halves (if desired)
  Candied cherry halves (if desired)

Preheat oven to 375 degrees. Combine in a small bowl the flour, soda and salt; set aside. Using larger bowl, combine softened margarine and both sugars; beat until very light and fluffy. Beat in eggs (one at a time) and vanilla. Add flour mixture; mix well. Stir in butterscotch chips and nuts. Drop dough into coconut. With lightly floured or greased hand, roll to coat with coconut. Form into balls. Bake at 375 degrees on ungreased cookie sheet for 10–12 minutes. Garnish each cookie with pecan half before baking if desired or place half candied cherry on each cookie as you remove from oven. Remove to cooling rack and allow to cool.

Jodie McCoy, Tulsa, Okla.

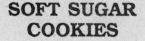

SOFT SUGAR COOKIES

- ½ cup butter *or* margarine
- 1½ cups white sugar
- 2 eggs
- 1 teaspoon vanilla
- 3 cups unsifted enriched flour
- 1 teaspoon salt
- ½ teaspoon baking powder
- ½ teaspoon baking soda
- 1 cup dairy sour cream

Cream butter or margarine with sugar; add vanilla. Add eggs and beat well. Mix flour, salt, baking powder and baking soda. Add to creamed mixture alternately with sour cream. You may add chocolate chips or raisins, or sprinkle with colored sugar, or sugar and cinnamon before baking. Drop on greased and floured cookie sheets. Bake at 400 degrees for 10–12 minutes.

I have made these cookies for a number of years for my children, and now grandchildren. The recipe is fast and easy.

Doris Mustard, Xenia, Ohio

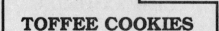

TOFFEE COOKIES
Makes 3 dozen

- 1½ cups flour
- 1 teaspoon baking powder
- ½ teaspoon salt
- ½ cup margarine
- ¾ cup packed brown sugar
- 1 egg
- 1 teaspoon vanilla
- 1 cup finely chopped Heath bars
- ⅓ cup coarsely chopped pecans

Mix egg, sugar, margarine and vanilla until smooth and creamy. Stir in dry ingredients. Blend in chopped candy bars and nuts. Drop by spoonfuls, 2 inches apart, on greased cookie sheet. Bake at 350 degrees for 12–15 minutes. Remove from cookie sheet. A great crunchy cookie!!

Jodie McCoy, Tulsa, Okla.

CARROT CHEDDAR COOKIES

- 1½ cups oats (quick *or* old-fashioned), uncooked
- 1 cup mild cheddar cheese (4 ounces), shredded
- 1 cup shredded carrots (or canned, no juice)
- ¾ cup all-purpose flour
- ⅔ cup soft butter *or* margarine
- ⅓ cup firmly packed brown sugar
- 1 egg, beaten
- ½ cup small raisins *or* chopped dates
- 1 teaspoon cinnamon
- 1 teaspoon vanilla
- ½ teaspoon salt
- ¼ teaspoon soda
- ⅛ teaspoon cloves

Combine all ingredients and mix well. Drop by rounded tablespoonfuls onto ungreased cookie sheet and flatten. Bake for 16–18 minutes at 350–375 degrees. Store tightly covered.

The small amount of sugar is more nutritious and permits those on low-calorie diets to enjoy.

Mabel E. Holsted, Stanton, Mich.

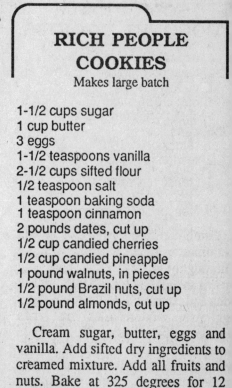

RICH PEOPLE COOKIES
Makes large batch

- 1-1/2 cups sugar
- 1 cup butter
- 3 eggs
- 1-1/2 teaspoons vanilla
- 2-1/2 cups sifted flour
- 1/2 teaspoon salt
- 1 teaspoon baking soda
- 1 teaspoon cinnamon
- 2 pounds dates, cut up
- 1/2 cup candied cherries
- 1/2 cup candied pineapple
- 1 pound walnuts, in pieces
- 1/2 pound Brazil nuts, cut up
- 1/2 pound almonds, cut up

Cream sugar, butter, eggs and vanilla. Add sifted dry ingredients to creamed mixture. Add all fruits and nuts. Bake at 325 degrees for 12 minutes.

Lucy Dowd, Sequim, Wash.

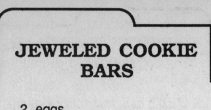

JEWELED COOKIE BARS

2 eggs
1 cup sugar
1 teaspoon vanilla
1 cup sifted flour
½ teaspoon salt
½ cup chopped, toasted blanched almonds
½ cup cut-up gumdrops
½ cup gumdrops for topping, cut up

Beat eggs until foamy; beat in sugar and vanilla. Sift together flour and salt; stir into creamed mixture. Fold in almonds and gumdrops. Spread in well-greased and floured 9-inch square pan. Sprinkle extra gumdrops over top of batter. Bake in 350-degree oven for 30–35 minutes until top has a dull crust. Cut into squares while still warm, then cool before removing from pan.

Mrs. W.T. Gore, Aztec, N.M.

OATMEAL-RAISIN COOKIES

3 eggs, well-beaten
1 cup raisins
1 teaspoon vanilla
1 cup shortening
1 cup brown sugar
1 cup granulated sugar
2½ cups flour
1 teaspoon salt
2 teaspoons soda
1 teaspoon cinnamon
2 cups oatmeal
½ cup chopped nuts

Combine eggs, raisins and vanilla. Let mixture stand for 1 hour or more. Thoroughly cream together shortening, brown and white sugars. Sift flour, salt, soda and cinnamon. Mix well; blend in egg/raisin mixture, oats and nuts. Dough will be very stiff.) Roll the dough into balls, the size of a large walnut; roll the balls in a cinnamon-sugar mixture (1 teaspoon cinnamon mixed with 1 cup sugar). Place on cookie sheet about 3 inches apart. Bake at 350

degrees for 10–12 minutes, or until lightly browned. Remove from oven and let cool a few minutes before removing from cookie sheet. These will keep several weeks, stored in a tightly covered container. Put waxed paper between layers of cookies. Let cool *completely* before closing container.

Jean Vincent, Grand Blanc, Mich.

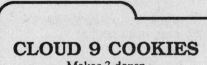

CLOUD 9 COOKIES

Makes 3 dozen

2 egg whites, stiffly beaten
⅔ cup sugar
⅛ teaspoon salt
1 cup chopped almonds
1 cup miniature chocolate chips

Preheat oven to 350 degrees for 15 minutes; turn off when putting cookies in oven. Fold sugar, salt, nuts and chips into stiffly beaten egg whites. Drop by teaspoonfuls onto a well-greased cookie sheet. Leave in oven 2½ hours or overnight, but do not open oven door until time to remove cookies. A good lunchbox or after-school snack.

Joy Shamway, Freeport, Ill.

ROLLED GINGER COOKIES

Makes 5 dozen

1 cup shortening
1 cup sugar
1 egg
1 cup molasses
2 tablespoons vinegar
5 cups sifted all-purpose flour
1½ teaspoons soda
½ teaspoon salt
2–3 teaspoons ground ginger
1 teaspoon cinnamon
1 teaspoon cloves

Cream shortening and sugar. Beat in egg, molasses and vinegar. Sift together dry ingredients; blend in. Chill 3 hours. Roll dough ⅛-inch thick on lightly floured board. Cut in shapes. Place 1 inch apart on greased cookie sheet. Bake at 375 degrees for 5–6 minutes. Cool slightly; remove to rack to cool completely.

Agnes Ward, Erie, Pa.

SCOTTISH BANANA COOKIES

Makes 5 dozen

⅔ cup butter
1 cup sugar
2 eggs
1 teaspoon almond flavoring
2¼ cups flour
2 tablespoons cornstarch
1 teaspoon baking powder
½ teaspoon baking soda
½ teaspoon salt
1½ cups mashed bananas

Cream together butter and sugar until light and fluffy. Add eggs, 1 at a time, and beat well after each addition. Add almond flavoring. Sift together flour, cornstarch, baking powder, baking soda and salt. Add alternately with mashed bananas.

Drop by teaspoonfuls onto greased cookie sheets. Bake in a 400-degree oven for 15 minutes.

Agnes Ward, Erie, Pa.

PECAN CRESCENT COOKIES

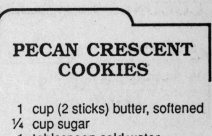

1 cup (2 sticks) butter, softened
¼ cup sugar
1 tablespoon cold water
1 teaspoon vanilla extract
2 cups unsifted all-purpose flour
1 cup finely chopped pecans
½ teaspoon salt
½ cup confectioners' sugar

In large bowl, with electric mixer or wooden spoon, blend butter, ¼ cup sugar, water and vanilla. Gradually stir in flour, pecans and salt until well-blended. Form dough into a ball; flatten to 1 inch thick. Wrap in plastic wrap; refrigerate 2 hours. Preheat oven to 375 degrees. Roll dough between palms, a tablespoon at a time, to make 2-inch rolls. Place rolls 2 inches apart on ungreased baking sheets; curve each to make a crescent. Bake 15 minutes to lightly golden. Cool slightly; roll in ½ cup confectioners' sugar. Serve with sherbet, if desired.

Edith Ruth Muldoon, Baldwin, N.Y.

ZEBRA COOKIES

Makes 4–5 dozen

- 1½ cups sugar
- ½ cup vegetable oil
- 1¼ teaspoons vanilla extract
- 3 eggs
- 1⅔ cups all-purpose flour
- ½ cup cocoa
- ½ tablespoon cinnamon
- 1½ teaspoons baking powder
- ¼ teaspoon salt
- 1 cup confectioners' sugar

In a mixing bowl combine sugar, oil and vanilla. Add eggs, 1 at a time; mix well. Stir in flour, cocoa, cinnamon, baking powder and salt. Cover; refrigerate 2 hours. Lightly grease baking sheet; set aside. Place confectioners' sugar in a shallow dish. Shape dough into 1-inch balls; roll in confectioners' sugar. Place 2 inches apart on baking sheet. Bake at 350 degrees for 11 minutes; cool on rack. (These cookies crack on top as they bake; thus the striped zebra look).

Gwen Campbell, Sterling, Va.

MRS. FIELD'S COOKIES

- 2 cups butter
- 2 cups granulated sugar
- 2 cups brown sugar
- 4 eggs
- 2 tablespoons vanilla
- 4 cups flour
- 5 cups oatmeal
- 1 teaspoon salt
- 2 teaspoons baking powder
- 2 teaspoons baking soda
- 1 (24-ounce) package chocolate chips *plus* 8-ounce Hershey bar
- 3 cups chopped nuts

Cream butter and sugars; add eggs and vanilla. Combine dry ingredients and add to creamed mixture. Add chips and grated Hershey bar. Add chopped nuts. Put on cookie sheet about 2 inches apart. Bake at 375 degrees for about 6 minutes.

Kit Rollins, Cedarburg, Wis.

DATE BARS

- 1 pound dates
- 1 cup walnut meats
- ½ cup flour
- ¼ teaspoon baking powder
- ¼ teaspoon salt
- 1 cup sugar
- 2 eggs
- ¼ cup melted butter
- Confectioners' sugar

Pit dates and cut into quarters. Mix together flour, baking powder, salt and sugar. Add dates and nuts to flour mixture. Beat eggs. Add melted butter and combine mixtures. Bake in 8 x 12-inch pan for 30 minutes in moderate oven of 350 degrees. When slightly cool, cut into bars. Roll each bar in confectioners' sugar.

Suzan L. Wiener, Spring Hill, Fla.

CANDIED ORANGE PEEL COOKIES

Makes 3 dozen

- 2 eggs
- ⅔ cup shortening
- 1 cup sugar
- ⅔ cup sour cream
- ½ cup candied orange peel
- 2⅓ cups all-purpose flour
- 2 teaspoons baking powder
- ¼ teaspoon salt
- ½ teaspoon baking soda

Beat together first 5 ingredients. Sift together dry ingredients; add to liquid ingredients. Drop by teaspoonfuls onto greased cookie sheet; press small piece of candied peel into top of each cookie. Bake at 375 degrees for 12 minutes, or until lightly browned.

Gwen Campbell, Sterling, Va.

UNBAKED COOKIES

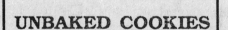

Mix together in a mixing bowl:
3 cups oatmeal
1/2 cup coconut
1/2 cup chopped nuts
4 tablespoons cocoa
1 (6-ounce) package chocolate
chips
1 teaspoon vanilla
Dash of salt

Then boil together for 3 minutes the following:
2 cups sugar
1 cup margarine
1/2 cup milk

Pour over the dry mixture; mix well. Drop by teaspoonfuls on waxed paper.

Ilene Ongman, Klamath Falls, Okla.

CHEWY WALNUT SQUARES

- 1 egg, beaten
- 1 cup brown sugar
- 1 teaspoon vanilla
- ½ cup flour
- ¼ teaspoon soda
- ¼ teaspoon salt
- 1 cup chopped walnuts

Grease an 8-inch square pan. Stir together egg, brown sugar and vanilla. Quickly stir in flour, baking soda and salt. Add walnuts. Spread in pan and bake at 350 degrees for 18 minutes. Cookies should be soft in center when taken from the oven. Leave in pan to cool. Cut into 2-inch squares.

Brenda Peery, Tannersville, Va.

PECAN SANDIES

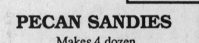

Makes 4 dozen

- ¼ cup soft margarine
- 1 (8-ounce) package softened cream cheese
- 1 egg
- 1 teaspoon pecan nut flavoring
- 1 (2-layer size) package dry cake mix
- 1 cup chopped pecans

Cream softened margarine and cream cheese. Add egg and flavoring. Beat well. Add dry cake mix; then add chopped pecans. Drop by teaspoonfuls onto greased cookie sheet. Bake in preheated 350-degree oven for 12 minutes, or until browned and done.

Marcia Mitchell, St. Joseph, Mo.

APPLESAUCE CHOCOLATE CHIP COOKIES

2 cups flour
1 teaspoon baking soda
1/2 teaspoon salt
3/4 cup margarine
1 cup light brown sugar
1 egg
1-1/2 teaspoons vanilla
1 cup applesauce
1 cup chocolate chips
1/2 cup chopped pecans

Combine dry ingredients together. Cream margarine and brown sugar until well-blended. Beat egg into mixture; add vanilla. Gradually add dry ingredients to creamed mixture and blend; fold in applesauce, chocolate chips and nuts. Drop by teaspoonfuls onto greased cookie sheets and bake in 375-degree oven for 10–12 minutes.

Jodie McCoy, Tulsa, Okla.

GRANDMA'S SUGAR-RAISIN COOKIES

Makes 6 dozen

1½ cups seedless raisins
1½ cups sugar
1 cup shortening
2 eggs
1 teaspoon vanilla
3 cups flour
1 teaspoon baking powder
1 teaspoon baking soda
½ teaspoon salt
½ teaspoon nutmeg
  Sugar

Simmer raisins in water to barely cover, until water is all absorbed. Set aside to cool. Cream sugar and shortening; add eggs and vanilla; beat thoroughly. Sift together the dry ingredients except last sugar, and add to creamed mixture. Stir in raisins. Roll dough into 1-inch balls; roll in sugar. Place balls 2 inches apart on greased cookie sheets; flatten with bottom of sugar-dipped glass. Bake at 400 degrees for 10 minutes until lightly browned.

Agnes Ward, Erie, Pa.

HALFWAY BARS

1 cup shortening
½ cup brown sugar
½ cup white sugar
2 egg yolks
1 tablespoon cold water
½ teaspoon baking soda
2 cups flour
2 egg whites
1 (6-ounce) package chocolate chips
1 cup brown sugar

Mix first 7 ingredients and pat into 13 x 9-inch pan. Sprinkle with chocolate chips; push chips into mixture. Beat egg whites until stiff and add 1 cup brown sugar. Spread over top of mixture. Do not touch sides of pan. Bake at 325 degrees until golden brown, about 35 minutes.

Mrs. George Brown, Lee, Fla.

DATE DAINTIES

1 cup chopped dates
1 stick margarine
1 egg
1 cup sugar
½ cup chopped pecans
  Rice Krispies (2 or more cups)
  Shredded coconut

Boil together dates, margarine, egg and sugar for 6–8 minutes, stirring constantly. Add nuts and Rice Krispies. Form into small balls. Roll in coconut.

Chris Bryant, Johnson City, Ind.

ORANGE SUGAR COOKIES

Makes 6 dozen

¾ cup shortening
1 cup sugar
2 eggs, beaten
2 teaspoons grated fresh orange peel
3½ cups flour
3 teaspoons baking powder
¼ teaspoon salt
½ teaspoon vanilla
⅓ cup milk

Cream shortening and sugar; add eggs. Combine sifted flour, baking powder and salt; sift together. Mix into the creamed mixture; add orange peel, vanilla and milk. Chill dough until easy to roll out. Cut out cookies into your desired shapes and bake at 375 degrees for 8–10 minutes.

Jodie McCoy, Tulsa, Okla.

LEMON-PINEAPPLE DROPS

Makes 4 dozen

½ cup shortening
2 eggs
1 (3-ounce) package lemon-flavored gelatin
1 (1-pound) package cake mix
1 (8¼-ounce) can crushed pineapple, well-drained

In mixing bowl, combine shortening and eggs. Blend in dry gelatin. Add half of dry cake mix. Beat at medium speed of mixer until fluffy. Add remaining cake mix. Blend on low speed, scraping sides of bowl constantly. Stir in pineapple. Drop rounded teaspoonfuls 2 inches apart on ungreased cookie sheet. Bake at 375 degrees for 10–12 minutes. Cool 1 minute on cookie sheet. Remove; cool on rack.

Shirley Viscosi, Worcester, Mass.

BASIC BUTTER COOKIES

Makes 30 cookies

1 cup all-purpose flour
½ cup cornstarch
½ cup confectioners' sugar
¾ cup (1½ sticks) real butter, room temperature
½ cup coarsely chopped walnuts

Preheat oven to 300 degrees. Sift first 3 ingredients into large bowl. Add butter and mix well. Stir in walnuts. Drop by teaspoonfuls onto baking sheets. Bake until cookies are lightly golden, about 20–25 minutes.

Note: Real butter is the secret of these buttery-tasting cookies.

Agnes Ward, Erie, Pa.

PUMPKIN CAKE BARS

Makes 24

4 eggs, well-beaten
2 cups cooked pumpkin or 1 (1-pound) can
1-1/2 cups sugar
1/4 teaspoon salt
1 teaspoon ginger
1 teaspoon cinnamon
1/2 teaspoon cloves
1 box yellow cake mix
1/2 cup butter, melted
1 cup chopped pecans

Mix eggs, pumpkin, sugar, salt, ginger, cinnamon and cloves together; pour into a 13 x 9-inch pan. Sprinkle dry cake mix on top. Drizzle melted butter over mix; spread chopped nuts over all. Bake at 325 degrees for 1 hour and 20 minutes. (Cover with foil loosely to keep from browning too soon for the first half of cooking time.) Cut into squares.

Marcella Swigert, Monroe City, Mo.

CHEWY PEANUT BARS

Crust:
1 cup flour
½ cup brown sugar, packed
½ cup butter

Topping:
1 cup brown sugar, packed
2 eggs
3 tablespoons flour
1 teaspoon baking powder
1 teaspoon vanilla extract
2 cups salted peanuts, whole or coarsely chopped

Crust: Put flour and sugar in a bowl; mix well. With a pastry blender cut in butter until mixture resembles coarse crumbs. Spread evenly in a greased 13 x 9-inch pan. Bake at 375 degrees for 8–10 minutes, or until

crust appears slightly firm in center. Cool.

Topping: Mix sugar and eggs until smooth. Stir in flour, baking powder and vanilla until well-blended. Stir in peanuts. Pour over crust. Bake at 375 degrees for 18–20 minutes, or until browned and edges are firm. (Center may be somewhat soft, but crusted over.) Cool; cut into bars.

Vickie Vogt, Kewaskum, Wis.

CHEESECAKE BARS

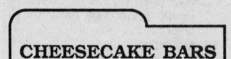

1 box Duncan Hines Golden Butter Recipe cake mix
1 egg
1 stick margarine
1 (8-ounce) package cream cheese
2 eggs
1 (1-pound) box confectioners' sugar

Blend together the first 3 ingredients. Crumble and press into greased oblong pan. Then mix next 3 ingredients together and spread on top of bottom layer. Bake at 350 degrees for 35–40 minutes, or until golden brown. Cool completely and cut into bars.

Sue Hibbard, Rochester, N.Y.

CASHEW DROPS

Makes 6–7 dozen

Cookies:
½ cup (1 stick) butter
1 cup firmly packed light brown sugar
1 egg
1 teaspoon vanilla extract
1¾ cups all-purpose flour
1 teaspoon baking powder
½ teaspoon baking soda
½ cup dairy sour cream
1 cup chopped salted cashews

Frosting:
¼ cup (½ stick) butter
2 cups confectioners' sugar
3 to 3½ tablespoons milk

Preheat oven to 375 degrees. For cookies, cream butter. Gradually add sugar; continue beating until blended. Beat in egg and vanilla. Combine flour, baking powder and soda. Add to creamed mixture alternately with sour cream; fold in cashews. Drop by rounded teaspoonfuls onto buttered cookie sheets. Bake 8–10 minutes. Remove to wire rack to cool. When cool, frost. For frosting, heat butter over low heat until light amber color. Remove from heat and stir in sugar and milk.

WALNUT MACAROONS

1 egg white
⅔ cup white sugar
⅛ teaspoon salt
¼ teaspoon almond extract
⅓ cup very finely chopped walnuts

Beat egg white very stiff, adding sugar slowly. Add salt very gradually while beating; still beating, add extract and chopped nuts. Drop by teaspoonfuls onto cookie sheet (Teflon or non-stick sheet if possible). Bake at 325 degrees for 15 minutes. Cool on rack.

Pearle M. Goodwin, South Ryegate, Vt.

CRISPY CORN-FLAKES COOKIES

3 cups cornflakes cereal
1 cup sugar
1 cup walnuts, coarsely chopped
¼ teaspoon almond extract
2 egg yolks, beaten
2 egg whites

Combine first 5 ingredients. Beat egg whites until stiff; fold into cornflakes mixture. Drop by tablespoonfuls onto a well-greased baking sheet. Bake at 350 degrees until pale amber. Allow to cool before removing from cookie sheet.

Gwen Campbell, Sterling, Va.

AGGRESSION COOKIES

6 cups oatmeal
3 cups brown sugar
3 cups (6 sticks) margarine
3 cups flour
3 teaspoons baking soda

Combine all ingredients and beat the daylights out of them! Drop onto ungreased cookie sheets and bake at 350 degrees for about 10 minutes.

Genevieve Gilham, Royal, Ark.

CHOCOLATE MACAROONS

Makes 6 dozen

1 (18.5-ounce) package devil's food cake mix with pudding
1 cup flaked coconut, toasted
½ cup regular oats, uncooked and toasted
¾ cup butter *or* margarine, melted
2 teaspoons vanilla
2 eggs, slightly beaten
6 (1.45-ounce) milk chocolate candy bars
¾ cup flaked coconut

Combine first 6 ingredients; chill 30 minutes. Drop by heaping teaspoonfuls 2 inches apart on ungreased cookie sheets. Bake at 350 degrees for 10 minutes. Immediately top each cookie with 1 chocolate square; spread to front; sprinkle cookies with coconut.

Mrs. Robert T. Shaffer, Middleburg, Pa.

PECAN BALLS

Makes 5 dozen

1 cup soft butter
½ cup granulated sugar *or* ½ cup confectioners' sugar
¼ teaspoon salt
1 teaspoon vanilla
2¼ cups flour
1 cup chopped pecans

Mix butter, sugar, salt and vanilla. Work in flour. The last bit of flour may be worked in with hands. Add nuts.

Chill dough. Roll into 1-inch balls. Place on ungreased baking sheet and bake at 350 degrees for 10–12 minutes, until set, but not browned. Roll in sifted confectioners' sugar while warm. Cool; roll again.

Betty Slavin, Omaha, Neb.

WALNUT CLUSTERS

Makes 50

¼ cup butter
½ cup sugar
1 egg, unbeaten
1¼ teaspoons vanilla
1½ squares unsweetened chocolate, melted
½ cup flour
¼ teaspoon baking powder
½ teaspoon salt
2 cups unbroken walnuts

Cream butter and sugar until fluffy. Add egg and vanilla; blend well. Stir in chocolate, then flour sifted with baking powder and salt. Add walnuts. Drop by teaspoonfuls onto greased baking sheet. Bake at 350 degrees for 10 minutes. Cookies should be soft, almost like candy.

Elizabeth S. Lawson, Delbarton, W.Va.

CHOCO SURPRISE COOKIES

Makes 8 dozen

1 cup all-purpose flour
1 teaspoon baking powder
1 teaspoon cinnamon
1 cup peanut butter (creamy)
½ cup margarine, softened
1 cup firmly packed brown sugar
2 eggs, well-beaten
1 (16-ounce) package milk chocolate stars (or Hershey Kisses with tips cut off)
Confectioners' sugar

Combine first 3 ingredients and set aside. Combine and cream until fluffy, the peanut butter, margarine, brown sugar and eggs. Add dry ingredients. Cover dough; chill 1 hour or overnight.

Shape 1 teaspoon dough around star; place on lightly greased cookie sheet or

on Teflon cookie sheet. Bake at 350 degrees for 9–11 minutes, or until lightly browned. Cool slightly on wire racks; then roll in confectioners' sugar. Cool completely before storing.

Mrs. Hobert Howell, Waco, Texas

STARLIGHT MINT SURPRISE COOKIES

Makes 4½ dozen

3 cups flour
1 teaspoon soda
½ teaspoon salt
1 cup butter
1 cup sugar
½ cup brown sugar
2 eggs
1 teaspoon vanilla
1 package chocolate mint wafers

Mix first 3 ingredients; set aside. Cream butter, sugars, eggs and vanilla. Add flour mixture. Cover and chill 2 hours. Enclose each chocolate mint wafer in 1 tablespoon dough. Place on greased cookie sheet, 2 inches apart. Top with pecan half. Bake for 10 minutes in a 375-degree oven.

Ann Sterzer, Lincoln, Neb.

CHERRY WINKS

Makes 2½ dozen

1 cup confectioners' sugar
1 cup butter, softened
1 teaspoon vanilla
1 egg
2 cups flour
2 tablespoons poppy seeds
½ teaspoon salt
Cherry preserves (⅓–½ cup)

Heat oven to 300 degrees. Beat confectioners' sugar and butter until fluffy. Add vanilla and egg; blend well. Stir in flour, poppy seeds, salt; mix well. Drop by rounded teaspoonfuls onto ungreased cookie sheets. With finger make imprint in center of each cookie. Fill with ½ teaspoon preserves. Bake at 300 degrees for 20–25 minutes, or until edges are light golden brown. Remove from cookie sheet immediately.

This is a very light and buttery cookie.

Vickie Vogt, Kewaskum, Wis.

BUTTERSCOTCH BARS

Makes about 4 dozen

4 eggs
6-ounce package brown sugar
2 cups buttermilk biscuit mix
2 cups chopped pecans
1 small package (6 ounces) butterscotch morsels
1 teaspoon vanilla

Beat eggs at medium speed of mixer until frothy. Gradually add sugar, beating until thick. Add remaining ingredients, stirring well. Spread batter in a greased and floured 13x9x2-inch pan. Bake in a preheated 325-degree oven for 45 minutes. Cool and cut into bars.

Mrs. Bruce Fowler, Woodruff, S.C.

FIG SQUARES

3 eggs
¾ cup sugar
1 teaspoon vanilla
1 cup flour
⅛ teaspoon salt
2 teaspoons baking powder
1 (8-ounce) package (1½ cups) figs, chopped
1 cup walnuts, chopped

Beat eggs until light. Add sugar and vanilla; mix well. Add sifted dry ingredients and mix well. Fold in figs and walnuts. Bake in greased 9-inch square pan at 350 degrees for 30 minutes. Cool; cut in squares; sprinkle with sifted confectioners' sugar. Serve these with hot spiced tea!

Eleanor V. Craycraft, Santa Monica, Calif.

SOUR CREAM DATE DREAMS

¼ cup shortening
¾ cup brown sugar
½ teaspoon vanilla
1 egg, beaten
1¼ cups flour
½ teaspoon soda
¼ teaspoon baking powder
⅔ cup dates, chopped
Walnut halves

¼ teaspoon salt
¼ teaspoon cinnamon
⅛ teaspoon nutmeg
½ cup sour cream

Cream together shortening, sugar and vanilla. Add egg; mix well. Sift together dry ingredients and add to shortening mixture alternately with sour cream. Stir in dates.

Drop by teaspoonfuls onto greased cookie sheet. Top each with a walnut half and bake at 400 degrees for about 8–10 minutes.

Eleanor V. Craycraft, Santa Monica, Calif.

RICH SHORTBREAD COOKIES

2 cups butter
1½ cups confectioners' sugar
2 teaspoons vanilla
4 cups flour
1 teaspoon salt
Candied cherries, if desired

Cream butter thoroughly. Add confectioners' sugar and vanilla; beat well. Add flour and salt; blend together. Form into several rolls and wrap each roll in waxed paper. Refrigerate overnight. Slice and put on ungreased baking sheets. At this point, you may decorate with red cherries. Bake for 20 minutes at 300 degrees.

Great for Valentine's Day festivities!!

Lillian Smith, Montreal, Quebec, Canada

COCONUT CREAM COOKIES

Makes 4¼–5 dozen

1 cup margarine
2 (3-ounce) packages cream cheese
1 cup sugar
¼ teaspoon salt
1 teaspoon vanilla
1 egg
2 tablespoons milk
2 cups flour
½ cup coconut
Pecan or walnut halves

Cream together first 7 ingredients

until fluffy. Stir in flour and coconut. Mix well. Drop by small spoonful onto greased cookie sheets. Top each cookie with nut half. Bake 20 minutes in 325-degree oven.

Jodie McCoy, Tulsa, Okl

BUTTERFINGER COOKIES

2⅔ cups flour
1 teaspoon baking soda
⅔ cup Crisco
½ teaspoon salt
1½ cups sugar
2 eggs
4 Butterfinger candy bars, chopped

Cream Crisco and sugar; beat in egg. Sift dry ingredients and sprinkle ove candy pieces. Mix well. Stir into eg mixture. Shape dough into rolls. Cove with foil or plastic wrap. Chill rolls. Cu into thin slices. Place slices on grease cookie sheet; bake at 375 degrees for 1 minutes. Remove from pan immedi ately.

Sue Thomas, Casa Grande, Ari

FRUIT-N-HONEY COOKIES

¼ cup brown sugar
½ cup honey
½ cup butter *or* margarine
2 eggs
1½ cups flour
½ teaspoon salt
½ teaspoon baking soda
1 teaspoon cinnamon
½ cup milk
½ cup raisins
½ cup ground nuts
¼ cup coconut

Cream brown sugar, honey and butter together in a mixing bowl. Add eggs. Sift together dry ingredients. Add to creamed mixture alternately with milk. Mix well. Stir in raisins, nuts and coconut. Drop by teaspoonfuls onto greased cookie sheet. Bake at 400 degrees for 6–8 minutes.

Mrs. E. O'Brien, Richmond, Va.

Crockpot
CLASSICS

CORNED BEEF AND CABBAGE

2 medium onions, sliced
1 (2 1/2-to 3-pound) corned beef
  brisket
1 cup apple juice
1/4 cup packed brown sugar
2 teaspoons orange peel, finely
  shredded
2 teaspoons prepared mustard
6 whole cloves
6 cabbage wedges

Place onions in crockpot. Trim away any fat that might be present on the corned beef brisket. If needed, cut brisket to fit into Crockpot; place on top of onions. In a bowl combine apple juice, sugar, orange peel, mustard, and cloves; pour over brisket. Place cabbage on top of brisket. Cover; cook on *low* setting for 10-12 hours or on *high* setting for 5-6 hours.

CROCK-STYLE BARBECUE BEANS
Serves 10-12

These beans are great additions to a meal or for take-alongs to potlucks. Fast and easy, these beans stay hot for travel.

8 cups water
3 cans pork and beans
1/4 teaspoon salt
1/4 teaspoon pepper
1/4 teaspoon minced onion
1 small onion, chopped
1/2 cup brown sugar

2/3 cup syrup
3 tablespoons white sugar

Combine water, pork and beans. Add remaining ingredients and stir well. Cook on *low* for six hours, *high* for less than six hours. Stir before serving.

COUNTRY ROAST AND VEGETABLES
Serves 6-8

1 roast, thawed
Several potatoes, canned sliced or
  whole
Several carrots
Green beans, corn (optional)
1 onion, sliced
1 cup water
1/4 teaspoon salt
1/4 teaspoon pepper
3 tablespoons butter or margarine
1/4 cup flour (optional)

Place roast in Crockpot. Add peeled potatoes, carrots, beans, corn, sliced onion, and butter. Add water and flour for gravy. Sprinkle with salt and pepper. Cook on *low* for 6-12 hours, *high* for less than 6 hours.

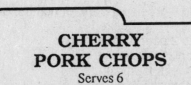

CHERRY PORK CHOPS
Serves 6

6 pork chops, cut 3/4-inch thick
1/4 teaspoon salt
1/4 teaspoon pepper
1/2 can cherry pie filling (1 cup)
2 teaspoons lemon juice

1/2 teaspoon instant chicken
  bouillon granules
1/8 teaspoon ground mace

Trim excess fat from pork chops. Brown pork chops in hot skillet with butter or oil. Sprinkle each chop with salt and pepper. Combine cherry pie filling, lemon juice, chicken bouillon granules, and ground mace in cooker. Stir well. Place pork chops in Crockpot. Cover. Cook on *low* for 4-5 hours. Place chops on platter. Pour cherry sauce over meat.

VEGETABLE BEEF SOUP
Serves 8

This meal-in-one is more than nutritious, it's delicious! Cook for dinner and keep it for lunches, weekends snacks, and light, late-night brunches.

1 pound ground beef
1 large can tomatoes, whole
1 can tomato soup
1 small onion, chopped
2 cups water
1 can lima beans, drained
1 can whole-kernal corn, undrained
1 cup sliced carrots
1 cup potatoes, cut up
1 cup diced celery
1/4 teaspoon salt
1/4 teaspoon pepper

Combine beef, tomatoes, soup, and onion in cooker. Add water, beans, and vegetables. Add salt, pepper, and other spices of preference. Stir well. Cook at lowest setting, 4 to 6 hours.

TENDER MEATBALLS IN MUSHROOM GRAVY
Serves 4-6

No running to the store for any of these ingredients; hamburger and mushroom soup are found in every kitchen. Simple and delicious; everyone likes meatballs.

1 pound hamburger
4 slices soft white bread
1 teaspoon salt
1/4 teaspoon pepper
1 tablespoon minced onion
1 can mushroom soup
1/3 cup water

Pull apart bread into small, dime-size pieces. Combine hamburger, bread, salt, pepper, and minced onion in large mixing bowl. Using a spoon, scoop out rounds of meat, or shape into several round, 2-inch balls by hand.

Brown meatballs in a hot skillet using a small amount of butter or oil. Turn them occasionally so all sides are browned. Place meat in cooker. Add soup and water. Cook on *low* for 6 to 12 hours, *high* for up to 6 hours.

CLASSIC SWISS STEAK
Serves 4-6

Super good, super simple, super anytime—for a family lunch, dinner, or for guests.

1 round steak
2 cups flour
1/4 teaspoon salt and pepper
2 tablespoons butter or shortening
1 (4-ounce) can tomato sauce
1 sliced onion
1 sliced green pepper

Cut steak into serving portions. Combine flour, salt, and pepper in medium-size bowl. Roll cut steaks in flour mixture, coating both sides. Melt shortening or butter in hot skillet. Brown meat on both sides, but do not cook. Place browned meat in Crockpot. Add tomato sauce, onion, and green pepper. Cook on *low* for 6 to 12 hours, or on *high* for up to 6 hours.

MINESTRONE SOUP
Serves 6–8

Minestrone soup bean mix*
1 onion, chopped
1 garlic clove
6–8 cups water
1 can tomatoes (about 2 cups)
Italian seasonings to taste (such as oregano, basil, rosemary, thyme, marjoram)
1 meaty ham bone
Spaghetti

Soak bean mix overnight. Rinse. Put in pot with all the other ingredients except spaghetti. Cook in Crockpot for about 6–8 hours on medium; on stove, simmer until beans are soft—several hours. About 15 minutes before serving, add a handful of uncooked spaghetti. Serve with Parmesan cheese.

*If minestrone soup mix is not available in your area, mix your own using several kinds of dried beans, barley and split peas. Use about 2 cups for the soup.

CINDY'S STUFFED PEPPERS

6 to 8 green peppers, or number of servings desired
1 to 2 pounds hamburger
1 onion, sliced
1/4 teaspoon salt
1/4 teaspoon pepper
1 egg
1 slice white bread
1 can tomatoes, whole

Combine hamburger, onion, salt, pepper, and egg in large mixing bowl. Pull apart bread into small pieces. Add to hamburger mixture. Clean and remove seeds and white membrane from green peppers. Stuff peppers with hamburger mixture.

For meat loaf, combine remaining meat into oblong ball. Place meat loaf and peppers in Crockpot. Pour tomatoes, undrained, over meat. Cook on *low* for 6 to 12 hours, *high* for less than 6 hours.

APPLE-RAISIN-TOPPED HAM
Serves 6

This recipe gives ham a new taste and look. Great for dinner, sandwiches, and leftovers.

1 (21-ounce) can apple pie filling
1/3 cup light raisins
1-1/2 pounds fully cooked ham, sliced about 2-3/4 inches thick
1/3 cup orange juice
2 tablespoons water
1 tablespoon lemon juice
1/4 teaspoon ground cinnamon

Combine pie filling, raisins, orange juice, water, lemon juice and cinnamon. Cut ham slice into six equal pieces. Place meat and apple mixture in crockery cooker by alternating layers of each, and ending with the apple mixture. Cover and cook on *low* for 4-5 hours. Serve with rice, if desired.

CROCKPOT APPLE BUTTER

8 cups cooked apples
4 cups sugar
½ cup vinegar
2 teaspoons cinnamon

Place in Crockpot and cook 6 hours on HIGH. This is a great recipe and smells great in the kitchen while cooking.

Thelma Hervey, Hedrick, Iowa

Desserts
DELICIOUS

CHOCOLATE NUT CRUNCH

2 cups vanilla wafer crumbs
1 cup chopped walnuts
1/2 cup butter or margarine
1 cup confectioners' sugar
3 egg yolks, well-beaten
1-1/2 (1-ounce) squares unsweetened chocolate, melted
1/2 teaspoon vanilla
3 egg whites, stiffly beaten

Combine crumbs and nuts; line bottom of 9-inch square pan with half of the crumb mixture. Thoroughly cream butter and sugar; add egg yolks. Add chocolate and vanilla. Mix well. Fold in stiffly beaten egg whites. Spread over crumb mixture. Top with remaining crumb mixture. Chill in refrigerator overnight. Cut in squares.

Ida Bloedow, Madison, Wis.

PEAR CRISP

2 (1-pound) cans pear halves with syrup
1/2 cup golden raisins
3/4 cup rolled oats
3/4 cup flour
1/2 cup brown sugar
1/4 cup melted butter
1 teaspoon cinnamon
1/2 teaspoon ground nutmeg

Place pears and raisins in 8 x 8-inch baking dish. Combine remaining ingredients; mix until crumbly. Sprinkle evenly over pears. Bake at 350 degrees until golden brown.

Leota Baxter, Ingalls, Kan.

MARBLE-TOP CHOCOLATE TARTLET

Crust:
1/3 cup margarine
1 cup sifted flour
1 (1-ounce) bar dark chocolate, grated
3-4 tablespoons water
Pinch of salt

Cut margarine into flour. Add salt. Stir in chocolate and sprinkle with water. Mix lightly until it holds together. Roll out and place in muffin tins; flute edges. Bake at 450 degrees for about 12 minutes.

Filling:
1 cup sugar
1 tablespoon unflavored gelatin
1 cup milk
2 egg yolks, beaten
1 cup chocolate chips
2 egg whites
1/4 cup sugar
1 cup heavy cream

2 tablespoons confectioners' sugar
1 teaspoon vanilla
Pinch of salt

Combine the sugar, gelatin, and salt; stir in milk and egg yolks. Add chocolate chips and stir over medium heat until it begins to boil. *Do not* boil. Stir until melted; cool; chill until set. Beat egg whites until foamy and gradually add confectioners' sugar. Whip cream, gradually adding 1/4 cup sugar until stiff. Fold beaten egg whites into cooled gelatin; alternately add this and a layer of whipped cream into baked pie crust. Swirl knife through to give a marbled effect. Chill until firm before serving. This makes a wonderful centerpiece.

DATE PUDDING

¾ cup sugar
1 (8-ounce) package pitted dates
1 cup chopped nuts
2 eggs
¼ cup milk
1 teaspoon baking powder
⅓ cup flour
Pinch salt
½ teaspoon vanilla
Butter

Note: Have all ingredients at room temperature.

In a mixing bowl, place chopped dates and nuts. Then add sugar, flour, salt and baking powder. Mix and add beaten eggs, milk and vanilla. Mix well again and spread evenly in a well-greased and floured aluminum baking pan, 7 x 11-inch. Dot all over the top with butter. Bake in 325-degree oven for 30–35 minutes. Do not overbake. Cool overnight in refrigerator, or can be frozen until ready to use.

Before serving cover with whipped cream (or topping). Cut into desired number of squares. Place a red maraschino cherry in center of green-tinted whipped cream for Christmas. Any other time, you can serve with plain whipped cream and walnut or pecan half in center.

Opal Hamer, St. Petersburg, Fla.

MOCHA FLUFF
Serves 4

1 envelope gelatin
¼ cup water
¼ cup sugar
¼ teaspoon salt
1½ cups hot, strong coffee
2 tablespoons lemon juice
2 egg whites, stiffly
   beaten

Soften gelatin in cold water. Add sugar, salt and hot coffee, stirring thoroughly to dissolve. Add lemon juice and cool. When nearly set, beat until stiff. Add egg whites and continue beating until mixture holds its shape. Turn into molds and chill.

Suzan L. Wiener, Spring Hill, Fla.

GOLD RUSH BROWNIES

2 cups graham cracker crumbs
1 can sweetened condensed
   milk
1 (6-ounce) package chocolate
   chips
½ cup chopped pecans

Mix together and put into an 8 x 8-inch pan (well-greased). Bake at 350 degrees for 30 minutes. Let brownies cool 10 minutes. Cut into squares and remove from pan.

Norma L. Farrar, Sullivan, Mo.

MILK DUD DESSERT

6 egg yolks
1 cup sugar
1 cup rusk crumbs
½ cup chopped walnuts
1 teaspoon vanilla
1 teaspoon baking
   powder
6 egg whites
4 small packages Milk
   Duds
¹/₂ cup milk

1 cup confectioners'
   sugar
2 tablespoons butter
½ pint whipping cream

Beat egg yolks; add sugar and beat again.

Mix together rusk crumbs, nuts, vanilla and baking powder. Add to egg mixture. Fold in stiffly beaten egg whites. Bake in 9 x 13-inch greased pan at 350 degrees for 30 minutes. Cool. Melt Milk Duds, milk, confectioners' sugar and butter until smooth, stirring constantly. Let stand until cool and creamy. Whip the cream; spread over baked portion. Pour sauce on top and refrigerate overnight.

FROZEN DESSERT

23 Ritz crackers
1 large box pistachio instant pudding
1 pint vanilla ice cream, softened
1/2 stick melted margarine
3/4 cup milk
1 small carton Cool Whip

Combine Ritz crackers and the margarine and press into a 9-inch pie plate and bake at 350 degrees for 8–10 minutes. Allow to cool. Combine pudding with milk and blend in softened ice cream. Pour into crust. Spread Cool Whip on top surface and freeze. Garnish with chopped nuts.

Jodie McCoy, Tulsa, Okla.

BABY RUTH CANDY BROWNIES

⅔ cup margarine
1 cup brown sugar
¼ cup light corn syrup
¼ cup smooth peanut butter
1 teaspoon vanilla
1 cup quick oatmeal

Topping:
1 (12-ounce) package chocolate

   chips
1 (6-ounce) package butterscotch chips
⅔ cup smooth peanut butter
1 cup salted Spanish peanuts

Combine margarine, sugar and syrup in saucepan. Stir over low heat until margarine melts and sugar dissolves. Add peanut butter and vanilla. Pour over oatmeal; mix well. Press into a greased 13 x 9-inch pan and bake at 375 degrees for 12 minutes. Melt chocolate and butterscotch bits. Add peanut butter and peanuts. Pour over baked mixture. Cool and cut into squares.

Shirley Viscosi, Worcester, Mass.

PECAN BUTTER-SCOTCH BROWNIES
Makes 24 squares

¼ cup vegetable oil
1 tablespoon dark molasses
½ cup brown sugar, firmly packed
½ cup pecans, chopped
2 cups all-purpose flour
2 eggs
2 teaspoons vanilla
¼ teaspoon salt
½ cup milk
½ teaspoon baking powder

Combine all ingredients; spread in a greased 8 x 8 x 2-inch pan. Bake at 350 degrees for 30 minutes; turn out of pan; cut into squares or bars while hot; place a whole pecan on each square.

Gwen Campbell, Sterling, Va.

HULA SALAD

2 packages lime gelatin
2 cups boiling water
1 (16-ounce) can crushed pineapple
   with syrup
1 pint sour cream
1 cup maraschino cherries
1/2 cup chopped Macadamia nuts
1/2 cup coconut

Dissolve gelatin in boiling water and allow to cool. Add pineapple and sour cream. Fold in cherries and nuts. Pour into serving dish and sprinkle with coconut. Refrigerate.

QUICK APPLE KUCHEN

1 cup flour
1 teaspoon baking powder
1 egg
½ cup sugar
⅓ cup milk
¼ cup butter, melted
2 cups sliced apples
¼ cup sugar
½ teaspoon cinnamon

Sift together flour and baking powder; set aside. Beat egg; add sugar. Add half of dry ingredients; mix well; add milk; add remaining dry ingredients. Mix well and stir in butter.

Turn into well-greased 9 x 9-inch pan. Arrange apple slices on top of batter. Sprinkle with mixture of sugar and cinnamon. Bake at 375 degrees for 30–35 minutes.

June Harding, Ferndale, Mich.

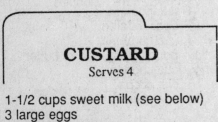

CUSTARD
Serves 4

1-1/2 cups sweet milk (see below)
3 large eggs
1/2 teaspoon vanilla
1/8 teaspoon nutmeg
1/8 teaspoon salt
Nutmeg, garnish

Beat or blend all ingredients until thoroughly combined. Pour into 4 custard cups and sprinkle with additional nutmeg. Set the custard cups in a pan of hot water. The water should come within 1 inch of the tops of the cups. Bake on oven shelf that is just below the oven center. Bake at 300 degrees for 1 hour, or until knife inserted in center comes out clean. Cool 20 minutes. Serve warm or cool to room temperature before serving, or chill in refrigerator and serve cold.

Sweet Milk:
2 cups reconstituted nonfat milk
2/3 cup raisins

Combine milk and raisins in a jar; cover and refrigerate at least overnight. Before using, shake the jar vigorously. Milk should be an ivory color. Strain the milk to remove the raisins, which will be mushy. Use milk as directed.

Note: It should be made at least one day in advance, but reaches peak sweetness after two or three days. (105 calories per serving)

EASY CHERRY COBBLER

2 cans tart cherries, undrained
1 package white cake mix
1 stick margarine, melted
1 cup nuts

Pour cherries in bottom of 9 x 13-inch pan, then sprinkle dry cake mix over cherries and *do not stir*. Pour melted margarine over cake mix; sprinkle nuts on top. *Do not mix.* Bake at 400 degrees for 30 minutes, or until set. Delicious topped with ice cream.

Denise Garcia, Salina, Kan.

LEMON REFRIGERATED DESSERT

Crust:
1 cup flour
1/2 cup margarine
1 cup finely chopped pecans

Mix flour, margarine and pecans together. Press into a 9 x 13-inch glass dish. Bake 20 minutes at 350 degrees. Cool.

Filling:
8 ounces cream cheese (room temperature)
1 cup confectioners' sugar
1 medium-size container Cool Whip
2 (1 1/2-ounce) packages instant lemon pudding
3 cups milk

Cream sugar and cream cheese. Fold in half of the Cool Whip and spread mixture over cooled crust. Blend pudding with milk until pudding begins to thicken. Spread on top of cheese mixture. Spread remaining Cool Whip over pudding mixture. Refrigerate until completely cooled and firm.

This can be prepared in advance. I often make it for family gatherings and reunions.

Flo Burtnett, Gage, Okla.

SIMPLY DELICIOUS EASY BROWNIES
Makes 25–30 bars

Grease a 9 x 13-inch baking pan. In large bowl, combine in order given:

1 cup butter *or* margarine
2 cups sugar
4 eggs (beating after each addition)
2 teaspoons vanilla
1½ cups all-purpose flour
½ cup plus 1 tablespoon cocoa
1 teaspoon salt

Mix well and add 1 cup chopped nuts, if desired. Put in pan; bake at 350 degrees for 30 minutes. Check at 25 minutes, if you like brownies chewy. Frost, if desired.

Audrey Reynolds, Lumberport, W.Va.

PASTEL BAVARIAN
Serves 7

1 (4-serving) package sugar-free gelatin, any flavor
3/4 cup boiling water
1/2 cup cold water
Ice cubes
1 (4-ounce) container Cool Whip topping, thawed

Dissolve gelatin in boiling water. Combine cold water and ice cubes to make 1-1/4 cups. Add to gelatin and stir until slightly thickened; remove any unmelted ice. Fold into whipped topping, blending well. Chill in individual dessert dishes or bowl until set, about 2 hours. (50 calories per serving)

Ida Bloedow, Madison, Wis.

CHERRY FRAPPÉ

1 small box cherry-flavored gelatin
1/2 cup boiling water
15 maraschino cherries
2 1/2 cups crushed ice
1 tablespoon maraschino cherry
　syrup

Put gelatin and boiling water in blender. Blend until gelatin is dissolved. Add cherries and syrup; continue to blend until mixture is fluffy. Add crushed ice and blend until mixture is the consistency of ice cream, about 3–4 minutes. Serve immediately in a cup or glass, or pour into 6-ounce paper cups and freeze for future use. Remove frozen frappés from freezer 15 minutes before serving. Top with mint, if desired.

This is a delicious treat for company, as well as your family.

Suzan L. Wiener, Spring Hill, Fla.

BRAN BLONDIES
Makes 36 squares

¾ cup flour, spooned lightly into
　cup
½ teaspoon baking powder
¼ teaspoon soda
¼ teaspoon salt
½ cup All-bran cereal
½ cup chopped walnuts *or*
　pecans
1 cup semisweet chocolate
　morsels
½ cup (1 stick) margarine
1 cup brown sugar (use part
　granulated, if desired)
1 large egg
1 teaspoon vanilla

Prepare a 9-inch square baking pan—spray with pan release, or grease and flour. (I foil-line and spray with pan release.)

Preheat oven to 350 degrees.

Into a small bowl measure flour, baking powder, soda, salt, All-bran, nuts and chocolate morsels; stir together; set aside. In a medium-size saucepan barely melt margarine. Remove from heat; stir in sugar. Add egg and vanilla; whisk or beat with fork to blend well. With a rubber spatula, stir in dry ingredients. Spread in prepared pan. Bake until cake tester comes out dry, about 20 minutes.

Especially good warm, while chocolate is still soft. Freeze extras; warm in microwave oven.

Note: For chocolate bars, combine only ⅔ cup chocolate morsels with dry ingredients. Melt remaining ⅓ cup morsels with margarine. Proceed as directed.

Mary Pledge Peterson, Cincinnati, Ohio

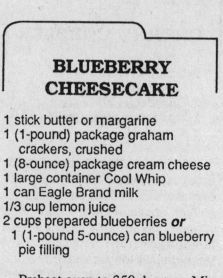

BLUEBERRY CHEESECAKE

1 stick butter or margarine
1 (1-pound) package graham
　crackers, crushed
1 (8-ounce) package cream cheese
1 large container Cool Whip
1 can Eagle Brand milk
1/3 cup lemon juice
2 cups prepared blueberries *or*
　1 (1-pound 5-ounce) can blueberry
　pie filling

Preheat oven to 350 degrees. Mix butter and graham crackers; press in bottom of oblong 9-inch glass dish to form crust. Bake 8-10 minutes until light brown. Cool. In large bowl combine cream cheese, Cool Whip, Eagle Brand milk and lemon juice; blend well. Pour into pie shell. Put blueberries on top. Refrigerate 3-4 hours before serving.

PUMPKIN FLAN
Serves 8

1/2 cup sugar
8 eggs
Sugar
1/4 teaspoon salt
2 (13 ounce) cans evaporated milk
2 teaspoons vanilla
1 cup canned pumpkin (not pie
　filling)
1 (8 ounce) can jellied cranberry
　sauce

Heat 1/2 cup sugar in heavy saucepan over medium heat until caramelized, stirring constantly. Pour caramel into 9x5-inch loaf pan; set aside. Beat eggs, 2/3 cup sugar, salt, evaporated milk, vanilla and pumpkin with wire whisk in large bowl until just blended but not frothy. Carefully pour pumpkin mixture into pan over caramel layer. Set pan inside large shallow baking pan. Place pans on oven rack and pour boiling water in outer pan to 1 inch. Bake at 350 degrees 1 hour or until knife inserted in center comes out clean. Cool on wire rack. Chill.

Just before serving, blend or process cranberry sauce until smooth. Loosen flan from sides of pan and invert onto serving plate. Cover top of flan with cranberry purée.

Bea Comas, Portland, Maine

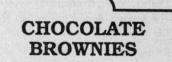

CHOCOLATE BROWNIES

2 cups sugar
2 cups flour
1 teaspoon soda
2 eggs, beaten
1 cup buttermilk
¼ pound margarine *or* butter
½ cup shortening
¼ cup cocoa
1 cup water

Sift flour, sugar and soda together in large bowl. Bring margarine, water, cocoa and shortening to a boil. Pour over flour and sugar, mix well. Add remaining ingredients. Pour into greased 15½ x 10½ x 1-inch pan. Bake at 350 degrees for 20–30 minutes, or until done.

Brownie Icing:
1 stick margarine *or* butter
¼ cup cocoa
6 tablespoons milk
4 cups confectioners' sugar,
　sifted
1 teaspoon vanilla
1 cup nuts, chopped

Mix first 5 ingredients well with mixer; fold in chopped nuts, and spread on brownies while hot. The icing melts a bit, but firms up again as it all cools. Brownies stay moist and are delicious!!

Dolores Warner, Thomasboro, Ill.

CHERRY BREAD AND BUTTER PUDDING

Serves 6

12 slices white bread
Butter
Cinnamon
1 (10 ounce) jar cherry preserves
4 eggs
2-2/3 cups milk
2 tablespoons sugar
1/4 teaspoon almond extract

Cut crusts from bread. Spread butter on one side of each slice. Arrange four slices in bottom of baking dish 8x8x2-inches. Sprinkle lightly with cinnamon. Spread about 2 teaspoons of preserves on each slice. Repeat, making two more layers. In medium bowl, beat eggs; add milk, sugar and extract and stir well until mixed. Pour over bread. Bake in preheated 325 degree oven for 1 hour. Refrigerate.

If preferred, serve warm from the oven.

Kit Rollins, Cedarburg, Wis.

CHICAGO PUMPKIN SLICES

1 large (2-pie) can pumpkin
1 (12-ounce) can evaporated milk
1 cup sugar
3 eggs
1 teaspoon cinnamon
½ teaspoon ginger
¼ teaspoon cloves
½ teaspoon salt
1 package Jiffy yellow cake mix
1½ sticks margarine, melted
1 cup coarsely ground nuts

Mix together first 8 ingredients; blend well. Put mixture into a 9 x 13 x 2-inch baking pan. Sprinkle top with package of Jiffy cake mix. Melt margarine and pour on top of mixture; sprinkle with ground nuts. Bake in a 350-degree oven for 50–60 minutes.

Joy Shamway, Freeport, Ill.

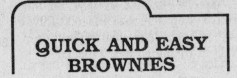

QUICK AND EASY BROWNIES

½ cup shortening
2 eggs
2 squares bitter chocolate
½ teaspoon baking powder
1 cup sugar
½ teaspoon salt
1 cup nuts, chopped
¼ cup flour
1 teaspoon vanilla

Melt chocolate and shortening together over hot water. Add sugar and eggs; beat thoroughly. Add vanilla and nuts. Mix baking powder and salt with the flour. Add to first mixture. Mix thoroughly. Pour into a greased 8 x 12-inch baking pan and bake 25 minutes in a moderate 350-degree oven.

Suzan L. Wiener, Spring Hill, Fla.

FROZEN FRUIT-MALLOW SQUARES

2 (3-ounce) packages cream cheese, softened
1 cup mayonnaise
1 (30-ounce) can fruit cocktail, drained
2 1/2 cups miniature marshmallows
1 cup chilled whipping cream
1/4 cup pecans, finely chopped

Combine cream cheese and mayonnaise; beat with an electric mixer, blending thoroughly. Stir in fruit cocktail, marshmallows and pecans. In a separate bowl, whip cream until soft peaks form; fold in fruit mixture. Pour into 12 x 7 1/2 x 2-inch glass dish or refrigerator tray. Cover and store in freezer until firm. Ten minutes before serving time, remove from freezer and allow to stand at room temperature. Cut into squares; serve at once.

Gwen Campbell, Sterling, Va.

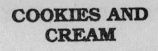

COOKIES AND CREAM

1 egg, well-beaten with mixer
2/3 cup–1 cup (as desired) confectioners' sugar
1 (8-ounce) container Cool Whip
8 ounces sour cream
*3/4 to 1 (1-pound) package Oreo cookies (crushed, with some pieces)

Add confectioners' sugar to egg; mix until smooth. Beat in sour cream. Fold in Cool Whip. Mix well. Add crushed cookies and stir well to combine. Cover and refrigerate overnight to soften cookie crumbs.

This is the same as that found in the dessert sections of the delis in stores. Any cream-filled sandwich cookie could be used.

*Using three-quarters of the cookies is my preference. Cookies swell when they set. It's all up to the individual's taste.

Lisa Hayden, Fostoria, Ohio

ORANGE-CREAM DESSERT

Serves 10–12

1 teaspoon shredded orange peel
1/2 cup orange juice
1/2 cup sugar
1 cup orange juice
1 prepared 10-inch sponge cake
1 cup whipping cream
1/4 cup sugar
1 teaspoon shredded orange peel
1 cup dairy sour cream

Combine 1 teaspoon peel, 1/2 cup orange juice and 1/2 cup sugar. Heat and stir until sugar dissolves. Add 1 cup orange juice; cool. Drizzle over top, bottom and sides of cake.

Combine whipping cream with 1/4 cup sugar and 1 teaspoon orange peel; beat until stiff peaks form. Fold into the sour cream until blended. Spread evenly over top and sides of cake. Chill several hours. (Sour cream in the frosting gives an unusual tang.)

Margaret Hamfeldt, Louisville, Ky.

APPLE ROLY POLY
Serves 6-8

2 cups prepared baking mix
1/2 cup honey
3/4 teaspoon cinnamon
1/4 teaspoon nutmeg
1/4 teaspoon cloves
3 tablespoons sugar
5 large tart apples, peeled, cored, finely chopped
2 tablespoons butter or margarine

Prepare biscuit mix as directed on package. On lightly floured board, roll dough into 1/4 inch oblong (about 10x12 inches). Spread with honey to within 1 inch of the edges of dough. Combine spices and sugar. Toss with apples. Spread apples evenly over the honey, and dot apples with butter. Roll up like a jelly roll and seal well. Bake in greased pan with sides at 350 degrees for 40 minutes. Slice and serve hot with whipped cream, hot lemon, or vanilla sauce.

COLONIAL BAKED APPLES
Serves 8

3 medium sweet potatoes
1/2 teaspoon finely shredded orange peel
2 tablespoons orange juice
1 tablespoon brown sugar
1 tablespoon butter or margarine
1/4 teaspoon nutmeg, ground
1/4 teaspoon salt
1 beaten egg
2 tablespoons milk
8 large cooking apples, peeled and cored
1/2 cup corn syrup
2 tablespoons lemon juice

Cook sweet potatoes, covered in enough boiling salted water to cover, for 25 to 35 minutes or until tender. Drain, peel, dice and mash with electric mixer on low speed until smooth. Should have about 1-3/4 cups mashed potatoes. Add orange peel, orange juice, sugar butter, nutmeg and salt. Add egg and milk; set aside. Remove a slice from top of each apple. Score apple by going around the outside surface with tines of a fork in circular pattern. Using pastry bag fitted with star tip, fill apples with sweet potato mixture. Place apples in 12 x 7-1/2 x 2-inch baking dish. Stir corn syrup and lemon juice together and pour over apples. Bake uncovered in 325 degree oven for 45 minutes or until tender, basting several times with the corn syrup mixture. Serve hot.

Leona Teodori, Warren, MI

BOILED APPLE DUMPLINGS

3 cups flour
4 teaspoons baking powder
1/2 teaspoon salt
2 tablespoons sugar
2 tablespoons vegetable shortening
1/4 cup milk
3 large tart apples
6 teaspoons sugar
Milk
Sugar

Sift baking powder, salt, and sugar with flour into bowl. Cut in shortening until mixture is in crumbs the size of peas. Stir in 1/4 cup milk. On floured board, roll dough to 1-1/2 inch thickness. Cut into six squares. Pare and core apples and cut in half. Place a half on each square of dough and sprinkle with 1 teaspoon sugar.

Pull the four corners of the dough together, dampen slightly, and press edges to seal. Tie each dumpling in a clean piece of white muslin. Drop dumplings into a large kettle of boiling water. Cook 20-25 minutes depending on size of apple. Serve with milk, cinnamon, and sugar, if desired.

Mrs. A. Dettmer, Canfield, OH

MAPLE APPLE BROWN BETTY
Serves 4

1-1/2 cups fine bread crumbs, toasted lightly
3/4 stick (6 tablespoons) unsalted butter
4 apples, peeled and diced
1/2 cup maple syrup
3/4 teaspoon cinnamon
Vanilla ice cream, as an accompaniment

Sprinkle bottom of well-buttered baking dish with one fourth of the crumbs; dot the crumbs with one fourth of the butter. Spread one third of apples over the crumbs. In a small bowl combine the syrup and cinnamon; drizzle one third of mixture over apples. Layer the remaining crumbs, butter, apples and syrup mixture, ending with a layer of crumbs and butter. Bake in a preheated 375 degree oven for 40 minutes or until apples are tender. Serve the dessert with ice cream, if desired.

Peggy Fowler Revels, Woodruff, S. C.

MARSHMALLOW APPLE CRISP
Serves 6

4 cups peeled, sliced apples
1/4 cup water
3/4 cup flour
1/2 cup sugar
1 teaspoon cinnamon
1/4 teaspoon salt
1/2 cup margarine
1/2 cup miniature marshmallows

Place apples and water in 8-inch square baking dish. Combine flour, sugar, cinnamon, and salt; cut in margarine until mixture is like coarse crumbs. Sprinkle over apples. Bake at 350 degrees for 35 to 40 minutes or until apples are tender. Sprinkle with marshmallows. Broil until lightly browned.

Barbara Beauregard-Smith, South Australia

STRAWBERRY MERINGUE TORTE

3 egg whites
1/2 teaspoon baking powder
1 cup sugar
10 squares or 10 soda crackers
    rolled fine
1/2 cup pecans, rolled fine
3 cups sliced strawberries
Cool Whip

Beat egg whites and baking powder until frothy. Gradually beat in sugar until whites are stiff. Fold in crackers and pecans. Spread in 9-inch pie pan, which has been greased thoroughly with butter. Bake 30 minutes in 300 degree oven.

Fill meringue tart with strawberries; top with Cool Whip when ready to serve.

Ruth Arnett, Fort Recovery, Ohio

STRAWBERRY ALMOND BUTTER

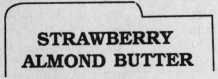

1/2 pound margarine
1 pound powdered sugar
1 pound strawberries
1/2 cup finely ground almonds

Cream butter with powdered sugar and work in the pound of hulled strawberries that have been forced through a colander. When well mixed, stir in almonds and pinch of salt, if desired.

For a change-of-pace dessert, strawberries with sour cream custard is a "conversation piece." This recipe will serve 6 and it looks delightful in a glass bowl that has been chilled.

FROZEN STRAWBERRY DESSERT

24 large marshmallows
1 (10-ounce) package frozen
    strawberries (thawed)
1 cup sifted flour
1/2 cup milk
1 envelope Dream Whip
1 stick margarine

Have margarine at room temperature. Cut margarine into flour to make crumbs. Press into bottom of 7x11-inch pan. Bake at 400 degrees until brown. Cool. Melt marshmallows in milk. Add strawberries and let cool. When cool, add prepared Dream Whip. Pour into crust and freeze. Best when eaten partially frozen.

I keep this dessert in the freezer for unexpected guests.

Charlene Stark, Riceville, Iowa

STRAWBERRY ALMOND FRITTERS

Strawberries
1 cup apricot jam
1 cup toasted almonds
1 cup cracker crumbs
2 eggs

Wash, hull, and dry strawberries on paper towel. Force apricot jam through coarse strainer. Finely chop toasted almonds and crush salted crackers until you have a cupful. Beat eggs slightly. Dip each berry in jam and roll in almonds. When all are coated, dip, two at a time, in egg and then crumbs. Chill. Before serving time, heat deep fat to 360 degrees and cook berries until they are golden brown. Serve at once, passing powdered sugar, if desired. These may be fried in skillet also.

Strawberries are not only for royalty, nor do we have to "sew a fine seam" to enjoy them. We are fortunate enough to have these delectable goodies available to us all year long. Whichever recipe you choose, it will add a noble note to your table.

STRAWBERRY GERMAN CREAM

Serves 6-8

1 (10-ounce) box frozen sliced
    strawberries, thawed
1 cup boiling water
1 (3-ounce) package strawberry
    gelatin
1 envelope dessert topping mix

Drain strawberries, reserving syrup. Pour boiling water over gelatin in bowl, stirring until gelatin is dissolved. Add enough cold water to reserved syrup to measure 1 cup; stir into dissolved gelatin. Chill until almost set. Prepare dessert topping mix as package directs. Beat gelatin until foamy. Fold gelatin and strawberries into topping mix. Pour into 1-quart mold. Chill until firm; unmold. Serve with sweetened whipped cream and garnish with strawberries.

Sharon M. Crider, Evansville, Wis.

FROSTY STRAWBERRY SUPREME

Serves 9-12

1 cup all-purpose flour
1/4 cup finely chopped pecans
1/4 cup brown sugar, packed
1/2 cup melted margarine
2 cups egg whites
1 (10-ounce) package frozen
    strawberries, partially thawed
2/3 cup white granulated sugar
2 tablespoons lemon juice
1 cup whipped cream or non-dairy
    whipped topping.

Combine flour, nuts, brown sugar, and melted margarine. Mix well and spread into 13x9-inch pan. Bake at 350 degrees for about 20 to 25 minutes, stirring to crumble. Combine egg whites, sugar, strawberries, and lemon juice in a large deep mixing bowl. Beat with electric mixer at high speed for 15 minutes. Fold in whipped cream or whipped topping. Place one-half the crumbs in bottom of the pan. Pour in strawberry mixture, then top with remaining crumbs. Freeze until firm. Cut into squares to serve. Top each serving with whipped topping, if desired. This is really a "Supreme" dessert.

Note: Use blueberries for a change of pace, adjusting to suit your own taste in regard to sugar.

Shirley Ann Crist, Marion, Ind.

CARAMEL CORN

Serves 6-8

6 toffee bars, (1-1/8 ounce each)
1/4 cup light corn syrup
8 cups popped popcorn
1 cup unsalted roasted peanuts

In heavy saucepan, heat toffee bars and corn syrup over low heat until melted, stirring often. Pour popcorn into large, deep pan. Add warm toffee mixture and peanuts. Toss well until popcorn is coated. Cool; break into chunks.

Children and adults all enjoy caramel corn.

Dorothy Garms, Anaheim, Calif.

CARAMEL CRUNCH

1 cup light brown sugar, firmly
    packed
1/2 cup butter or margarine
1 (6 ounce) package chocolate
    chips
1 cup coarsely chopped nuts

Combine sugar and butter in saucepan; boil 7 minutes. Melt chocolate chips in saucepan over low heat. Spread nuts over bottom of buttered 8x8 inch pan. Pour butter and sugar mixture slowly over nuts. Pour melted chocolate over top. Cool. Cut into pieces.

Sharon M. Crider, Evansville, Wis.

DATE NUT BALLS

Cook together for 5 minutes:
1 stick margarine
1 cup sugar
1 egg, beaten
1 (8 ounce) package dates, cut up
Pinch of salt

Remove from heat and cool.
Add:

1 cup chopped nuts
2 cups Rice Krispies
1 teaspoon vanilla

Stir well and shape in small balls. Roll in flaked coconut.

Jean Baker, Chula Vista, Calif.

EASTER EGG CANDY

1 cup hot mashed potatoes
2 tablespoons butter
1 cup shredded coconut
1 teaspoon vanilla
3 - 1 pound boxes confectioners'
    sugar
1 - 8 ounce package of chocolate
    chips
1/8 cake paraffin

Combine potatoes and butter; stir in coconut and vanilla. Add sugar gradually, mixing well after each addition. Form into egg shapes, using 1 tablespoon mixture for each egg; place on waxed paper. Let harden for 1-3 days. Melt chocolate over hot water; dip eggs into chocolate, using 2 spoons. Place on waxed paper to harden. Chopped nuts, candied fruits, or peanut butter may be used instead of coconut.

Allie Fields, Pensacola, FL

EASTER PEANUT BUTTER EGGS

2 eggs, well beaten
1/8 teaspoon salt
1-1/2 to 2 cups peanut butter
4-5 cups powdered sugar
1 teaspoon vanilla
1 Hershey chocolate bar
1 - 6 ounce package chocolate chips

Mix the eggs, salt, peanut butter, sugar, and vanilla in order listed. Form dough into egg shapes. Melt the chocolate bar and the chocolate chips in a double boiler. Dip egg shapes into chocolate mixture. Arrange on waxed paper until set.

Sally Thompson, Louisville, KY

ICE CREAM SANDWICHES

Makes 15

32 graham cracker squares
2 tablespoons milk
1 tablespoon cornstarch
1 tub Creamy Deluxe ready to spread
    frosting (any flavor)
1-1/2 cups chilled whipping cream.

Line 13x9x2 inch pan with aluminum foil. Arrange 16 graham crackers on foil, cutting about 6 of the squares to completely cover foil. Mix milk and cornstarch in large bowl; stir in frosting and whipping cream. Beat on medium speed, scraping bowl constantly, 2 minutes. Beat on high speed until thick and creamy; scrape bowl occasionally. Beat about 3 minutes. Spread over graham crackers in pan. Arrange remaining graham crackers over frosting mixture, cutting about 6 of the squares to completely cover mixture. Cover and freeze until firm, about 8 hours. Cut into 2-1/2 inch squares.

Agnes Ward, Erie, PA

HOMEMADE MARSHMALLOWS

2 cups granulated sugar
3/4 cup water
2 tablespoons gelatin
1/2 cup cold water
1 teaspoon vanilla
1/2 teaspoon salt
Cornstarch
Confectioners' sugar

Mix granulated sugar with 3/4 cup water. Simmer to soft ball stage. Remove from fire. Soften gelatin in cold water. Place on large platter. Pour hot syrup over softened gelatin. Stir until dissolved. Let stand until partially cooled; whip until thick and white, and mixture will nearly hold its shape. Add vanilla and salt. Pour into straight sided pans lined with equal parts of cornstarch and confectioners' sugar, mixed together. Let stand in cool place until firm (not in ice box). Cut into squares with scissors and dust with confectioners' sugar.

Jennie Lien, Stoughton, WI

OLD-FASHIONED RICE PUDDING
Serves 6

1 quart skim milk
1 teaspoon Sweet 'N Low sugar
   substitute
1/4 cup raw white rice
1 tablespoon butter
1/4 teaspoon salt
1/4 teaspoon nutmeg
1 teaspoon vanilla

Preheat oven at 325 degrees. In a lightly greased 1-1/2 quart casserole, combine all ingredients. Bake uncovered, stirring frequently, for the first hour. The complete cooking time is 2-1/2 hours. This may be served topped with low-calorie whipped cream or crushed fruit. (115 calories per serving)

Judy Codenys, LaGrange, Texas

FIGGY PUDDING
Serves 8-10

1-1/2 cups all-purpose flour
1 teaspoon baking powder
1/2 teaspoon baking soda
1/2 teaspoon cinnamon
1/2 teaspoon nutmeg
1/2 teaspoon ginger
1 cup chopped cranberries
1 cup shredded carrots
1 cup packed brown sugar
1/2 cup cooking oil
1/2 cup honey
2 beaten eggs

In a large bowl, combine dry ingredients. In a bowl, combine carrots, cranberries, brown sugar, oil, honey, and eggs. Add carrot mixture to dry ingredients. Pour into greased 7-cup mold. Bake in a 325-degree oven for 30 to 40 minutes or until it tests done. Serve with Orange Hard Sauce (recipe follows).

Orange Hard Sauce:
Makes 1/2 cup

1/4 cup butter, softened
1 cup sifted confectioners' sugar
1/4 teaspoon shredded orange peel
1 tablespoon orange juice

Beat butter and sugar together in a small bowl. Beat in peel and juice until well-blended. Spoon into small serving bowl. Chill.

Marcella Swigert, Monroe City, Mo.

PARTY PUNCH BOWL DESSERT

1 box yellow cake mix
2 large boxes strawberry gelatin
2 large containers Cool Whip
2 large (10-ounce) packages frozen
   sliced strawberries
2 large packages regular vanilla
   pudding (*not* instant)
Fresh strawberries for garnish

Use 2 (8-inch) round layer cake pans and a clear glass punch bowl. Make cake according to box directions. Cool; cut layers horizontally by pulling string through so you have 4 layers. Make vanilla pudding according to package directions and let cool. Mix 2-1/2 cups boiling water with 2 packages strawberry gelatin to dissolve. Add the 2 packages of partially thawed berries. Put in refrigerator until mixture thickens—but do not let it get too firm.

To assemble:
In the punch bowl add 1/4 of the gelatin mixture.
First layer of cake, 1/4 more gelatin, spread a layer of Cool Whip, then a layer of pudding.
Second layer of cake, gelatin, Cool Whip, pudding
Third layer of cake, gelatin, Cool Whip, pudding
Fourth layer of cake only, topped with thick layer of Cool Whip. Garnish with fresh, sliced berries. You can make this the night before but *do not* put last layer of Cool Whip on until an hour or so before serving. Use large serving spoon to scoop out servings. Prepare for raving reviews on appearance and taste!

Mary Fuller, Warren, Ohio

CARAMEL TOPPED RICE CUSTARD
Serves 6

12 caramel candies
2-1/4 cups milk, divided
2 cups cooked rice, cooled
4 eggs
1/3 cup packed brown sugar
1 teaspoon vanilla extract
1/4 teaspoon salt

Combine caramels and 1/4 cup milk in small saucepan. Cook, stirring, over medium-low heat until caramels melt. Pour equal amounts into 6 buttered, 3/4-cup custard cups. Spoon 1/3 cup rice into each cup. Blend remaining ingredients; pour evenly into each cup. Place cups in shallow pan, containing 1 inch water. Bake at 350 degrees for 45 minutes, or until custard is set. Loosen custard with knife and invert onto dessert plates. Garnish with chopped nuts or coconut, if desired. Serve warm.

STRAWBERRIES WITH SOUR CREAM CUSTARD

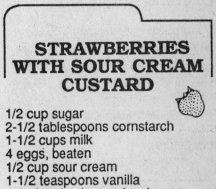

1/2 cup sugar
2-1/2 tablespoons cornstarch
1-1/2 cups milk
4 eggs, beaten
1/2 cup sour cream
1-1/2 teaspoons vanilla
1-2 pints fresh strawberries
   (washed, hulled and halved)

Combine sugar and cornstarch in medium saucepan. Gradually, stir in milk and cook over medium heat, stirring constantly until it boils. Boil and stir 1 minute. Remove from heat. Blend milk mixture *into egg mixture* in saucepan. Add sour cream and vanilla; beat with whisk until well blended. Cool *immediately* by placing in a bowl of ice cold water for a few minutes. Cover and chill thoroughly. To serve, spoon custard sauce over strawberries. Will literally melt in your mouth.

Strawberry Almond Fritters are also completely different from the usual.

CHOCOLATE DELIGHT

Crust:

1/2 cup chopped pecans
1-1/2 cups flour
1-1/4 sticks margarine

Melt margarine; add flour, nuts, and mix well. Pat into 9x13-inch pan. Bake 20-25 minutes at 350 degrees until slightly brown.

First layer:

1 cup powdered sugar
1 medium size Cool Whip
1 (8 ounce) cream cheese

Mix powdered sugar and cream cheese; blend well. Add 1 cup of Cool Whip; spread over crust.

Second layer:

2 (6 ounce) boxes instant chocolate
   pudding mix
3 cups milk

Combine pudding mix and milk. Pour mixture over first layer.

Third layer:

Spread remaining Cool Whip over top. Make dessert 24 hours before serving and refrigerate, but do not freeze.

Beulah Schwallie, Cincinnati, Ohio

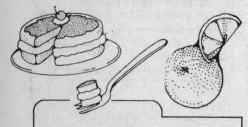

LEMON DELIGHT

Serves 12-15

1-1/2 cups flour, sifted
1-1/2 sticks margarine
1/2 cup chopped pecans
1 - 8 ounce package cream cheese
1 cup sifted powdered sugar
1 - 9 ounce container frozen whipped
   topping
2 - 6 ounce packages instant lemon
   pudding mix
2 tablespoons lemon juice
3 cups milk
1/2 cup chopped pecans

Blend together flour, margarine and 1/2 cup pecans. Press into a 13 x 9 inch pan. Bake 20 minutes at 350 degrees. Cool.

Blend together cream cheese, powdered sugar, and 1/2 of 9 ounce carton of whipped topping. Spread over crust. Combine 2 packages instant lemon pudding mix with 2 tablespoons lemon juice and 3 cups milk. Pour over previous layer. When firm, top with remainder of whipped topping. Sprinkle with 1/2 cup pecans. Chill overnight and keep in refrigerator. A delightful tasting dessert.

Barbara Beauregard-Smith, Northfield, South Australia

APPLE DUMPLING DESSERT

1 can (10) country-style refrigerator
   biscuits
2 cups thinly sliced peeled apples
1/2 cup packed brown sugar
1/2 cup evaporated milk
1/2 cup dark corn syrup
1/4 cup margarine

Preheat oven to 375 degrees.
Grease an 8-inch square baking dish. Separate biscuits into 10 individual ones. Place on bottom of buttered baking dish. Arrange apple slices over top.

In small saucepan combine all remaining ingredients and bring to a boil, stirring constantly. Pour hot syrup mixture over apples and biscuits. Bake at 375 degrees for 25-35 minutes or until golden brown and biscuits are done in the center. Serve warm.

For extra goodness, top with whipped cream.

Jodie McCoy, Tulsa, OK

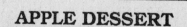

APPLE DESSERT

1 box yellow cake mix
1/2 cup margarine

1/2 cup coconut
2-1/2 cups sliced apples
1/2 cup sugar
1 teaspoon cinnamon
1 cup sour cream
1 egg

Put yellow cake mix, margarine and coconut in bowl and mix like you would for pie crust. Pat into ungreased 13 x 9 inch pan. Bake 10 minutes at 350 degrees. Mix sugar, cinnamon, and apples and put over baked crust. Blend the sour cream and egg; drizzle over top. Bake at 350 degrees for 25 minutes. You can use any flavor cake mix or any kind of fruit. This is a really delicious dessert you will enjoy.

Barbara Smith, Northfield, South Australia

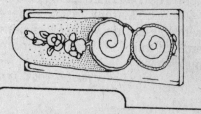

BANANA SPLIT DESSERT

First layer:

2 cups graham cracker crumbs
1/2 cup sugar
1 stick melted margarine
   Mix and spread in bottom of 11 x 14-inch casserole.

Second layer:

2 egg whites, stiffly beaten
1 stick softened margarine
1 (1-pound) box powdered sugar

Beat with mixer for 10 minutes, spread over crumbs.

Third layer:

Slice 2-3 bananas over sugar mixture.

Fourth layer:

Spread 1 large can crushed pineapple, drained, over banana layer.

Fifth layer:

Spread 1 large or 2 small cartons Cool Whip over pineapple.

Sixth layer:

Sprinkle chopped pecans and maraschino cherries over all.

Marcella Swigert, Monroe City, MO

Foreign
& EXOTIC

RED CABBAGE ROLLS
Makes 8 rolls

1 medium head of red cabbage, with the center core removed
2 tablespoons butter
1 cup bread crumbs
1 egg
3 tablespoons oil
2 cups clear meat stock or bouillon
3 small onions, minced
1 pound ground pork mixed with beef
Salt & pepper to taste
4 tablespoons all-purpose flour
1/3 cup half-and-half

Bring a large pot of salted water to full boil. Plunge the head of red cabbage into the boiling water. Let it cool for 5 minutes, carefully removing outer leaves. Repeat until all leaves are removed. In a small skillet, melt butter. Add onion; sauté until shiny. In a large bowl, combine bread crumbs, ground meats, sautéed onion, egg, salt, and pepper. Divide mixture into 8 portions. Take 2 cabbage leaves at a time, placing one leaf inside the other. Spread one portion of the mixture over surface (be sure to stop short of the edges). Roll up into a roll. Repeat with remaining cabbage and mixture. Heat oil in a large fry pan. Add cabbage rolls; sauté gently.

Dissolve flour in stock or bouillon; add to fry pan. Cover and cook gently over low heat for 40 minutes; stirring occasionally. Add salt and pepper to taste. Add the half-and-half; stir to blend. Place on a warm serving dish.

Spoon sauce over cabbage rolls. Serve mashed potatoes or rice, and a tossed salad.

Marie Fusaro, Manasquan, N.J.

CHICKEN WITH DUMPLINGS A LA ITALIANO

Soup:
3 quarts water
1 whole chicken, 2-1/2 to 3 pounds
1 onion
2-3 teaspoons salt
Parsley leaves

Egg Dumpling Mixture:
6 eggs
1/2 cup grated Parmesan cheese
1/2 cup Italian bread crumbs
1/2 teaspoon salt
Pinch black pepper
Few sprigs parsley, chopped
1/2 pound ground chuck

Soup:
Rinse chicken, and put into pan with 3 quarts boiling water; add onion, salt, and parsley; boil for 1-1/2 hours. Let stand awhile, then strain into another pan. Serve chicken separately.

Dumplings:
Blend dumpling mixture well. Put soup on to boil again and drop the dumpling mixture into the boiling soup by tablespoonfuls. Make ground chuck into shape of small marbles and drop into the soup; cook for 10 minutes. Serve hot with extra grated cheese.

Leona Teodori, Warren, Mich.

SOPA RANCHERA (RANCH-STYLE SOUP)
Serves 4

1/4 cup chopped onion
1 tablespoon cooking oil
4 cups chicken broth
1/4 cup long grain rice
1/4 cup tomato purée
1/4 teaspoon salt
Dash pepper
1 cup frozen peas

In saucepan cook onion in hot oil until tender, but not brown. Stir in chicken broth, rice, tomato purée, salt, and pepper. Bring to a boil. Reduce heat; cover and simmer for 25 minutes. Stir in frozen peas; simmer, covered, for 5 minutes longer.

Mrs. Robert Shaffer, Middleburg, Pa.

MEXICAN SOUFFLE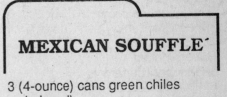

3 (4-ounce) cans green chiles (minced)
2 cups grated Monterey cheese
2 cups grated medium-sharp cheddar cheese
6 large eggs
1 cup flour
4 cups milk
Salt and pepper to taste

Butter bottom of 3-quart soufflé dish. Layer chiles and cheeses in bottom. Beat eggs, flour, milk, seasonings, and pour over chiles and cheeses. Bake at 350 degrees for 1 hour. Let stand 5 minutes before serving.

GERMAN-STYLE BEANS
Serves 6

4 slices bacon
½ cup onion, chopped
1½ tablespoons sugar
1½ tablespoons flour
¼ teaspoon celery seed
½ teaspoon salt
2 (15½-ounce) cans green and shelled beans
⅓ cup vinegar

Cook bacon until crisp; remove and drain bacon. Add onion to bacon drippings. Cook until tender. Add sugar, flour, celery seed and salt. Cook until bubbly. Drain beans; reserve ⅓ cup liquid. Add bean liquid and vinegar to flour mixture. Stir; add beans. Simmer about 10–15 minutes, or until slightly thickened and thoroughly heated. Crumble bacon and add to beans.

Leota Baxter, Ingalls, Kan.

APPLE STRUDEL (GERMANY)
Serves 8

2 cups sifted flour
3 teaspoons baking powder
1/2 teaspoon salt
3 tablespoons sugar
1/4 cup shortening
2/3-3/4 cup milk
Butter, melted
1 teaspoon cinnamon
3/4 cup apples, chopped
1/2 cup brown sugar
1 tablespoon cream or half-and-half
Confectioners' sugar
1/2 teaspoon vanilla

Sift flour with the baking powder, salt, and 3 tablespoons of sugar. Cut shortening into the dry ingredients until evenly distributed; add milk to make soft dough. Turn onto a lightly floured board and knead gently. Roll dough into a rectangular shape, which is 1/4-inch thick. Brush melted butter over the top surface of rectangle. Combine the cinnamon, 1/2 cup sugar, and apples. Cover the dough's surface with apple-cinnamon mixture. Roll in jelly roll fashion to enclose the fruit filling. Place on a greased cookie sheet; shape the roll into the form of a semicircle. Bake at 400 degrees for 30 minutes. Sprinkle brown sugar over the top during the last 15 minutes of baking time. Combine remaining ingredients for icing. Frost strudel and sprinkle with nuts, if desired.

Zenana Warren, Bloomville, Ohio

EUROPEAN TORTE SQUARES

½ pound butter (2 sticks)
1 cup sugar
6 egg yolks
2 cups flour
1 teaspoon salt
1 teaspoon baking powder
Grape jelly

Cream butter and sugar. Add the 6 egg yolks and cream well. Sift flour, salt and baking powder; add to creamed mixture. Pat this mixture on a cookie sheet and spread top surface with grape jelly. Top this with icing (recipe follows).

Icing:
6 egg whites
1 cup ground nuts
1 cup sugar

Beat egg whites until they hold peaks. Add nuts and sugar; blend well. Use this on top of torte. Cut in squares and bake for 30 minutes at 375 degrees.

Jen Lien, Stoughton, Wis.

MEXICAN STUFFED GREEN PEPPERS

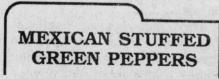

6–8 large green peppers
1 pound bulk sausage, or 1 pound ground beef
1/2 cup green onion, chopped
1 can chili beef soup
1/2 cup tomato juice
1/2 cup Monterey Jack cheese, grated
1 (12-ounce) can Mexicorn, drained
1 cup cooked rice
1 cup tortilla chips, crushed

Slice off tops of peppers; remove seeds; rinse insides of peppers. Place peppers in a 2-quart casserole; cover and microwave on HIGH for 7–10 minutes. Let stand 4 minutes.

Place sausage and onion in a 2-quart casserole; microwave on HIGH for 4–6 minutes; stir twice. Drain and break up meat. Stir in soup, tomato juice, cheese, Mexicorn and rice. Mix well and spoon into peppers; cover and microwave on (70 percent) MEDIUM HIGH for 7–9 minutes, or until hot. Sprinkle with tortilla chips.

ENGLISH STEAMED FRUIT PUDDING
Serves 8

1/4 pound (1 stick) butter
1/2 cup sugar
1 egg
1 1/2 cups flour
1/2 teaspoon baking soda
1/4 teaspoon ground nutmeg
1/4 cup buttermilk
3 cups berries or other diced fruit

Cream butter and sugar until smooth. Beat in egg. Sift together flour, baking soda and nutmeg. Add to butter mixture, along with buttermilk. (Batter should be firm, but still a little sticky.) With floured hands line a 4-cup mold with 2/3 of the dough. Fill with the fruit. Top with the rest of dough and smooth with a spatula. Cover mold tightly with foil. Place on a steamer rack. Cover and steam over medium heat, 2 1/2–3 hours, or until pastry is done. Cool 15 minutes, then unmold onto a serving platter. Slice to serve and accompany with heavy cream or whipped cream.

I acquired this recipe several years ago from an Englishman, who said this was his favorite dessert. It has brought rave reviews every time I have served it. I've used various fruits but raspberries, apricots and blueberries are my favorites. It freezes well.

Roxanne E. Chan, Albany, Calif.

Holiday
SPECIALS

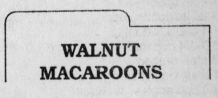

GOOEY CHOCOLATE CAKE
Serves 16

1 cup buttermilk
1 cup vegetable oil
2 eggs
2 cups flour
2 cups sugar
1 tablespoon baking soda
1/2 teaspoon salt
1/2 cup cocoa
1 cup strong hot coffee

Mix together the buttermilk, oil and eggs. Set aside. In separate bowl, sift together flour, sugar, soda, and salt, if desired. Add cocoa to dry mixture. Combine buttermilk mixture and dry ingredients, beat about 2 minutes. Slowly add the hot coffee, beating well. Bake in greased and floured 9x13-inch baking pan at 350 degrees for 35-40 minutes.

Frosting:
3-4 (1-ounce) squares unsweetened chocolate
3 tablespoons margarine
1 (1-pound) box confectioners' sugar
3-6 tablespoons strong coffee

Over low heat, melt chocolate and margarine (for very dark, use 4 squares). Cool slightly and beat in confectioners' sugar. Add 3 tablespoons coffee and beat; add remaining coffee to make the proper consistency for spreading. Cake may be frosted as a single layer or cut in half and frosted as layer cake.

Another "love token" is a Praline Cake, equally as delicious, and it will serve 12—if cut carefully.

HOLIDAY GARLAND HAM
Serves 20

5 pounds precooked ham
  Whole cloves
1 cup brown sugar, firmly packed
½ cup maple-flavored syrup
¼ cup Dijon mustard
1 tablespoon cornstarch
1 (20-ounce) can crushed pineapple with juice
  Vegetable Garland (recipe follows)

Score ham; stud with cloves. Place on rack in shallow baking pan; bake at 350 degrees for 2 hours. Combine sugar, maple syrup and mustard; use ¾ cup glaze mixture to baste ham during last 40 minutes of baking. In saucepan, blend remaining glaze mixture, cornstarch and pineapple with juice. Cook until sauce thickens; serve extra glaze as sauce over slices of ham.

Vegetable Garland:
2 (15-ounce) cans whole baby carrots
4 ears corn, quartered
2 acorn squash, cut into serving pieces
1 butternut squash, cut into serving pieces

Cook corn and squash separately in salted, boiling water; cook corn 5 minutes; squash, 15–20 minutes.

To serve: Place ham on large platter; arrange vegetables in a garland around the ham.

Gwen Campbell, Sterling, Va.

EGGNOG COOKIES
Makes 6 dozen

1 cup butter
2 cups sugar
1 cup eggnog
1/2 teaspoon nutmeg
1 teaspoon baking soda
5-1/2 cups sifted flour

Cream butter and sugar until light and fluffy. Add eggnog, nutmeg, and soda; mix well. Add enough flour to make stiff dough. Chill. Roll to 1/8-inch thickness on lightly floured pastry cloth and cut with Christmas cookie cutters. Brush with slightly beaten egg white and decorate with candied fruits or colored sugar. Bake at 375 degrees for 8-10 minutes, or until lightly browned.

Jenni Lien, Stoughton, Wis.

WALNUT MACAROONS

1 egg white
2/3 cup white sugar
1/8 teaspoon salt
1/4 teaspoon almond extract
1/3 cup very finely chopped walnuts

Beat egg whites very stiff, adding sugar slowly. Add salt, very gradually while beating; still beating, add extract and chopped nuts. Drop by teaspoonfuls onto cookie sheet (teflon or non-stick sheet if possible). Bake at 325 degrees for 15 minutes. Cool on rack.

Pearle M. Goodwin, South Ryegate, Vt.

ELF OVEN-FRIED CHICKEN
Serves 4

10 (24 ounces) chicken breasts
2 cups dairy sour cream *or* plain yogurt
¼ cup lemon juice.
4 teaspoons Worcestershire sauce
2 teaspoons celery salt *or* ground celery seed
2 teaspoons paprika
4 garlic cloves, finely chopped *or*
½ teaspoon garlic powder
2 teaspoons salt
½ teaspoon pepper
2 teaspoons poultry seasoning
2 teaspoons parsley
½ cup margarine, melted
Cornflakes crumbs

Cut chicken breasts in half. Wipe dry; remove skin and excess fat. In large bowl, combine all ingredients except margarine and cornflakes; stir well. Add chicken, making sure each piece is covered well. Let stand overnight in refrigerator. Remove chicken pieces from mixture; blot off excess with dry towel. Dip each piece in melted margarine, then roll in cornflakes crumbs. Place chicken in single layer on shallow pan. Sprinkle with additional parsley. Bake at 375 degrees for 25–30 minutes, or until chicken tests done.

Marcella Swigert, MonroeCity, Mo.

JAPANESE FRUITCAKE
Makes one 3-layer, 8-inch cake

3 cups flour, divided
1 teaspoon cinnamon
1 teaspoon allspice
1 teaspoon nutmeg
1 teaspoon cloves
1 teaspoon baking powder
1 cup butter
2 cups sugar
4 eggs
1 cup milk

1 cup jam
1 cup seedless raisins
1 cup chopped nuts
Frosting (recipe follows)

Sift 2 cups flour with spices and baking powder. Mix remaining 1 cup flour with raisins and nuts.

Cream butter and sugar in another bowl. Add eggs, one at a time, beating well after each addition. Add flour/spice mixture to creamed mixture alternately with milk. Add jam, raisins and nuts to mixture and mix well.

Pour batter into three 8-inch cake pans which have been greased and floured. Bake in a preheated 350-degree oven for 35 minutes. Cool completely before completing cake with *Frosting*.

Frosting:
2 cups flaked coconut
Grated rind and juice of 3 oranges
1 small can crushed pineapple
2 1/2 cups sugar
2 tablespoons flour

Combine all ingredients in a saucepan; mix well. Stirring constantly, cook until thick. Cool. Spread between cooled cake layers and on top and sides of cake.

Margaret Cotton, Franklin, Va.

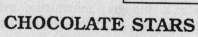

CHOCOLATE STARS
About 8 dozen

1-1/2 cups sifted flour
1-1/2 cups unblanched almonds, grated
1 teaspoon grated lemon peel
1 cup butter
1-1/2 cups sugar
2 egg yolks
4 squares (1 ounce each) unsweetened chocolate, melted and cooled

Mix flour, nuts and rind. Cream butter, add sugar gradually, cream until fluffy. Add egg yolks, chocolate, and mix well. Add flour mixture gradually, mix. Roll 1/8 inch thick on floured board and cut with floured 2-3/4 inch star-shaped cutter. Bake on ungreased cookie sheets in preheated 350 degree oven about 8 minutes.

Mrs. Kit Rollins, Cedarburg, Wis.

FESTIVE COCOA CARDS
Yield: 12 cookies

1 cup butter or margarine, softened
1/2 cup sugar
3/4 cup molasses or dark corn syrup
1 egg
1 teaspoon vanilla extract
3/4 cup flour
1/2 cup cocoa
1/2 teaspoon baking soda
Tubes of red and green frosting

In large bowl, cream butter and sugar until light and fluffy. Beat in molasses, egg and vanilla. Combine flour, cocoa and baking soda. Stir into butter mixture until well blended. Chill 1 hour. On a lightly floured surface, roll dough into a 12 x 15-inch oblong. Cut into twelve 3 x 5-inch oblongs. Place on greased cookie sheets. Bake in 350 degree oven 10-12 minutes or until firm to the touch. Cool on cookie sheets. Write names or greetings on cookies.

Roberta Wiggin, Mechanicville, N.Y.

EASY FRUIT CAKE

1 box spice cake mix
1 (8 ounce) jar mixed fruit and peels
1 (4 ounce) jar candied cherries
1 (4 ounce) jar candied pineapple
1 cup golden light raisins
2 eggs
1 cup pecans
1 cup walnuts
Pineapple juice in place of water for cake mix
1/4 cup dates, chopped
1/4 cup prunes, chopped

Mix cake mix with eggs and pineapple juice. Flour fruits and nuts and add to cake batter. Pour into two bread pans that have been buttered and dusted with flour. Fill 3/4 full. Bake at 350 degrees for 1-1/2 hours or until done.

Leona Teodori, Warren, Mich.

MINCEMEAT SQUARES

Makes 24 bars

2-1/2 cups flour
1-1/2 teaspoons baking soda
1/2 teaspoon salt
1-1/2 cups quick cooking rolled oats
1 cup firmly packed dark brown sugar
3/4 cup (1-1/2 sticks) butter or margarine
1 (16 ounce) jar prepared mincemeat

Sift flour, baking soda and salt into large bowl. Stir in rolled oats and brown sugar until blended. Cut in butter or margarine with pastry blender until mixture is crumbly. Pat half the mixture into greased 11x7x1-inch baking pan. Spread mincemeat on top. Sprinkle remaining oat mixture over and press into mincemeat. Bake in moderate oven at 375 degrees for 25 minutes or until topping is golden. Cool in pan on wire rack 15 minutes.

With sharp knife, cut 3 times lengthwise and 5 times crosswise to make 24 bars. Remove from pan with spatula and store, layered between wax paper, in metal tin with tight-fitting lid.

Melba Bellefeuille, Libertyville, Ill.

CHRISTMAS PUDDING SAUCE

Serves 10-12

1 cup sifted powdered sugar
2 egg yolks, well beaten
1/2 cup melted butter
1 teaspoon vanilla or 2 tablespoons sherry
1 cup heavy cream, whipped

Gradually stir powdered sugar into beaten egg yolks. Beat in butter, vanilla or sherry. Fold in whipped cream. Serve with hot pudding.

NOTE: Leftover sauce can be stored, covered in refrigerator. Beat well before using.

Agnes Ward, Erie, Pa.

HALLOWEEN PUMPKIN CHIFFON

Serves 9

1 tablespoon gelatin
¼ cup cold water
3 eggs, separated
¼ cup sugar
1¼ cups canned *or* cooked pumpkin
½ cup 2 percent milk
1 teaspoon pumpkin pie spice
Dash of salt, if desired
13 packets Equal brand low-calorie sweetener
12 graham cracker squares
¼ teaspoon cinnamon

Soak gelatin in cold water. Beat egg yolks slightly in an enamel pan or top of double boiler. Add sugar, pumpkin, milk, pumpkin pie spice and salt. Cook over low heat or hot water, but not boiling. Stir in gelatin until dissolved. Chill. When pumpkin mixture is beginning to set, whip egg whites until stiff, but not dry. Add 12 packets of Equal and beat just until mixed. Fold egg whites into pumpkin mixture. Line bottom of 8-inch square baking pan with 9 graham crackers. Spread pumpkin mixture evenly in pan. Make crumbs from the 3 remaining graham crackers; add 1 packet Equal and cinnamon. Mix and spread over top of pumpkin. Chill until firm. Cut into 9 equal squares.

Peggy Fowler, Woodruff, S.C.

WALNUT GLAZE

(for fruit cakes)

2 tablespoons butter, melted (do not substitute)
2 tablespoons honey
1 cup finely-chopped walnuts

Combine honey and butter. Blend. Add walnuts and stir. Chill. Spread onto ripened fruit cake the day of serving. Can also be used as an ice cream topping.

Pearle M. Goodwin, South Reygate, Vt.

CHRISTMAS EGGNOG CHERRY NUT LOAF

2-1/2 cups all-purpose flour
3/4 cup sugar
1 tablespoon baking powder
1 teaspoon salt
1 egg, beaten
1 recipe of homemade eggnog (recipe follows)
1/3 cup oil
1/2 cup chopped walnuts or pecans
1/2 cup chopped maraschino cherries, red and green

In mixing bowl, stir together flour, baking powder and salt. Mix egg, eggnog and oil. Stir in dry ingredients mixing well. Fold in nuts and cherries after they have been coated with flour. Pour into greased and floured 8x4x2-inch loaf pans. Bake at 350 degrees for 40-50 minutes or until tests done. Cool for 10 minutes before removing from pans.

Homemade Eggnog:

1 cup light cream
1/4 cup sugar
1/4 teaspoon ground nutmeg

Beat all ingredients together.

Carmen Bickert, Dubuque, Iowa

IRISH EGGY MASHED POTATOES

Serves 3

2 cups mashed potatoes
1 egg
Salt and pepper to taste
1 teaspoon dried parsley flakes *or*
1 to 2 tablespoons fresh minced parsley
Paprika

Whip egg and combine with mashed potatoes and a little salt, pepper, and parsley flakes. Put into a baking dish; sprinkle paprika over the top and bake at 350 to 375 degrees for 25 minutes. Serve hot from the baking dish.

WHITE CHRISTMAS PIE

Makes 2 pies

1 tablespoon gelatin
1 cup sugar
4 tablespoons flour
1/2 teaspoon salt
1-1/2 cups milk
3/4 teaspoon vanilla extract
1/4 teaspoon almond extract
1/2 cup whipping cream, whipped
3 egg whites
1/4 teaspoon cream of tartar
1-1/2 cups moist shredded coconut
2 baked 9-inch pie shells

Soften gelatin in 1/4 cup cold water, set aside. Combine 1/2 cup sugar, flour and salt in saucepan, stir in milk, bring to boil over low heat, stirring constantly. Boil 1 minute, remove from heat. Stir in softened gelatin, cool until partially set. Pour into large bowl. Beat with rotary beater until smooth. Blend in vanilla and almond extracts, fold whipped cream into custard. Beat egg whites until soft peaks form, add cream of tartar and 1/2 cup sugar, beating until stiff. Fold into custard mixture. Carefully fold in 1 cup coconut. Spoon into cooled pie shells. Sprinkle with remaining coconut. Chill for 2 hours or until set. Remove from refrigerator 20 minutes before serving.

Melba Bellefeuille, Libertyville, Ill.

CHRISTMAS BRAID BREAD

1-1/2 packages or cakes yeast
1/8 cup water, warm
1/4 teaspoon sugar
1/2 cup milk, scalded
1/4 cup sugar
1 teaspoon salt
1/4 cup margarine, softened
3 cups flour
1 egg
1/2 cup raisins
1/8 teaspoon cinnamon

Dissolve yeast in water, add 1/4 teaspoon sugar. Mix all ingredients. Knead 10 minutes. Let dough rest 10 minutes, covered. Let dough rise to double, then punch down, dividing dough into 3 equal balls. Roll into three strips the same length. Braid loosely, place on cookie sheet. Let rise until double in size. Bake at 350 degrees for 35 minutes. While warm drizzle with glaze.

Glaze:
1/2 cup powdered sugar
1 teaspoon margarine, softened
1 tablespoon water

Mix all ingredients well. Drizzle over bread.

Pearl Stevenson, Lafayette, Ind.

GREEK CHRISTMAS BREAD

1 package dry yeast
1/4 cup warm water
1/3 cup sugar
1 teaspoon ground cardamom
1/4 teaspoon salt
1 egg
1/4 cup milk
1/4 cup vegetable oil
1-1/2 cups whole wheat flour
1 cup all-purpose flour
1/4 cup raisins
1/4 cup walnuts
1/4 cup citron

Dissolve yeast in warm water. Combine sugar, cardamom, salt, egg, milk and oil in large bowl, mix well. Add yeast mixture, flour, raisins, nuts and citron, mix well. Add enough extra flour to make soft dough. Turn dough onto floured surface, knead until smooth and elastic, about 5 minutes. Shape into round loaf. Place round loaf onto lightly-oiled 8-inch round cake pan. Cover with damp towel, let rise in warm draft-free place until doubled, about 1 hour. Bake at 350 degrees for 35-40 minutes or until brown.

Marie Fusaro, Manasquan, N.J.

CHRISTMAS PINWHEEL COOKIES

Makes 3 dozen

¼ cup chopped red candied cherries
¼ cup chopped green candied cherries
½ cup chopped walnuts
½ cup shortening
¾ cup sugar
1 egg
1 tablespoon milk
1 teaspoon vanilla
1¼ cups flour
½ teaspoon baking powder
¼ teaspoon salt

Coarsely grind cherries and walnuts and set aside for filling. Cream shortening and sugar together. Add egg; beat well. Stir in milk and vanilla. Sift together flour, salt and baking powder. Stir into creamed mixture. If necessary, chill dough to handle easier. Roll out on lightly floured board or pastry sheet into a 10-inch square, ¼ inch thick. Sprinkle with cherries and nuts; roll up as for jelly roll; roll in waxed paper; chill thoroughly. Cut into ¼-inch slices and place on greased baking sheets. Bake at 400 degrees for 10–12 minutes.

Judy Haffner, Auke Bay, Alaska

SANTA'S STUFFED CELERY

Makes 15 appetizers

1 (2¼-ounce) can deviled ham
1 (3-ounce) package cream cheese, softened
½ teaspoon prepared mustard
½ teaspoon chili sauce
4 stalks celery, cut into 3-inch pieces
Pickle relish

Blend cream cheese, deviled ham, mustard and chili sauce. Stuff celery with the mixture. Top with pickle relish for garnish.

Judy Haffner, Auke Bay, Alaska

PORTUGUESE FRUIT CAKE

2/3 cup packed brown sugar
2/3 cup shortening
2 eggs
1/3 cup honey
1/3 cup light molasses
1/4 cup apple cider or apple juice
1-1/2 cups all-purpose flour
1/2 teaspoon baking powder
1/2 teaspoon salt
1/4 teaspoon ground cinnamon
1/4 teaspoon ground cloves
2/3 cup pitted dates, chopped
2/3 cup raisins
2/3 cup chopped almonds
1/3 cup chopped candied cherries
1/3 cup chopped candied pineapple
1/3 cup chopped candied citron
2 tablespoons all-purpose flour
1/2 cup powdered sugar
1 slightly beaten egg white

In large mixer bowl, cream brown sugar and shortening. Beat in eggs, honey, molasses, and apple cider or apple juice. Stir together 1-1/2 cups flour, baking powder, salt, cinnamon and cloves. Coat dates, raisins, almonds, cherries, pineapple and citron with remaining 2 tablespoons flour. Stir flour mixture into creamed mixture, fold in fruits and nuts. Grease a 9x9x2-inch baking pan, line bottom with waxed paper. Spread batter evenly in pan. Place pan with batter on the top oven shelf. Place another pan on bottom oven shelf and fill with hot water. Bake at 300 degrees for 1 hour and 25 minutes. Cool cake in pan. Remove from pan. Wrap and store cake overnight. Frost cake with mixture of sifted powdered sugar and egg white.

Leona Teodori, Warren, Mich.

HOLIDAY CRANBERRY MOUSSE

Serves 8

1 (20 ounce) can crushed pineapple in juice

1 (6 ounce) package strawberry gelatin
1 cup water
1 (1 pound) can whole berry cranberry sauce
3 tablespoons fresh lemon juice
1 teaspoon fresh grated lemon peel
1/4 teaspoon ground nutmeg
2 cups dairy sour cream
1/2 cup chopped pecans

Drain pineapple well, reserving all juice. Add juice to gelatin in 2 quart saucepan. Stir in water. Heat to boiling, stirring to dissolve gelatin. Remove from heat. Blend in cranberry sauce. Add lemon juice, lemon peel and nutmeg. Chill until mixture thickens slightly. Blend sour cream into gelatin mixture. Fold in pineapple and pecans, pour into 2-quart mold. Chill until firm. Unmold onto serving plate.

Melba Bellefeuille, Libertyville, Ill.

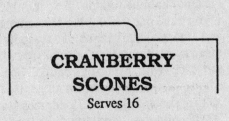

CRANBERRY SCONES

Serves 16

2-1/2 cups all-purpose flour
2-1/2 teaspoons baking powder
1/2 teaspoon baking soda
3/4 cup cold butter or margarine, cut into small pieces
1 cup coarsely-chopped cranberries
2/3 cup granulated sugar
3/4 cup buttermilk

Preheat oven to 400 degrees. Have an ungreased large cookie sheet ready. Mix flour, baking powder and soda in large bowl. Cut in butter with pastry blender until mixture resembles coarse crumbs. Stir in cranberries and sugar, then buttermilk just until blended. Cut dough in half. On lightly-floured surface with lightly floured finger tips, press half the dough into 8-inch circle about 1/2 inch thick. Cut into 8 wedges. Place on cookie sheet 1/2 inch apart. Bake 12-15 minutes until puffed and lightly brown. Remove to rack, and repeat with remaining dough. Serve warm.

Edna Askins, Greenville, Texas

ALMOND SNOWBALL COOKIES

Makes 5 dozen

½ cup butter or margarine
¼ cup evaporated milk
½ teaspoon grated lemon rind
1¾ cups sifted flour
¾ cup sugar
½ teaspoon salt
1 cup finely chopped almonds
6 tablespoons confectioners' sugar
½ pound candied cherries

Cream butter; beat in milk, a little at a time, until all is blended with butter. Add lemon rind. Sift flour with sugar and salt; gradually add to butter mixture. Add nuts; mix well. Pinch off pieces of dough, about a teaspoon. Flatten dough in palm of hand. Place a cherry on dough; pinch dough up around cherry completely. Roll between palms. Place on lightly greased, floured cookie sheet. Bake at 375 degrees for 12 minutes. Roll in confectioners' sugar while still warm.

Mrs. Don Shamway, Freeport, Ill.

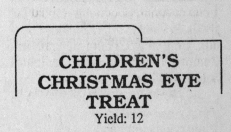

CHILDREN'S CHRISTMAS EVE TREAT

Yield: 12

1 box rainbow colored flat-bottomed ice cream cones
1 (9 ounce) box white cake mix
1/4 cup red cherries, chopped
1/4 cup green cherries, chopped
1/2 box miniature chocolate covered mint patties

Place ice cream cones in a 12-cup muffin tin. Prepare cake mix according to package directions; fold in green and red cherries. Half fill each cone with cake batter. Bake 350 degrees for 25-30 minutes; remove from oven. While still hot, place 3 to 4 mint patties on top of each cupcake. They will melt and run down inside of the cone.

Mrs. Gwen Campbell, Sterling, Va.

CANDLESTICK BARS

1 (14 ounce) package gingerbread
   mix
1 (8 ounce) can applesauce
1/2 cup raisins
1 (4 ounce) jar chopped mixed
   candied fruits and peels
1 (14 ounce) package white creamy
   frosting mix
2 tablespoons lemon juice

Combine gingerbread mix and apple sauce, beat 2 minutes at medium speed or 2 minutes with spoon. Stir in raisins, fruits and peels. Spread in 15-1/2x10-1/2x1-inch jelly roll pan. Bake 375 degrees for 15 minutes. Prepare frosting and add lemon juice, substituting lemon juice for half the liquid. Spread on cooled bars. Decorate with red and yellow gum drops to look like a candle. Use red candy for candle and yellow candy for flame.

Melba Bellefeuille, Libertyville, Ill.

KRIS CRINKLES

3 ounces unsweetened chocolate
2 cups walnuts, finely ground
1 cup sugar
2 eggs
Dash salt
2 tablespoons flour
1 teaspoon cinnamon
1/4 teaspoon nutmeg
1/2 teaspoon cloves
1/4 cup white bread crumbs, finely
   crushed
Confectioners' sugar

Preheat oven to 325 degrees. Melt chocolate and add walnuts. Add sugar, eggs, and salt. Remove to mixing bowl and add flour and spices; mix well. Add bread crumbs, mix. Shape into small balls and roll in confectioners' sugar. Bake on greased cookie sheets for about 12 minutes or until tops of cookies crinkle and crack. Remove and roll in confectioners' sugar again and cool.

Suzan L. Wiener, Spring Hill, Fla.

MINCEMEAT PEEK-A-BOOS
Makes 6 dozen

1½ cups butter *or* margarine,
   softened
¾ cup granulated sugar
¾ cup packed brown sugar
1 egg
¼ cup milk
4½ cups all-purpose flour
¾ teaspoon baking soda
¾ teaspoon salt
1¼ cups prepared mincemeat
¼ cup orange marmalade

Cream butter or margarine and sugars; beat in egg and milk. Stir together flour, soda and salt; stir into creamed mixture. Wrap and chill dough. On floured surface roll *half* the dough at a time, ⅛-inch thick; cut with 2½-inch round cookie cutter. Cut small hole in center of half the rounds (use a thimble if you have one). Combine mincemeat and marmalade. Place 1 teaspoon mincemeat mixture on each plain round; top each with a cut-out round. Seal edges with fork. Place on ungreased baking sheet; bake at 375 degrees for 10–12 minutes. Cool on wire rack. Wrap; label; freeze, if desired.

Diantha Susan Hibbard, Rochester, N.Y.

HERMITS

1 cup sugar
1/2 cup salad oil
2 1/2 cups flour
1/2 teaspoon nutmeg
1 teaspoon baking soda
1 teaspoon cinnamon
1/2 cup milk
1/2 cup molasses
1 cup raisins

Mix in order given. Blend well. Place in greased 9x13-inch pan and bake at 350 degrees for about 25 minutes. Do not overbake. When you remove from the oven, sprinkle with sugar.

Pearle M. Goodwin, South Ryegate, Vt.

CRANBERRY COOKIES
Yield: 2 dozen

1/2 cup butter or margarine
1 cup sugar
3/4 cup brown sugar, packed
1/4 cup milk
2 tablespoons orange juice
1 egg
3 cups sifted flour
1 teaspoon baking powder
1/4 teaspoon soda
1/2 teaspoon salt
1 cup chopped nuts
2-1/2 cups (12 ounce package)
   fresh cranberries, chopped

Preheat oven to 375 degrees. Cream butter and sugar together, beat in milk, juice and egg. Sift together flour, baking powder, soda and salt. Combine with creamed mixture, blend well. Stir in cranberries and nuts. Drop by teaspoonfuls on greased cookie sheet. Bake at 375 degrees for 10-15 minutes.

Edna Askins, Greenville, Texas

HOLIDAY ANGEL TOWER

1 package angel food cake mix
1 (1 pound 2-1/2 ounce) jar mincemeat
1 (8 ounce) package cream cheese,
   softened
1/4 cup walnuts, chopped
2 cups heavy cream, whipped and
   sweetened

Prepare and bake angel food mix as directed on package. Cool. Slice into three layers. Blend mincemeat, cream cheese and nuts. Spread mixture between layers, and put layers together. Cover and refrigerate several hours or overnight. Frost with whipped cream before serving. Store in refrigerator.

Judy Haffner, Auke Bay, Alaska

FRUITCAKE COOKIES

Makes 150–170 cookies

2 pounds dates
½ pound candied cherries
½ pound candied pineapple
½ pound shelled almonds
½ pound shelled Brazil nuts
2½ cups sifted flour
1 teaspoon baking soda
1 teaspoon salt
1 teaspoon cinnamon
1 cup butter
1½ cups sugar
2 eggs

Discard date pits and cut dates in chunks. Quarter cherries. Slice pineapple in thin slivers. Blanch almonds; chop coarsely and toast until golden. Chop Brazil nuts. Sift flour, baking soda, salt and cinnamon together. Preheat oven to 400 degrees. Work butter until soft and creamy. Add sugar gradually; continue working until smooth. Beat in eggs thoroughly. Stir in sifted flour mixture, all fruits and nuts. Drop by teaspoonfuls on ungreased cookie sheet. Bake 10 minutes; do not overbake. Cookies are best when soft in texture. Remove from sheet.

Leona Teodori, Warren, Mich.

CANDY CANE COOKIES

Makes 30

¾ cup butter *or* margarine, softened
¾ cup sugar
1 egg
½ teaspoon vanilla
½ teaspoon peppermint extract
2 cups flour
½ teaspoon salt
¼ teaspoon baking powder
⅓ cup flaked coconut
1 teaspoon red food coloring

Cream butter and sugar; beat in egg, vanilla and extract. Sift flour with salt and baking powder; stir into creamed mixture. Divide dough in half. Stir coconut into 1 portion; blend food coloring into remaining dough. Cover; chill doughs for 10 minutes.

Divide each dough into 30 balls; keep half of each dough chilled until ready to use. With hands, roll each ball into 5-inch rope. For each cane, pinch together 1 end of red rope and 1 end of white rope; twist ropes together. Pinch together remaining ends. Place on ungreased cookie sheet; curve to form cane. Leave space between canes, as they expand during baking. Repeat with remaining balls. Bake at 375 degrees for 10 minutes.

Kit Rollins, Cedarburg, Wis.

MINCEMEAT SQUARES

Makes 24 bars

2½ cups flour
1½ teaspoons baking soda
½ teaspoon salt
1½ cups quick-cooking rolled oats
1 cup firmly packed dark brown sugar
¾ cup (1½ sticks) butter *or* margarine
1 (16-ounce) jar prepared mincemeat

Sift flour, baking soda and salt into large bowl. Stir in rolled oats and brown sugar until blended. Cut in butter or margarine with pastry blender until mixture is crumbly. Pat half the mixture into greased 11 x 7 x 1-inch baking pan. Spread mincemeat on top. Sprinkle remaining oat mixture over and press into mincemeat. Bake in moderate oven at 375 degrees for 25 minutes, or until topping is golden. Cool in pan on wire rack for 15 minutes.

With sharp knife, cut 3 times lengthwise and 5 times crosswise to make 24 bars. Remove from pan with spatula and store, layered between waxed paper, in metal tin with tight-fitting lid.

Melba Bellefeuille, Libertyville, Ill.

TRADITIONAL PUMPKIN PIE

3 eggs
1/2 teaspoon salt
2/3 cup brown sugar
1/3 cup sugar
1-1/2 cups milk (evaporated milk may be used)
1-1/2 cups cooked pumpkin
2 teaspoons cinnamon
1 teaspoon ginger
1/2 teaspoon nutmeg
1/8 teaspoon allspice
1 unbaked 9-inch pastry shell

Beat eggs; stir in salt, sugar and milk. Add pumpkin and spices. Mix well; pour into pastry shell. Bake at 425 degrees for 35-45 minutes or until center firms up.

Agnes Ward, Erie, Pa.

CHRISTMAS BISCUITS

2 cups butter
4 cups sugar
4 eggs
1 teaspoon baking soda
1 cup sour cream
Sifted flour

Cream butter and sugar; beat in eggs, one at a time. Dissolve soda in sour cream; stir into creamed mixture. Add enough flour to make an easily-handled dough; chill overnight. Roll dough out thin on floured board; cut with round cookie cutter. Place on baking sheet and bake at 350 degrees for 10-12 minutes.

Agnes Ward, Erie, Pa.

SAINT NICHOLAS COOKIES

1 cup butter
2 cups sugar
1 cup shortening
½ cup sour cream
½ teaspoon soda
4 cups flour
½ teaspoon cloves
1 teaspoon cinnamon
½ cup chopped nut meats

Cream together first 3 ingredients. Blend together sour cream and soda. Add to first mixture. Sift remaining ingredients and add. Stir in nut meats. Press into loaf pan and chill overnight. Slice; place on cookie sheet and bake in 350-degree oven for about 10–12 minutes.

Leona Teodori, Warren, Mich.

SPICED BANANA FRUIT CAKE

3-1/2 cups sifted flour
4 teaspoons baking powder
1 teaspoon salt
1/2 teaspoon soda
2 teaspoons cinnamon
2 teaspoons ginger
1 teaspoon nutmeg
1-1/3 cups shortening
1-1/3 cups sugar
4 eggs, beaten
2 cups mashed ripe banana
1-1/2 cups chopped nuts
1 cup raisins
4 cups diced candied fruits

Sift dry ingredients. Cream shortening. Gradually blend in sugar. Beat in eggs. Add flour mixture alternately with banana. Mix raisins, nuts and candied fruits into batter. Turn into two well greased and floured 9-inch bread pans. Bake at 300 degrees for 2 hours or until done.

Judy Haffner, Auke Bay, Alaska

HOLIDAY MINCEMEAT UPSIDE DOWN CAKE

1-1/2 cups sugar
3/4 cup unsalted butter
3-1/2 cups all-purpose flour
1-1/2 cups sweet milk
3-1/2 teaspoons baking powder
3 eggs
1-1/2 cups mincemeat
1-1/2 cups apples, chopped
1/2 cup fresh orange juice
1/2 cup sugar
2 tablespoons melted butter
1/2 cup brown sugar, firmly packed

Cream butter and sugar; beat in eggs. Add milk, flour and baking powder. Set aside. In bottom of baking pan melt butter and brown sugar; place mincemeat mixture over this. Pour cake batter over all. Bake 375 degrees for 40 minutes. On cake plate, turn cake upside down. To serve: cut into squares; serve with whipped cream.

Gwen Campbell, Sterling, Va.

JOLLY GOOD PLUM CAKE
Serves 12

2 cups all-purpose flour
1 teaspoon baking soda
1 teaspoon nutmeg
1/2 teaspoon salt
1-1/2 cups sugar
1 cup salad oil
3 eggs
1 cup buttermilk
1 (7-1/2 ounce) jar junior plums
1 teaspoon vanilla
1 cup chopped walnuts

Preheat oven to 350 degrees. Sift together flour, baking soda, nutmeg and salt. In large bowl, combine sugar and oil. Add eggs and beat well. Alternately add sifted ingredients and buttermilk; mix well. Add plums and vanilla, stirring to blend. Fold in chopped walnuts. Spoon batter into greased 13x9x2-inch baking pan. Bake 45 minutes or until done. Let cool in pan. Cut into squares in pan.

Bobbie Mae Cooley, Bowen, Ill.

WITCHES' ORANGE COOKIES

1 egg
1/2 cup margarine
1/2 cup orange juice
2 teaspoons orange rind
2 cups sifted flour
1/2 teaspoon salt
1/2 teaspoon baking powder
1 teaspoon cinnamon
1/2 cup chopped nuts
1/2 cup raisins

Beat egg well. Add margarine, orange juice and rind; set aside. Sift flour, salt, baking powder and cinnamon together. Combine with egg mixture. Fold in nuts and raisins. Drop by teaspoon on lightly greased cookie sheet. Bake at 375 degrees for 15 minutes, or until lightly browned. Enjoy!

PUMPKIN MUFFINS

1½ cups sifted flour
1 teaspoon salt
2 teaspoons baking powder
½ cup sugar
½ teaspoon nutmeg
½ teaspoon cinnamon
¼ cup margarine, softened
1 egg
½ cup cooked pumpkin
⅓ cup milk
⅓ cup raisins

Sift flour, salt, baking powder, sugar, nutmeg and cinnamon together. Set aside. Combine margarine, egg, pumpkin and milk. Add to flour mixture. Fold in raisins. Fill muffin tins and bake at 400 degrees for 20 minutes.

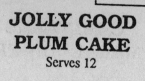

SNOWFALL CAKE

1 round sponge cake
2 packages instant vanilla custard
Snowfall cream (recipe follows)
Candied fruits
1/2 cup confectioners' sugar, sifted

Cut cake into 3 equal layers; place waxed paper between layers; chill. Prepare custard filling; chill. When chilled, spread 1/2 the custard on first layer; top with second layer and cover with remaining custard; top with last layer. Cover entire cake with Snowfall Cream; gently press candied fruits on sides and in 2 rounds on top of cake. Gently "snowfall" the confectioners' sugar across top of cake and add candied fruits.

Snowfall Cream:
4 cups whipping cream
4-8 tablespoons powdered sugar

Whip cream until soft peaks form; beat in sugar until stiff peaks form.

Gwen Campbell, Sterling, Va.

CHRISTMAS MACAROON PIE

2 dozen macaroons, dried thoroughly
1/2 cup soft butter
1/2 cup milk
2 slightly-beaten eggs
1/3 cup sugar
Pinch of salt
1/2 envelope unflavored gelatin
1/4 cup cold water
1 cup heavy cream, whipped
1/4 cup finely-chopped pecans
4 large marshmallows, cut fine
1 slice canned pineapple, cut fine
2 ounces candied cherries

Make crust from crushed macaroons and butter. Press into 9-inch pie plate. Make custard of next 5 ingredients over low heat. Soak gelatin in cold water and add to hot custard, stirring until gelatin dissolves. Allow to cool, then fold in fruits, nuts and marshmallows. Pour into pie shell and chill.

Julie Habiger, Spearville, Kan.

NOEL ROASTED CHESTNUT BREAD

2 (13-3/4 ounce) packages hot roll mix
1-1/4 cups warm milk
2 eggs
1/4 cup honey
1/2 teaspoon cinnamon
1/2 teaspoon nutmeg
1 cup canned roasted chestnut purée
2 tablespoons honey
2 tablespoons almonds, flaked

Prepare hot roll mix according to package directions; beat in eggs, honey and spices. Let rise 30 minutes. Turn onto floured surface; knead roasted chestnuts gently into dough. Place in round 1-1/2-quart ovenproof casserole; allow to rise until double in volume. Bake at 375 degrees 40-50 minutes until deep golden brown. Loosen from casserole; cool on wire rack. While still warm, brush bread with honey; sprinkle with flaked almonds.

Gwen Campbell, Sterling, Va.

CHRISTMAS CARROT LOAF
Makes 1 loaf

1-1/4 cups sifted flour
1/2 cup sugar
1/2 teaspoon baking powder
1/2 teaspoon soda
1 teaspoon cinnamon
1/2 teaspoon nutmeg
1/2 teaspoon ginger
1/4 teaspoon salt
2 eggs, beaten
1/4 cup oil
1/4 cup milk
1 cup shredded carrots
3/4 cup coconut
1/4 cup maraschino cherries, chopped and drained
1/4 cup raisins
1/4 cup chopped pecans.

Sift flour, baking powder and soda together with spices in large bowl. Combine eggs, oil and milk in bowl, mix well. Add dry ingredients, beat well. Stir in remaining ingredients. Turn into greased loaf pan. Bake at 350 degrees for 50-60 minutes.

Melba Bellefeuille, Libertyville, Ill.

MINCEMEAT BREAD
Makes 2 loaves

1 (9 ounce) package dry mincemeat
1 cup whole wheat flour
2 cups sifted flour
3/4 cup sugar
4 teaspoons baking powder
1 teaspoon salt
1 egg, beaten
1 cup evaporated milk or half-and-half

Crumble mincemeat into saucepan; add 1/2 cup water. Bring to boil, stirring constantly. Cook about 4 minutes; cool. Blend flours, sugar, salt and baking powder together. Combine egg and evaporated milk; add flour mixture, mixing until smooth. Fold in mincemeat. Place in 2 greased loaf pans. Bake at 350 degrees for about 45 minutes or until it tests done. May be glazed, if desired, after cooling.

Agnes Ward, Erie, Pa.

CANDLESTICK BARS

1 (14-ounce) package gingerbread mix
1 (8-ounce) can applesauce
1/2 cup raisins
1 (4-ounce) jar chopped mixed candied fruits and peels
1 (14-ounce) package white creamy frosting mix
2 tablespoons lemon juice

Combine gingerbread mix and applesauce; beat 2 minutes at medium speed or 2 minutes with spoon. Stir in raisins, fruits and peels. Spread in 15½ x 10½ x 1-inch jelly roll pan. Bake at 375 degrees for 15 minutes. Prepare frosting and add lemon juice, substituting lemon juice for half the liquid. Spread on cooled bars. Decorate with red and yellow gumdrops to look like a candle. Use red candy for candle and yellow candy for flame.

Melba Bellefeuille, Libertyville, Ill.

PUMPKIN COOKIES

1 cup brown sugar
1 cup cooked pumpkin
½ cup Mazola oil
2 cups sifted flour
1 teaspoon vanilla
1 teaspoon baking soda
1 teaspoon baking powder
½ teaspoon salt
½ teaspoon cinnamon
½ teaspoon nutmeg
½ cup raisins
½ cup nuts
⅔ cup orange slices (candy), finely chopped

Mix all ingredients together. Drop by spoonfuls onto greased cookie sheet. Bake at 375 degrees for about 10 minutes.

Marcella Swigert, Monroe City, Mo.

Meat DISHES

ROAST DUCK WITH CHERRIES AND MADEIRA
Serves 4

1 (5-pound) duckling
Salt

Lemon juice
1 clove garlic, cut
1 (1-pound) can bing cherries, pitted
2 tablespoons Madeira wine
2 tablespoons sugar
2½ cups Brown Sauce (recipe follows)

Rub duck with salt, lemon juice and garlic. Roast at 350 degrees on 1 side for 30 minutes; turn duck on other side; roast 30 minutes more. Pour off fat; turn duck breast side up; roast another 1½ hours; continue to pour off fat. Drain liquid from cherries; simmer juice and Madeira wine for 10–15 minutes. Return cherries to liquid; add sugar; simmer. Add Brown Sauce, cherries and liquid; bring to a gentle boil. To serve, pass Cherry-Madeira Sauce with carved slices of roast duck.

Brown Sauce:
2 tablespoons butter *or* margarine
3 tablespoons flour
1½ cups boiling water
2 tablespoons beef bouillon granules
½ teaspoon brown gravy coloring

Melt butter in a saucepan; let brown. Add flour; cook until browned. Stir in 1½ cups boiling water; add bouillon granules and gravy coloring; simmer until hot and bubbling.

Gwen Cambpell, Sterling, Va.

DIFFERENT PIZZA

3/4 cup spaghetti or pizza sauce
1/2 pound pork sausage
4-ounce package refrigerated crescent rolls
1 cup cooked brown rice
1/4 cup shredded mild cheddar cheese
1/2 cup shredded mozzarella cheese
4 eggs
1/4 cup milk
1/2 teaspoon salt
1/8 teaspoon pepper
2 tablespoons grated Parmesan cheese

Brown sausage and drain. Mix with cooked brown rice. Place crescent rolls in lightly greased electric skillet. Spoon sauce and rice mixture over rolls. Top with cheddar and mozarella cheese. Pour beaten eggs, milk and salt and pepper mixture over this. Sprinkle with Parmesan cheese and bake in 300-degree skillet for 30 minutes.

Cut into wedges and serve.

Monica W. Cox, Cleveland, Miss.

SUNDAY NIGHT SCRAMBLED EGGS

1/2 pound bulk sausage (or smoked, summer)
1 onion, chopped
1/2 bell pepper, chopped
1 (17-ounce) can cream-style corn
1 cup grated Velveeta cheese
4 beaten eggs
1/4 cup milk

Brown sausage; pour off any grease. Add remaining ingredients and stir until eggs are set and cheese melted. If desired, sauté onion and pepper before adding other ingredients. Just the thing to have after Sunday's "honey-do chores."

BARBECUED RIB CHOPS
Serves 8

1 (5/8-ounce) package Italian salad dressing mix
1 (6-ounce) can tomato paste
8 lamb-rib chops, 3/4-inch thickness

Combine salad dressing mix and tomato paste; spread in thin layer over top side of chops. Broil 3 to 4 inches from source of heat, or cook on outdoor grill, 5-7 minutes. Turn; brush second side with sauce; cook 5 minutes longer, or until desired degree of doneness.

Marcella Swigert, Monroe City, Mo.

SAUSAGE-APPLE LOAF

2 eggs
½ teaspoon rosemary, crushed
½ teaspoon salt
¼ teaspoon ground sage
¼ teaspoon pepper
¼ teaspoon dry mustard
1 cup dry bread crumbs
1 cup thick applesauce
1 onion, finely chopped
2 pounds sausage meat

Preheat oven to 350 degrees. Lightly grease a 9 x 5 x 3-inch pan and line the bottom with greased waxed paper. In a large bowl beat eggs with seasonings and mustard. Stir in bread crumbs, applesauce and onion. Add half the sausage meat and work with your hands, or a fork, until evenly mixed. Work in remaining meat and firmly press into pan with palm of your hand. Lay a sheet of foil over top and bake in center of oven for 1 hour. Remove foil and drain off fat. Continue baking, uncovered, for 45 minutes more. Let cool in pan 5 minutes before turning out. This is excellent hot or cold.

Lillian Smith, Montreal, Quebec, Canada

HAMBURGER ROYAL
Serves 6

1 pound lean ground beef
1 medium onion, chopped
1 medium bell pepper, chopped
12-ounce can vacuum-packed corn with pimientos and peppers (Mexican-style)
15-ounce can tomato sauce

Cook hamburger, onion and green pepper until hamburger is brown and onion and green pepper are limp. Add corn and tomato sauce. Simmer for 15 minutes until heated through. Serve over hamburger buns.

Mary F. Speece, Lakeland, Fla.

SOUR CREAM TUNA LOAF

1 (13-ounce) can tuna, drained
6 slices white bread, crumbled
2 tablespoons instant minced onion
1 (2-ounce) jar chopped pimiento
2 cans cream of mushroom soup
½ cup grated cheddar cheese
3 eggs
1 tablespoon lemon juice
½ teaspoon salt
¼ teaspoon pepper
1 (16-ounce) carton sour cream

In large bowl, mix tuna, bread, eggs, onion, lemon juice, salt, pepper, pimiento and only 8 ounces (half) of the sour cream. Mix well; place in greased loaf pan. Bake at 350 degrees for 45 minutes until set.

Sour Cream Sauce:
Heat mushroom soup and desired amount of cheese (½ cup or more) until bubbly. Remove from heat and blend in remaining sour cream. Slice loaf and spoon over each serving.

J.L. Rede, Tucumcari, N.M.

BUTTER CRUST CHICKEN

1 frying chicken, cut up or parts
2 sticks margarine
1-1/2 teaspoons salt
1/2 cup flour
Paprika

Melt margarine; add salt and flour to make a medium-thick paste. Dip chicken and place on a cookie sheet. Sprinkle with paprika. Bake at 350 degrees for 1 hour, or until chicken is brown and tender. The chicken does not have to be turned while baking.

Marilyn Thomas, Carlisle, Ind.

SPARERIBS L'ORANGE
Serves 4

3 pounds spareribs, cut into serving pieces
3 tablespoons water

Basting sauce:
1 (6-ounce) can frozen orange juice
2 tablespoons water
1/2 cup brown sugar, firmly packed
1 tablespoon liquid smoke
2 tablespoons fresh lime juice
1 tablespoon white vinegar
1/2 cup honey
1 tablespoon Dijon mustard
1/4 teaspoon salt
1/8 teaspoon pepper
3 green onions, sliced, for garnish
Orange slices for garnish

In a baking pan, place ribs meaty side up; sprinkle with 3 tablespoons water. Bake 375 degrees for 30 minutes; drain off fat. In a saucepan combine all basting ingredients. Simmer 5 minutes; pour over ribs. Reduce heat to 350 degrees; bake 50 minutes; baste occasionally. To serve, sprinkle with sliced green onions; place orange slices around ribs.

Gwen Campbell, Sterling, Va.

CHICKEN CHOW MEIN

1 or 2 onions, chopped
1 green pepper, chopped
2 cups chicken
2 cups soup or bouillon
3 tablespoons soy sauce
2 or 3 tablespoons cornstarch

Sauté vegetables for 5 minutes. Add chicken. Add cornstarch to the soup or bouillon; then add to vegetables and chicken. Add soy sauce. Cook until thick and clear. Serve over rice. Garnish with tomatoes and serve with Chinese noodles.

Karen Donchez, Bethlehem, Pa.

GOLDEN GLAZED CHICKEN
Serves 4

2 chicken breasts, split and skinned
Salt and pepper
Paprika
1 tablespoon diet margarine
4 slices onion
4 slices orange
2 tablespoons cornstarch
1 teaspoon instant chicken bouillon
1 tablespoon orange juice *or* water
Snipped parsley

Arrange chicken breasts in 8- or 9-inch round glass baking dish with thicker portion toward edge of dish. Sprinkle with salt, pepper and paprika. Divide margarine into fourths; place pieces atop each breast. Top each with onion and orange slices. Cover with waxed paper. Microwave on HIGH for 10–12 minutes, or until chicken is done, rotating dish once. Let stand 5 minutes. Combine cornstarch, bouillon and orange juice in 1-cup glass measure. Drain juice from chicken into cornstarch mixture; mix well. Microwave on HIGH, uncovered, 45 seconds to 1 minute, or until mixture boils and thickens, stirring once. Spoon onto chicken breasts. Garnish with parsley. (170 calories per serving)

Mrs. Olen Begley, West Salem, Ohio

MARINATED PORK CHOPS
Serves 6

6 pork chops
3/4 cup honey
1/2 cup white vinegar
1/4 cup soy sauce
1/2 teaspoon ginger
1/4 teaspoon or less garlic powder

Place pork chops in 13x9-inch baking dish. Combine remaining ingredients; pour over pork chops. Cover and refrigerate for about 8 hours.

Remove from refrigerator; let stand 30 minutes. Bake in marinade, covered, at 350 degrees for 1 hour, or until meat is tender.

Flo Burtnett, Gage, Okla.

BEEF ROLL-UPS
Serves 6

2 pounds ground beef
1 cup shredded cheddar cheese
2/3 cup chopped onion
1/4 cup ketchup
2 tablespoons Parmesan cheese
2 tablespoons Worcestershire sauce
1/4 teaspoon pepper
1 teaspoon salt
2 eggs
12 strips bacon

Combine beef, cheese, onion, ketchup, Parmesan cheese, Worcestershire sauce, salt, pepper, and eggs. Mix well and divide in half. Shape each half into an 11-inch roll. Place beef roll on one end of bacon strips. Roll up, using waxed paper as an aid so that roll is wrapped with bacon. Cut into 6 patties. Secure bacon ends with toothpicks. Place on broiler rack; repeat with other roll. Broil 7 inches from source of heat.

Whole beef rolls can be baked, if you wish. Bake at 375 degrees for 40 minutes.

Diantha Susan Hibbard, Rochester, N.Y.

HAWAIIAN CHICKEN

5 deboned chicken breasts, diced
1 (16-ounce) can crushed pineapple
2 cups fresh pineapple chunks
1 green pepper, diced
1-1/2 cups brown sugar
1/2 cup lemon juice
2 tablespoons cornstarch

In a saucepan, combine pineapple including syrup, peppers, and brown sugar. Bring to a boil. Remove from heat and add lemon juice and corn starch. Mix well. Add diced chicken and heat throughly.

FOIL-WRAPPED PICNIC DINNERS
Serves 4

1-1/2 pounds round steak
2 packages frozen peas and carrots
4 medium potatoes, pared
1 package frozen broccoli, tops only
Salt and pepper to taste
1 (10-1/2-ounce) can cream of mushroom soup
1 envelope dry onion soup mix
8 cherry tomatoes

Cut meat into 1-inch pieces. Place frozen peas, carrots, and broccoli in colander; run cold water over all just until separated; drain. Tear off 4 pieces of heavy-duty aluminum foil, each 18 x 15 inches. On center of each piece, place meat, peas, carrots, potatoes, and broccoli tops. Sprinkle with salt and pepper to taste. Stir together mushroom soup and onion soup mix; spoon soup mixture over meat and vegetables. Place cherry tomatoes on top of mixture; wrap securely in foil; place on hot coals. Cook 50-55 minutes, or until meat is tender.

Gwen Campbell, Sterling, Va.

NO-FRILLS HENS ON THE GRILL
Serves 4

Marinade:
1/2 cup olive oil
1/2 cup fresh orange juice
2-1/4 tablespoons soy sauce
1/2 cup wine vinegar
1/4 teaspoon liquid hot sauce
1/2 teaspoon Worcestershire sauce
1/4 teaspoon thyme
1/4 teaspoon salt
1/4 teaspoon pepper
4 Cornish game hens

Combine marinade ingredients; pour into oblong glass dish. Place hens in marinade; marinade 4 to 5 hours; turn occasionally. Place hens on grill over hot coals; baste with marinade frequently. Cook about 1 hour.

Gwen Campbell, Sterling, Va.

SALMON LOAF FOR TWO
Serves 4

- 2 cups canned salmon, boned and flaked
- 1 egg
  Liquid from salmon, plus milk to make ¾ cup
- 1½ cups cracker crumbs
- 1 tablespoon lemon juice
- 1 teaspoon chopped onion
- ⅛ teaspoon salt
- ⅛ teaspoon pepper

Heat oven to 350 degrees. Grease a 9 x 5 x 3-inch loaf pan. Blend egg into flaked salmon. Stir in remaining ingredients. Spoon into pan. Bake 45 minutes, or until top is brown and crisp.

Flo Burtnett, Gage, Okla.

CHICKEN RICE POCKETS
Serves 8–10

- 1/3 cup long-grain rice
- 1/2 teaspoon instant chicken bouillon granules
- 1-1/2 cups cooked chicken, chopped
- 2 or 3 small tomatoes, seeded and chopped
- 1 avocado, peeled, seeded and chopped
- 1 cup frozen chopped broccoli, cooked and drained
- 1 hard-cooked egg, chopped
- 1/2 cup shreddid cheddar cheese
- 1/4 cup sliced olives
- 1/2 cup mayonnaise
- 1 tablespoon Dijon-style mustard
- 2 teaspoons honey
- 1/4 teaspoon celery salt
- 1/8 teaspoon pepper
- 4 or 5 large pita bread rounds, halves

In saucepan bring 2/3 cup water to boiling. Stir in rice and bouillon granules. Reduce heat. Cover and simmer for 20 minutes, or until tender and water is absorbed. Meanwhile, combine chicken, tomatoes, avocado, broccoli, egg, cheese and olives. Add cooked rice. Stir together mayonnaise, mustard, honey, celery salt and pepper. Pour over rice mixture; toss to coat. Cover and chill. Spoon about 1/2 cup into each pita bread half.

Laura Hicks, Troy, Mont.

OVEN STEAK DINNER

- 1-1/2 pounds round steak, 1/2-inch thick
- 4 medium carrots
- 4 medium potatoes, pared and cut in half
- 1 can cream of mushroom soup
- 1 envelope dry onion soup mix
- 1 package frozen peas

Heat oven to 450 degrees. Cut meat into pieces. Place peas in colander; run cold water over them until they break apart. Drain. Tear off 4 pieces heavy-duty aluminum foil, each 18 x 15 inches. On center of each piece place 1 carrot thinly sliced, 1 potato cut into quarters, and 1/4 of the meat. Stir together soup and soup mix; spoon over meat and top with peas. Wrap securely; place on ungreased baking sheet. Bake 50-60 minutes, or until tender.

Donna Holter, West Middlesex, Pa.

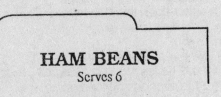

HAM BEANS
Serves 6

- 1 pound navy beans
- ½ cup onions, chopped
- 1 meaty ham bone
- 3 cups water
  Salt and pepper to taste

Soak beans in water to cover overnight. Rinse and put into Crockpot or other pan along with other ingredients. Celery and carrots may be added, if desired. Simmer 6–8 hours in a Crockpot on medium, or for a shorter length of time on the stove. When beans are soft, they are done. Serve with chopped raw onions and corn bread.

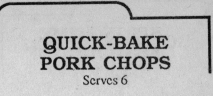

QUICK-BAKE PORK CHOPS
Serves 6

- 6 pork chops
- 2 teaspoons salt
- 3 tablespoons melted shortening
- 1 cup uncooked long-grain rice
- 3/4 teaspoon chili powder
- 1/2 cup chopped green pepper
- 1/2 cup tomatoes
- 6 green pepper rings
- 3/4 cup shredded processed American cheese

In a large skillet, brown pork chops in shortening for 20 minutes. Drain off excess fat. Add chili powder, salt, and pepper; sprinkle over meat. Add rice and chopped green pepper; spoon canned tomatoes over chops and rice. Cover skillet and cook over low heat for 30-35 minutes, stirring occasionally. Add in pepper rings; cover and cook for 5 minutes longer. Sprinkle top with cheese and cover until cheese melts.

Suzan L. Wiener, Spring Hill, Fla.

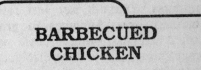

BARBECUED CHICKEN

Boil cut-up fryers 15 minutes in water seasoned with bay leaves. Drain off water, and combine with sauce.

Sauce:
- 1-1/2 tablespoons oil
- 1 stick margarine
- 4 tablespoons soy sauce
- 3 tablespoons lemon juice
- 2 tablespoons Worcestershire sauce
- 1/4 to 1 teaspoon liquid smoke
- 1 clove crushed garlic
- 1-1/2 teaspoons vinegar
- Dash salt and pepper

Combine and simmer 5 minutes. Pour sauce over chicken, and marinate 1 hour to overnight. Cook on barbecue grill for 10-12 minutes, or until brown, basting with sauce. (The marinade will become jellied if chilled overnight.) This method saves time in barbecuing and chicken is absolutely delicious!!

Rose Pickens, Eugene, Ore.

SPRINGTIME CASSOULET OF LAMB
Serves 6

4 cups lamb shoulder, cubed
1 tablespoon vegetable oil
1 clove garlic, minced
4 cups beef broth (bouillon)
3 1/4 cups water, divided
4 carrots, sliced
3 ribs celery, sliced
1 parsnip, sliced
1 bay leaf
1 1/2 tablespoons paprika
2 ounces medium noodles
1 1/2 cups frozen Italian green beans
1 cup frozen green peas
1 jar small white onions, with liquid
1 can Great Northern beans
1 tablespoon all-purpose flour

Cut lamb into 1/2-inch cubes. In Dutch oven heat oil. Add lamb and brown on all sides; add garlic; cook 5 minutes. Add broth, 3 cups water and next 5 ingredients. Bring to a boil; reduce heat; cover and simmer for 35 minutes. Discard bay leaf. Add noodles; simmer 5 minutes. Add green beans and peas. Bring to a boil; simmer 5 minutes, or until vegetables and noodles are tender. Gently stir in the small onions and beans. In a small bowl, blend together flour and remaining 1/4 cup water. Add to the cassoulet, stirring until thickened.

Gwen Campbell, Sterling, Va.

SWISS STEAK
Serves 4

1½ pounds round steak (about 1 inch thick)
¼ cup all-purpose flour
Salt and pepper to taste
3 tablespoons vegetable oil
1 large (6-ounce) onion, sliced
1 large rib celery, sliced

½ pound mushrooms, sliced
1 clove garlic, finely chopped
1 (8-ounce) can stewed tomatoes
¼ teaspoon dried, crushed basil
¼ teaspoon dried, crushed oregano
¼ teaspoon dried, crushed thyme

Trim excess fat from steak. With the edge of a heavy saucer or a meat mallet pound flour into both sides of steak. Sprinkle with salt and pepper. In a large skillet heat oil; add steak. With medium-high heat brown meat well on both sides. Place steak in a baking dish (12 x 8 x 2-inch). In the drippings in the skillet, lightly cook onion, celery, garlic and mushrooms. Stir in tomatoes, basil, oregano and thyme. Pour over steak; cover lightly with foil. Bake at 300 degrees for 1¼–1½ hours, or until tender.

Marion A. Jones, Pottsville, Pa.

SHISH KABOBS

1 pound lamb steak, 3/4-inch thickness
4 slices canned pineapple
Water-pack tomato wedges
Green pepper wedges
Onion
1/4 pound mushrooms
1-1/2 tablespoons cooking oil
2 tablespoons minced onion
3 tablespoons lemon juice
1/2 teaspoon salt

Cut lamb into 1-inch squares and marinate for several hours in oil, lemon juice, minced onion, and salt. Drain lamb and alternate on 4 metal skewers with mushroom caps, 1-inch pieces of pineapple, as well as tomato and green pepper wedges. Broil 4 inches from broiler for about 12-15 minutes turning several times, or place on barbecue grill and cook until desired doneness.

Suzan L. Wiener, Spring Hill, Fla.

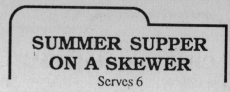

1 (6-ounce) can frozen orange juice concentrate
1/2 cup honey
1/4 cup crystallized ginger, finely chopped
1/4 teaspoon marjoram leaves
2 pounds chicken, veal, beef, or pork, cut into 1-inch cubes
1 acorn squash, cut into 2-inch pieces
4 apples, unpeeled and quartered
12 plump prunes

Mix orange juice concentrate, honey, ginger, and marjoram. Place meat in shallow glass dish; pour orange juice mixture over meat. Cover; refrigerate several hours; turn meat occasionally. Cook squash in boiling, salted water 10 minutes; drain. Remove meat from marinade; reserve marinade. On 6 skewers, alternate meat, squash, apples, and prunes. Place on grill 3 inches from coals. Cook 30 minutes, or until meat is brown, and squash, apples, and prunes are tender. Turn and baste frequently with reserved marinade. Can be served over hot fluffy rice, if desired.

Gwen Campbell, Sterling, Va.

BUDGET CHICKEN AMERICANA
Serves 4

2 pounds chicken parts
1/4 cup margarine
1 (10-1/2-ounce) can cream of mushroom soup
1/4 teaspoon thyme
1/4 teaspoon rosemary
1/4 teaspoon ground sage
1/2 cup water
12 small pearl onions

Brown chicken in margarine. Stir in soup, thyme, rosemary, sage and water. Bring to a boil; reduce heat; simmer 10 minutes. Add onions; simmer gently for 40 minutes, or until chicken is fork tender.

Gwen Campbell, Sterling, Va.

CHICKEN SUPREME

4 split chicken breasts *or* 8 chicken filets
6 tablespoons margarine
1/2 cup diced onions
1/2 cup diced green peppers
1/2 cup diced celery
8 ounces sharp, grated cheddar cheese
1 can cream of chicken soup
1 can cream of celery soup

Brown chicken in melted margarine in frying pan. Put chicken in a 9 x 13-inch pan. Sauté celery, green pepper and onion in margarine. Add cream of celery and cream of chicken soup. Dilute with 2 cans water. Let come to boil and pour over chicken. Cover and bake at 375 degrees for 2 hours. With 30 minutes of baking time remaining, sprinkle cheddar cheese over chicken and continue baking, uncovered.

Elizabeth Svitek, Canonsburg, Pa.

SALMON LOAF
Serves 5–6

1 (1-pound) can salmon
2 tablespoons melted butter
2 egg yolks
1 teaspoon Worcestershire sauce
½ teaspoon salt
½ cup milk
½ cup soft bread crumbs
1 teaspoon lemon juice
2 egg whites, stiffly beaten

Remove bones from salmon; add all ingredients, except egg whites. Fold in egg whites carefully. Place in greased loaf pan (8½ x 4½ x 2½-inch) and bake in a 350-degree oven until brown. Serve with cream of mushroom sauce made by heating 1 can cream of mushroom soup with 1 teaspoon Worcestershire sauce.

Shari Crider, Stoughton, Wis.

BROILED FISH DINNER

4 haddock fillets (1 pound total)
4 tomatoes
2 medium potatoes, boiled and sliced
2 tablespoons melted butter *or* margarine
1 tablespoon melted fat
Salt and pepper

Place a piece of waxed paper in broiler pan. Place fish, skin side down, on paper. Brush with melted fat; sprinkle with salt and pepper. Set broiler pan in oven so that fish is 3 inches from heat. Cut tomatoes in halves; spread melted butter over each half; sprinkle with salt and pepper.

After fish has broiled 10 minutes, put tomatoes and potatoes around fish; broil 10 minutes more.

Diane Holmes, Brooksville, Fla.

HAM LOAF
Serves 12

3 pounds smoked ham
2 pounds lean fresh pork
3 eggs
1½ cans tomato soup
1 teaspoon paprika

Have ham and pork ground at the market or store. Beat eggs; add tomato soup and paprika; mix with ground meat. Place mixture in a loaf pan and bake in a 350-degree oven for 1½ hours.

Place baking pan in hot water to bake.

Ham Sauce:
1 cup mayonnaise
1 cup whipped cream
⅓ cup prepared mustard

Add mustard to mayonnaise. Fold in whipped cream just before serving.
Lucy Dowd, Sequim, Wash.

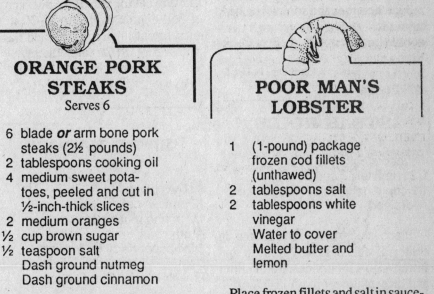

ORANGE PORK STEAKS
Serves 6

6 blade *or* arm bone pork steaks (2½ pounds)
2 tablespoons cooking oil
4 medium sweet potatoes, peeled and cut in ½-inch-thick slices
2 medium oranges
½ cup brown sugar
½ teaspoon salt
Dash ground nutmeg
Dash ground cinnamon

Cook steaks in skillet with cooking oil until browned. Sprinkle with salt. In a 9 x 13-inch baking dish arrange sweet potatoes. Thinly slice one of the oranges; place on top of potatoes; cover with steaks. Squeeze remaining orange; add water to juice to measure ½ cup. Combine juice, brown sugar, salt and spices. Pour over steaks. Bake, covered, at 350 degrees for 45 minutes. Uncover; bake 30 minutes more.

Leota Baxter, Ingalls, Kan.

POOR MAN'S LOBSTER

1 (1-pound) package frozen cod fillets (unthawed)
2 tablespoons salt
2 tablespoons white vinegar
Water to cover
Melted butter and lemon

Place frozen fillets and salt in saucepan with cold water to just cover. Bring to boil; lower heat and cook 10 minutes. Drain. Cover again with cold water and white vinegar. Bring to boil. Lower heat and cook 10 minutes more. Drain.

Serve, dipping each bite into melted butter and lemon. Tastes just like lobster with no salt or vinegar taste.

I squeeze lemon juice directly into the hot melted butter.

Madeline Darrow, Warren, Mich.

PEPPER STEAK WITH RICE
Serves 4

1 pound lean beef steak, 1/2-inch thickness
2 tablespoons margarine
Garlic powder
1 (10-ounce) can beef broth
1 cup sliced green onions, including tops
2 green peppers, cut into strips
2 tablespoons cornstarch
1/4 cup water
1/4 cup soy sauce
2 large, fresh tomatoes (cut into wedges)

Cut meat into 1/4-inch-wide strips. In large skillet, brown meat in melted margarine. Add garlic powder and beef broth. Cover and simmer 20 minutes. Stir in onions and green peppers. Cover and simmer 15 minutes.

Blend cornstarch, water and soy sauce. Stir into meat mixture. Cook and stir until thickened.

Add tomatoes and stir until heated; serve over rice. (This recipe earlier won a third prize in Illinois Beef Cook-off.)

Barbara Lindholm, Pekin, Ill.

STEAK ROLLS

4 cubed steaks
1/2 cup finely diced celery
1/2 cup mushrooms, chopped and drained

Place celery and mushrooms in center of cubed steaks. Roll up and fasten with 4 toothpicks. Roll in flour and brown slowly in oil in skillet.
Combine:
1 package onion soup mix
1/2 cup ketchup
1/4 teaspoon garlic powder
1/4 teaspoon Worcestershire sauce
1 1/2 cups water

Take steaks out of skillet. Arrange in a baking dish; pour sauce over top surface of steaks. Bake at 350 degrees for about 1 to 1 1/2 hours, or until done.

Dorothy Dayle Hare, Fremont, Neb.

BUTTER-HERB BAKED FISH

½ cup butter *or* margarine
⅔ cup crushed saltine crackers
¼ cup grated Parmesan cheese
½ teaspoon *each* basil leaves, oregano leaves and salt
¼ teaspoon garlic powder
1 pound frozen sole, perch *or* flounder fillets, thawed and drained (Fresh fish may be used.)

Preheat oven to 350 degrees. In 13 x 9-inch baking pan, melt butter in preheated oven, 5–7 minutes. Meanwhile, in a 9-inch pie pan combine cracker crumbs, Parmesan cheese, basil, oregano, salt and garlic powder. Dip fish fillets in melted butter, and then in crumb mixture. Arrange fillets in baking pan. Bake near center of 350-degree oven for 25–30 minutes, or until fish is tender and flakes with a fork. Serve immediately.

Peggy Fowler Revels, Woodruff, S.C.

LIVER KABOBS
Serves 4

4 slices bacon
12 ounces calves liver
1/2 pound mushrooms
4 tomatoes
2 tablespoons oil for broiling
Salt
Freshly ground black pepper

Cut bacon slices in half and flatten with the edge of a knife and roll up. Trim liver and cut into cubes. Trim mushrooms and slice tomatoes in half. Thread 4 skewers with alternate liver cubes, bacon rolls, mushroom caps and halved tomatoes. Brush kabobs with oil and season with salt and pepper. Put under a moderately hot broiler and cook for 10–15 minutes, turning occasionally.

Suzan Wiener, Spring Hill, Fla.

SEAFOOD QUICHE

1 quart heavy cream
5 eggs
1 clove of garlic, crushed
1 teaspoon celery seed
¾ cup cheddar cheese (chopped)
¼ pound *each* of shrimp, crabmeat and scallops
Butter
¼ cup Parmesan cheese
Paprika
1 (9-inch) unbaked pie shell

Pour heavy cream in saucepan and heat to simmer or tiny bubbles. Remove from heat. In a large bowl whisk together eggs, garlic and celery seed; add to heavy cream. Place cheddar cheese in bottom of pie crust; set aside. Sauté all seafood in a large skillet or saucepan with butter. When seafood has cooked about 8 minutes, place over cheese. Then pour cream mixture over all ingredients in the pie crust. Sprinkle with Parmesan cheese and paprika. Bake at 350 degrees for approximately 30 minutes, or until knife comes out clean.

Sheila Symonowicz, Loganville, Pa.

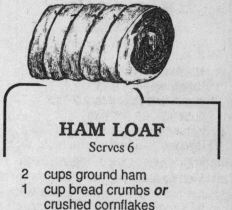

HAM LOAF
Serves 6

2 cups ground ham
1 cup bread crumbs *or* crushed cornflakes
1 egg
1 cup shredded carrots
1 cup milk

Grind ham coarsely in a meat grinder, then mix with other ingredients. Form into loaf and bake in a loaf pan at 350 degrees for 45 minutes. Pineapple slices sprinkled with brown sugar may be added as a garnish and baked with the loaf for the last 15 minutes.

ATLANTIC COAST CRABMEAT BAKE

Serves 3

1½ cups light cream
½ pound crabmeat
1 teaspoon prepared mustard
1 cup onion, minced
1 teaspoon liquid hot sauce
1¼ tablespoons butter *or* margarine
1 cup bread crumbs
1 egg, beaten
2 teaspoons fresh lemon juice
¼ teaspoon salt
¼ teaspoon pepper
Cracker crumbs for topping
Butter *or* margarine for topping

In a large saucepan heat the cream and the next 10 ingredients. Place mixture in an ovenproof casserole; cover with cracker crumbs; dot with butter. Bake 400 degrees, 15 minutes until crumbs are golden and crispy.

Gwen Campbell, Sterling, Va.

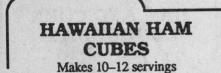

HAWAIIAN HAM CUBES

Makes 10–12 servings

1 (10-ounce) jar orange marmalade
1 tablespoon soy sauce
1 pound ham, cut into 1/2-inch cubes
1 (8-ounce) can pineapple chunks, drained
1 large green pepper, cut into 1/2-inch squares

Mix marmalade and soy sauce in a 2-quart casserole. Stir in remaining ingredients until well-coated. Cover with a tight-fitting lid or plastic wrap.

Microwave on HIGH, 100 percent power, for 10 minutes, or until hot and bubbly. Stir halfway through the cooking time.

If desired, prepare recipe right in a dish to fit a chafing dish. Remove from microwave oven and elegantly serve at a party.

Marie Fusaro, Manasquan, N.J.

MEDITERRANEAN BAKED FISH

Serves 4

2 pounds tomatoes
1 tablespoon vegetable oil
3/4 cup chopped onion
1/2 cup diced green pepper
1 garlic clove, crushed
1 teaspoon salt
1 teaspoon grated orange peel
1/2 teaspoon thyme leaves, crushed
1/4 teaspoon fennel seed
1/16 teaspoon ground black pepper
1-1/2 pounds fish fillets

Use tomatoes held at room temperature until fully ripe. Preheat oven to 350 degrees. Cut tomatoes into 1/4-inch cubes (makes about 4 cups); set aside. In a medium saucepan heat oil until hot. Add onion, green pepper, and garlic. Sauté until onion is transparent, about 5 minutes. Add salt, orange peel, thyme, fennel, black pepper, and reserved tomato. Simmer, uncovered, stirring frequently for 15 minutes. Spoon half of the tomato mixture into a 13x9x2-inch baking pan. Arrange fish in a single layer over sauce. Spoon remaining tomato mixture on fish. Cover and bake until fish flakes easily with a fork, about 20 minutes. (209 calories per serving)

Sally Jones, Indianapolis, Ind.

CLAM CAKES

1 pint of clams, chopped
1 teaspoon baking powder
1 cup milk
2 eggs
2 cups flour
½ teaspoon salt
½ cup clam juice
Fat for frying

Mix flour, baking powder and salt; set aside. Beat eggs; add milk and clam juice. Add chopped clams, then flour mixture. Mix well. Drop by large spoonfuls into hot fat (or onto grill). When browned remove from fat and drain on paper towel or brown paper. Serve hot.

Mrs. Stanley Thims, Falmouth, Maine

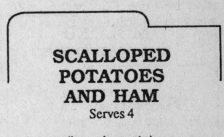

PINEAPPLE HAM

3 ounces ground *or* finely chopped ham
¼ teaspoon mustard
1 tablespoon mayonnaise
1 tablespoon pineapple juice
3 slices canned pineapple, drained
Cauliflower sprigs for garnish

Mix together chopped ham, mustard, mayonnaise and pineapple juice.

Then arrange the 3 pineapple slices on a baking tray and cover with ham mixture. Bake in 350-degree oven for 15 minutes.

This is a delicious recipe which my whole family loves!

Suzan L. Wiener, Spring Hill, Fla.

SCALLOPED POTATOES AND HAM

Serves 4

4 medium-size potatoes
Slices of leftover ham
Flour
Margarine
1 to 1½ cups milk
Salt and pepper to taste

Peel potatoes and cover with cold water. Heat oven to 350 degrees. Grease 2-quart baking dish. Layer ham slices in bottom of dish. Slice potatoes in thin slices to cover ham. Sprinkle potato layer with 1 tablespoon flour, salt and pepper to taste, and dot layer with 1 tablespoon margarine. Repeat, making 2 more layers. Pour milk over potatoes until it can be seen through the top layer. Bake covered for 45 minutes. Uncover and bake for 20–30 minutes more until top has browned.

BEEF ROULADEN

8 slices round steak (6 x 3 x ¼ inch)
Salt and pepper to taste
8 strips bacon, uncooked
Mustard
8 lengthwise slices carrots
8 lengthwise slices pickle
8 tablespoons chopped onion
2 tablespoons flour
¼ cup sour cream

Season meat with salt and pepper. On each slice of round steak lay 1 strip bacon, a little mustard, 1 slice carrot and 1 slice pickle. Sprinkle 1 tablespoon onion along length. Roll up and fasten with toothpicks or skewers. Fry in fat until brown. Cover with water and simmer 1½–2 hours, covered. Test for doneness with fork. To make gravy, add flour, sour cream and a little water to juices in pan. Season to taste.

June Harding, Ferndale, Mich.

MOLDED SHRIMP RING

1 (3-ounce) package lemon gelatin
1½ cups boiling water
½ cup ketchup
1 small can shrimp
1 cup chopped celery
1 teaspoon grated onion
1 cup cooked peas
10 stuffed olives, sliced

Dissolve gelatin in boiling water. Add ketchup and let set until slightly congealed. Then add remaining ingredients. Mix well and pour into mold. Let set until firm. Serve with the following:

Dressing:
½ cup mayonnaise
2 tablespoons cream
1 hard-cooked egg, cut up fine

Mix all ingredients together.

Mrs. Roy G. Carlson, Sycamore, Ill.

BAKED YOGURT CHICKEN
Serves 4

2-1/2–3 pounds chicken, cut up
Salt and pepper
6 tablespoons butter *or* margarine
2 tablespoons flour
1 tablespoon paprika
2 cups plain yogurt
1/4 pound fresh mushrooms, sliced
2 tablespoons fresh lemon juice
2 tablespoons chopped fresh dill or parsley

Wash chicken pieces and wipe dry. Add salt and pepper. In a large pan, melt 4 tablespoons butter; fry chicken until golden brown. Remove to buttered, shallow baking dish. Sprinkle flour and paprika into pan juices and cook, stirring for 1 minute. Stir in yogurt and mix well. Spoon over chicken. Sauté mushrooms in remaining 2 tablespoons butter and lemon juice for 1 minute and spoon over chicken. Sprinkle with dill. Bake, covered, at 325 degrees for about 1-1/4 hours, or until chicken is tender.

Laura Hicks, Troy, Mont.

BOILED HAM DINNER
Serves 4–6

1 ham bone with chunks of meat
3–4 carrots
4–6 small whole onions
3–4 potatoes
1 bay leaf
6 peppercorns and cloves
Water to cover
1 small head of cabbage

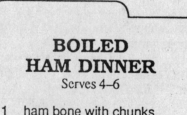

Cook ham in large pot with carrots and potatoes (peeled and cut into chunks), peeled onions, bay leaf, peppercorns, cloves and water. Simmer until carrots are tender. On the stove, that would be about 1½ hours; in a slow cooker on medium setting, about 6. Add cabbage, cut into wedges, and cook for 20 more minutes.

BAKED HAM IN A BLANKET
Serves 12-15

1 (12-to 15-pound) ham
4 cups flour
1 cup brown sugar
2 tablespoons ground cloves
2 tablespoons cinnamon
2 tablespoons mustard
1 teaspoon black pepper
Water or cider

Have a butcher cut off small end of ham. Trim off rind and excess fat. Place in open roasting pan with fat side up. Combine remaining ingredients, adding enough liquid to make stiff dough. Roll into sheet to cover ham over top, ends, and sides. It is not necessary to add water to pan in which ham is baked. Place in cold oven. Bake at 300 degrees, allowing 25 minutes per pound of ham.

HAM AND CORN CROQUETTES
Serves 4

1 cup cream-style corn
2 tablespoons green pepper, chopped
1 cup ground ham
½ cup dried bread crumbs
1 egg, beaten

Mix all ingredients in saucepan. Heat to boiling. Cook for a minute or 2 to let the egg thicken. Remove from heat and chill.

When mixture is cold, shape into patties and dip into more dried bread crumbs, then in 1 egg beaten with 2 tablespoons water, then in crumbs again. They may be put back into the refrigerator until you are ready to fry them, or fry at once. Fry 2 at a time in deep fat until brown. Serve with a sauce made from canned mushroom soup diluted with a little milk and heated.

FILET MIGNON TETA-A-TETA

Valentine's Dinner for 2

4 tablespoons butter
2 tablespoons shallots, minced
1 clove garlic, whole
1 tablespoon Worcestershire sauce
1 teaspoon soy sauce
2 (6-ounce each) Filets Mignons
3 ounces brandy
1 tablespoon cashew nuts, coarsely
  chopped

Heat 2 tablespoons butter in skillet; add shallots and garlic; sauté over medium heat for 5 minutes. Remove and discard garlic. Increase heat to high, add Worcestershire sauce and soy sauce; place filets in pan. Let cook 3 minutes on each side, turning once for slightly rare. Transfer filets to warm dish. Deglaze pan with brandy and then ignite with a match (be careful of flames). Remove pan from heat, swirl in remaining butter to thicken sauce. Pour over filets and top with cashew nuts. Serve immediately.

Marie Fusaro, Manasquan, NJ

SPANISH RICE STEAKS

Serves 4

4 cube steaks
1 cup all-purpose flour
1/2 cup vegetable oil
Salt and pepper to taste
1 onion, sliced
1 (5 ounce) can Spanish rice
1/4 teaspoon sugar
2 teaspoons parsley flakes

Coat steaks with flour. In skillet, brown steaks in oil. Transfer to lightly greased 9 inch square baking dish. Season with salt and pepper; set aside. Saute onions slices; add Spanish rice and sugar; mix well. Spoon rice mixture over steaks; sprinkle with parsley flakes.

Gwen Campbell, Sterling, VA

FRUITED POT ROAST

4 pounds chuck roast or pot roast
2 tablespoons margarine
1-1/2 teaspoons salt
1/8 teaspoon pepper
1 cup apple juice
1 cup dried apricots
1 cup pitted prunes
1 cup tart apples, pared and sliced
2 cinnamon sticks, or 1/4 teaspoon
  ground cinnamon

Brown meat in margarine. Pour off the drippings. Season with salt and pepper. Cover and simmer in Dutch oven (or bake at 350 degrees) for 2-2-1/2 hours, or until tender.

Turn meat over and add fruit. Continue cooking for 30 minutes or until apples are tender. Serve on a warm platter, surrounded by the fruit.

Mrs. L.W. Mayer, Richmond, VA

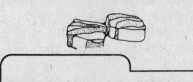

MOCK STROGANOFF

Serves 6

1/4 cup onion, chopped
1 tablespoon margarine, melted
2 tablespoons oil, any kind (except
  olive oil)
Salt to taste
3 cups cubed, cooked beef
1 can (10-3/4 ounces) condensed
  tomato soup
1 can (3 or 4 ounces) chopped mushrooms
1 (8 ounce) can peas, drained
1 teaspoon sugar
1 cup dairy sour cream
Hot cooked and buttered noodles of
  your choice

Saute onion in oil and margarine in a large frying pan; add beef and brown lightly. Stir in tomato soup, mushrooms, peas, sugar, and salt. Cover mixture, simmer 20 minutes to blend flavors. Stir in sour cream; heat just to boiling point (Don't let sauce boil, as sour cream may curdle). Serve over buttered hot noodles.

Marie Fusaro, NJ

GLAZED BEEF PINWHEEL ROLL

1 pound lean ground beef
1/4 teaspoon salt
1/4 teaspoon pepper
1 onion, chopped fine
1 egg
1 tablespoon milk
1 cup soft bread crumbs
1-1/2 cups raw carrots, shredded
2 tablespoons fresh parsley, minced
Chili Glaze (recipe follows)

Mix all ingredients, except carrots and parsley. Wet rolling pin; roll beef mixture on a sheet of wax paper to make a rectangle 6 inches wide and 1/2 inch thick. Spread with mixture of carrots and parsley. Roll as for jelly roll. Place in a shallow baking pan, uncovered. Spread top of roll with chili glaze. Bake at 350 degrees for 1 hour.

Chili Glaze:

Combine 1/2 cup chili sauce with 1/2 cup water, 1 tablespoon corn syrup, and 1 tablespoon Worcestershire sauce.

Gwen Campbell, Sterling, Va.

BEEF BEER BALLS

1 pound ground beef
1/4 to 1 teaspoon ground cloves, depending upon taste
1/2 teaspoon salt
1/4 teaspoon black pepper
1/2 teaspoon Accent seasoning
1/2 cup catsup
2 tablespoons Worcestershire sauce
12 ounces of beer

Mix ground beef, ground cloves, salt, pepper and Accent. Form into small balls about the size of walnuts. Brown well. Mix catsup, Worcestershire sauce and beer in separate pan. Simmer for 10 minutes. Drain fat from meatballs, add sauce. Cover; simmer 2 hours. Serve on toothpicks.

Ruby Jo Keplin

Micro-MAGIC

CHEESY MICROWAVE LASAGNA
Serves 6–8

1/2 pound lasagna noodles
2 (8-ounce) cans tomato sauce
1 (6-ounce) can tomato paste
1 tablespoon oregano
2 teaspoons basil
1/4 teaspoon garlic powder
1 pound ground beef, cooked and drained
2 cups cottage cheese
1 egg
1 tablespoon parsley flakes
1 (6-ounce) package sliced mozzarella cheese
1 (6-ounce) package cheddar cheese
1/2 cup grated Parmesan cheese

In the bottom of baking dish place 1 tablespoon oil, noodles and water to cover. Microwave on HIGH for 8 minutes. Drain noodles. In large bowl mix tomato sauce, paste, oregano, basil, 1/2 teaspoon salt and garlic powder. Spread 1/2 cup sauce over bottom of baking dish. Mix beef with remaining sauce. In small bowl mix cottage cheese, egg and parsley. Layer 3 noodles, half of cottage cheese mixture, half of mozzarella and cheddar cheese, half of sauce in baking dish. Repeat layers. Sprinkle Parmesan cheese over top. Cover with waxed paper, microwave on HIGH for 20–26 minutes, rotating dish 1/4 turn every 8 minutes. Let stand 10 minutes before cutting. Can be made ahead and refrigerated. Add 4–6 minutes to cooking time.

Mrs. Merle Mishler, Hollsopple, Pa.

CHICKEN KIEV
Serves 4–6

2/3 cup melted butter
3/4 cup dry bread crumbs or crushed cornflakes
3 tablespoons grated Parmesan cheese
1 teaspoon basil
1 teaspoon oregano
1/2 teaspoon garlic salt
1/4 teaspoon salt
4 chicken breasts, deboned and skinned
Pepper to taste

Sauce:
1/2 cup apple juice or white wine
1/2 cup chopped green onion
1/4 cup chopped fresh parsley
Reserved butter

Melt butter in glass mixing bowl in microwave for 40 seconds on HIGH. Dip chicken breasts in melted butter. Set aside melted butter after dipping chicken.

Combine bread crumbs, cheese, spices, salt and pepper. Dip chicken in crumb mixture to coat. Arrange chicken in 13 x 9 x 2-inch glass baking dish. Microwave on HIGH for 9 minutes. Rotate dish 1/2 turn; cook approximately 9 minutes longer, or until fork-tender.

Combine sauce ingredients, including reserved butter, and pour over chicken. Cover with waxed paper and microwave for 3–5 minutes on 70 percent power or 1-1/2–2 minutes on HIGH. Let stand, covered, for 5–6 minutes. Spoon sauce over chicken and serve hot. Garnish with paprika and parsley.

Carolyn Griffin, Macon, Ga.

CAULIFLOWER AND CARROT MEDLEY
Serves 8

1 head cauliflower or 1 (20-ounce) package frozen cauliflower florets
4 cups carrot slices, 1/4 inch thick
2 tablespoons water
1/4 teaspoon Dijon-style mustard
1 cup chicken broth
1/2 cup sour cream
3 tablespoons flour
1-1/4 cups grated cheddar cheese, divided
2 green onions, sliced

Place cauliflower, carrots and onions in a 3-quart casserole. Add 2 tablespoons water. (If using frozen vegetables, do not add water.) Cover and cook with HIGH power, 14–15 minutes. Let stand for 8–10 minutes without removing cover.

In large blender jar mix broth, mustard, sour cream and flour until smooth. Pour into a 4-cup measure and microwave with HIGH power, 4–5 minutes, until thick, stirring twice. Add 1 cup cheese and stir until melted.

Drain vegetables and add sauce; stir to coat vegetables with sauce. Sprinkle remaining cheese on top. Microwave with HIGH power, 4–5 minutes, until cheese melts and vegetables are heated through.

Yvonne Schilling, Wauwatosa, Wis.

FESTIVE LEMON PULL-APARTS

Makes 24 rolls

1/4 cup butter *or* margarine
1/2 cup chopped nuts
1/3 cup chopped maraschino cherries, patted dry with paper towel
1 (3-1/2-ounce) package instant lemon pudding mix
1 (16-ounce) loaf frozen white bread dough, thawed
1/2 cup flaked coconut

Place butter in 1-cup glass measure and cook on HIGH for 30–40 seconds, or until melted. Spoon half of butter into 8-inch square casserole. Set aside remaining butter. Sprinkle nuts, cherries, and 3 tablespoons pudding mix over butter in baking dish. Cut bread dough into 24 pieces and roll each into a ball. Combine remaining pudding mix and coconut in a shallow dish. Dip each ball into melted butter; then roll in coconut mixture. Place in baking dish. Sprinkle remaining coconut mixture over dough. Cover with plastic wrap. Microwave on WARM (10 percent) for 8 minutes. Let stand 10 minutes. Repeat once or twice, or until dough is doubled in size. Preheat conventional oven to 350 degrees. Remove plastic wrap and bake rolls 15–20 minutes, or until golden brown. Invert onto serving plate and serve warm.

Mrs. A.S. Warren, Charlotte, N.C.

CHEESE AND BACON STRATA

5 slices bread, toasted and buttered
2 cups cheddar cheese, grated
4 eggs
1 1/2 cups half-and-half
1/2 teaspoon salt
1 teaspoon dry mustard
4 slices bacon, cooked and crumbled
1/2 teaspoon paprika
Dash of pepper

Cut toast into 1-inch cubes. Spread toast cubes and cheese in a deep tube pan. Combine eggs, half-and-half, salt and mustard; pour over the bread-cheese layer. Cover and refrigerate at least 4 hours. Sprinkle with bacon, paprika and pepper. Cover with waxed paper and microwave on MEDIUM (50 percent) power for 16-18 minutes; rotate dish if necessary. Let stand 5 minutes before serving.

Here is a hot, refreshing tea without the spices.

VEGETARIAN ASPARAGUS DELIGHT

Serves 2

1 (16-ounce) can asparagus spears, drained (reserve liquid)
1 (3-ounce) can sliced mushrooms, drained (reserve liquid)
1 (1-1/4-ounce) package cheese sauce mix
1 tablespoon onion flakes
1 hard-cooked egg, chopped
1/4 cup (1 ounce) shredded cheddar cheese
2 tablespoons slivered almonds
Paprika

In 2-cup glass measure, add enough water to reserved liquids to equal 1 cup. Stir in cheese sauce mix and onion. Cook on HIGH 3–3-1/2 minutes, or until thickened; stir occasionally. Add mushrooms, egg and shredded cheese. Arrange asparagus in 9 x 5 x 3-inch loaf dish. Pour on cheese mixture. Sprinkle with almonds and paprika. Cook, covered with waxed paper, at HIGH 4–5 minutes, or until bubbly.

Let stand 5 minutes before serving.

Mrs. Merle Mishler, Hollsopple, Pa.

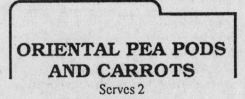

ORIENTAL PEA PODS AND CARROTS

Serves 2

1/4 cup water
1 tablespoon soy sauce
1 teaspoon cornstarch
Dash crushed red pepper
1 medium carrot, thinly sliced
2 teaspoons water
3 ounces frozen pea pods
2 tablespoon broken walnuts
1 teaspoon butter *or* margarine

Stir together 1/4 cup water, soy sauce, cornstarch and crushed red pepper. Microwave, uncovered, on HIGH (100 percent power) for 1–1-1/2 minutes, or until thick and bubbly, stirring every 30 seconds.

Put carrot in casserole dish. Sprinkle with 2 teaspoons water. Microwave, covered, on HIGH (100 percent power) for 2-1/2 minutes. Drain. Toss together carrot, pea pods and walnuts. Add butter or margarine. Microwave, covered, on HIGH (100 percent power) for about 1-1/2 minutes, or until the vegetables are crisp-tender. Toss with soy sauce mixture.

Laura Hicks, Troy, Mont.

RAINBOW VEGETABLES WITH CHEESE SAUCE

Serves 6

Butter
Paprika
1/2 cup herb-seasoned stuffing mix
1 cup cauliflower
1 cup broccoli florets
1 cup carrots, thinly sliced
Cheese Sauce (recipe follows)

Butter a 10-inch tube pan; sprinkle paprika on bottom; scatter stuffing mix on paprika. Press vegetables gently on top of stuffing mix, alternating vegetables. Cover; microwave 8–10 minutes on HIGH. Invert onto serving dish; drizzle with hot cheese sauce.

Cheese Sauce:
1 (10-1/2-ounce) can cheddar cheese soup
2 tablespoons water

Blend soup and water in a 2-cup measuring cup. Microwave 3 minutes on MEDIUM; stir after 1-1/2 minutes.

Gwen Campbell, Sterling, Va.

BAKED CHICKEN
Serves 4

2 cups boiling water
1 cup bulgur wheat
1 teaspoon instant chicken bouillon
  granules
1/8 teaspoon pepper
2 tablespoons butter *or* margarine
1/4 cup fine dry seasoned bread
  crumbs
2 tablespoons grated Parmesan
  cheese
1/4 teaspoon garlic powder
1/8 teaspoon paprika
2 whole medium chicken breasts
  (about 1-1/2 pounds total),
  skinned, deboned and halved
  lengthwise

To cook bulgur, in a 1-quart micro-wave-safe casserole combine water, bulgur, bouillon granules and pepper. Microwave, covered, on 100 percent power or HIGH for 4–5 minutes, or until bulgur is done, stirring once.

In a 1-cup glass measure cook butter, uncovered, on HIGH for 45–60 seconds, or until melted. In a shallow dish combine bread crumbs, cheese, garlic powder and paprika.

Brush the meaty side of each chicken piece with some of the melted butter or margarine; coat the same side with some of the crumb mixture. Place chicken, crumb side up, on a microwave-safe rack in a 12 x 7-1/2 x 2-inch microwave-safe dish. Sprinkle with the remaining butter or margarine.

Cover loosely with waxed paper. Cook on HIGH for 6–7 minutes, or until chicken is tender, giving the dish 1/2 turn once. Serve with bulgur mixture.

Note: If you wish to eat at different times, stir together the crumb mixture in advance and keep it in your refrigerator. Then, you can coat a halved chicken breast and cook it in less than 10 minutes.

Marcella Swigert, Monroe City, Mo.

IMPERIAL CRAB CARIBBEAN
Serves 6

3 (6-1/2 or 7-1/2-ounce) cans
  crabmeat, drained
1/4 cup mayonnaise
1/4 cup sour cream
1/4 cup peanuts, chopped finely
1 teaspoon pimiento, chopped
1/4 teaspoon salt
1/2 teaspoon Worcestershire sauce
2-1/2 drops liquid hot sauce
6 pineapple slices, drained
2/3 cup cornflakes crumbs
1 tablespoon vegetable oil
1/4 cup cornflakes crumbs

In a bowl combine mayonnaise, sour cream, peanuts, pimiento and seasonings. Add to crabmeat; mix lightly.

In a 12 x 7-1/2 x 2-inch lightly buttered microwave dish, place pineapple slices that have been coated on both sides with cornflakes crumbs. Place 1/3 cup crab mixture on top of each pineapple slice. Combine oil and crumbs; sprinkle over top of crab mixture. Microwave on HIGH for 5 minutes.

Gwen Campbell, Sterling, Va.

CRAB COQUILLE
1 serving

1-1/2 teaspoons margarine
1 green onion (with top), thinly sliced
1/2 teaspoon cornstarch
1/4 cup half-and-half
1 teaspoon lemon juice
Dash of salt
Dash of white pepper
1/3 cup cooked crabmeat
2 mushrooms, thinly sliced
1 tablespoon dry bread crumbs
2 teaspoons grated Parmesan
  cheese
1-1/2 teaspoons margarine, melted

Place 1-1/2 teaspoons margarine and the onion in 2-cup measure. Microwave, uncovered, on HIGH for 1–2 minutes, or until crisp-tender. Mix cornstarch. Stir in half-and-half, lemon juice, salt and pepper.

Microwave, uncovered, about minute, stirring after 30 seconds, un thickened. Stir in crabmeat and mus rooms. Spoon into shell-shaped dish 12-ounce, shallow casserole. Mix bre crumbs, cheese and 1-1/2 teaspoo margarine. Sprinkle over top. Co loosely and microwave, 1–2 minut or until hot.

Barbara Nowakowski, North Tonawan

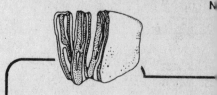

TURKEY ALMONDINE
Serves 4–6

1/2 cup slivered almonds
2 teaspoons butter *or* margarine
2 cups (8 ounces) sliced fresh mushrooms
3 green onions, sliced
2 tablespoons butter *or* margarine
1-1/2 tablespoons cornstarch
1 tablespoon instant chicken bouillon
  granules
1 tablespoon soy sauce
1/4 teaspoon garlic powder
1 cup water
2 cups cubed cooked turkey
1 (6-ounce) package frozen pea
  pods, thawed and halved
1 (2-ounce) can chopped pimiento,
  drained
6 baked patty shells

Combine almonds and butter in smal glass baking dish. Microwave on HIGH uncovered, for 2–3 minutes, or unti toasted, stirring twice. Set aside. Com bine mushrooms, onions and butter i 1-1/2-quart shallow casserole. Micro wave on HIGH, uncovered, 3–4 min utes, or until mushrooms are almos tender, stirring once. Stir in cornstarch bouillon, soy sauce, garlic powder and water. Microwave on HIGH, uncov ered, for 2–3 minutes, or until mixtur boils and thickens, stirring twice. Sti in turkey, pea pods and pimiento. Cove and microwave on HIGH for 4–5 min utes, or until heated through, stirring once. Spoon into patty shells; top wit almonds.

Mrs. A.S. Warren, Charlotte, N.C

STIR-FRY STEAK TERRIYAKI
Serves 2

'4 pound round steak
tablespoons light soy sauce
-2 tablespoons lemon juice
tablespoon brown sugar
teaspoons cornstarch
2 cup onion, thinly sliced
cup sliced mushrooms
2 cup green pepper, chopped
garlic clove, minced
tablespoon oil

Cut steak into 1/8-inch strips (cuts
est when meat is partially frozen).
lake a marinade of soy sauce, lemon
ice, brown sugar and cornstarch. Add
eat to marinade and let stand 15–20
inutes, or longer. In a 9-inch pie plate
ombine oil, garlic and onion. Micro-
ave on HIGH (100 percent power) for
minutes. Move onions to center of pie
ate. Remove meat from marinade
ave marinade). Arrange meat around
nions. Cover tightly; microwave on
IGH for 2 minutes. Stir meat and
nions together. Add mushrooms, green
ppers, 1/4 teaspoon ginger and mari-
de sauce and stir. Cover tightly;
icrowave on HIGH for 2 minutes,
irring once. Serve over rice.
*ote: Use slotted spoon when remov-
g meat from marinade sauce.*

Karen Blunt, Mason City, Iowa

CURRIED CHICKEN AND APPLES
Serves 4–6

4 cup apple juice
ablespoon lemon juice
ablespoons chopped parsley
easpoon curry powder
2 teaspoon salt
2 teaspoon paprika
8 teaspoon pepper
1/2–2 pounds chicken breast,
   deboned and skinned
nedium-size Golden Delicious
   apples, cored and sliced into rings
easpoon cornstarch

Combine apple juice, lemon juice,
parsley, curry powder, salt, paprika and
pepper. Marinade chicken 1 hour.
Remove chicken from marinade; reserve marinade. Microwave chicken on
HIGH for 3 minutes; turn 1/4 turn after
2 minutes. Let stand 5 minutes. Slice
chicken. Add cornstarch to 1/4 cup
marinade. Alternate chicken and apple
rings on microwave-proof platter; brush
with marinade mixture. Microwave on
HIGH for 2 minutes. Brush chicken
and apples and turn 1/4 turn. Microwave 1–2 minutes longer. Remove from
microwave and let stand 5 minutes.
Add remaining marinade to basting
mixture in 2-cup measure; microwave
on HIGH for about 6 minutes, or until
mixture comes to a boil.
*Note: Turkey breast can also be used
instead of chicken.*

Leona Teodori, Warren, Mich.

SWISS SCALLOPED CORN
Serves 6

1 tablespoon butter
1/4 cup unseasoned dry bread
   crumbs
Dash paprika
3 slices bacon
2 (16-ounce) cans whole-kernel corn,
   drained
1 cup shredded Swiss cheese
1 (5-1/4-ounce) can evaporated milk
1 egg
1 tablespoon flour
1/2 teaspoon onion powder
1/8 teaspoon pepper

Place butter in small bowl. Microwave at HIGH 45–60 seconds. Stir in
crumbs and paprika. Set aside. Arrange
bacon on rack. Cover with paper towel.
Microwave at HIGH for 3 minutes until
bacon is crisp; crumble into a 1-1/2-
quart casserole. Stir in corn and Swiss
cheese. In small mixing bowl, blend
remaining ingredients. Stir into corn
mixture. Microwave at MEDIUM for
about 12–14 minutes until cheese melts,

stirring occasionally. Sprinkle with
bread crumb mixture. Microwave at
MEDIUM for about 2 minutes until
hot.

Mrs. Merle Mishler, Hollsopple, Pa.

RYE AND MUSTARD ENGLISH MUFFIN BREAD
Makes 2 loaves

3-1/2 cups unsifted all-purpose flour,
   divided
1-1/2 cups unsifted rye flour
2 packages dry yeast
1 tablespoon sugar
2 teaspoons salt
1/4 teaspoon baking soda
1 tablespoon caraway seeds, optional
2 cups milk
1/2 cup water
2 tablespoons Dijon-style mustard
Cornmeal

In a large bowl combine 1-1/2 cups
all-purpose flour, rye flour, yeast, sugar,
salt, baking soda and caraway seeds.

In a 1-quart measure, microwave
milk, water and mustard on HIGH
power, using probe if available, until
very warm (120–130 degrees). Add to
dry ingredients and beat well. Stir in
remaining flour to make a stiff batter.

Spoon batter into 2 microwave-proof
(8-1/2 x 4-1/2 *or* 9 x 5-inch) loaf pans
that have been greased and sprinkled
with cornmeal. Sprinkle tops with cornmeal. Cover and let rise in warm place
for 45 minutes, or until doubled.

Microwave each loaf individually
on HIGH power for 6-1/2 minutes.
Surface of loaf will be flat and pale in
color. Turn out onto racks to cool. Slice
bread and toast as you would for English muffins.

TIP: Use your microwave to proof
your bread by microwaving 1 cup water
on HIGH power for 6–7 minutes. Place
bread loaves in microwave with hot
water; close door and let rise. This will
help to shorten rising time.

Yvonne Schilling, Wauwatosa, Wis.

SCALLOP MILANGE
Serves 2

1/2 pound scallops
2 stalks celery, cut into 1/2-inch pieces
1/2 of a sweet red *or* green pepper, cut into 3/4-inch squares
2 teaspoons cornstarch
1/4 teaspoon salt
1/8 teaspoon dried basil, crushed
Dash pepper
2/3 cup milk
1 cup cooked rice
1/2 cup shredded Swiss cheese
1 tablespoon dry white wine

In a 1-1/2-quart dish combine scallops, celery and pepper squares. Microwave, covered, on 100 percent power or HIGH for 4–5 minutes, or until scallops are nearly done, stirring once. Drain and set aside.

In the same dish combine cornstarch, salt, basil and pepper. Stir in milk. Microwave, uncovered, on 100 percent power or HIGH for 1-1/2–2 minutes, or until thick and bubbly, stirring every minute.

Gently stir in rice, cheese, wine, scallops and vegetables. Spoon mixture into 2 (15-ounce) casseroles. Microwave, uncovered, on 100 percent power or HIGH for 1 minute, or until heated thoroughly.

Laura Hicks, Troy, Mont.

SEAFOOD SPLASH
Serves 4

1 (6-ounce) package frozen crabmeat and shrimp
2 cups shredded potatoes *or* 12 ounces frozen hash brown potatoes, thawed
1 tablespoon butter
2 green onions, sliced, including tops
1 (10-3/4-ounce) can condensed cream of celery soup
3/4 cup sour cream
1 tablespoon lemon juice
1/4 teaspoon garlic salt
1/2 cup cheddar cheese
Paprika, if desired

Partially thaw frozen crabmeat and shrimp. Combine in 1-1/2-quart glass casserole potatoes, butter and onions. Cover with casserole lid. Microwave on HIGH for 4-1/2–5-1/2 minutes, or until potatoes are almost tender, stirring once. Stir in celery soup, sour cream, lemon juice and garlic salt. Add seafood. Cover and microwave on HIGH for 5 minutes, or until hot. Stir well.

Sprinkle with cheese and sprinkle with paprika, if desired. Microwave, uncovered, on HIGH 2-1/2 minutes.

Angela Biggin, Lyons, Ill.

CONE CAKES

Prepare your favorite cake recipe *or* box mix. Using ice-cream cones with flat bottoms, fill each cone with 2 tablespoons of prepared batter. When cooking more than 2 cones at a time, arrange cones in a circle.

Microwave on HIGH (100 percent) until surface springs back when lightly touched. Always check for doneness at minimum suggested time. If cones are not done at the same time, remove the baked cones and continue cooking the remaining cones. Cool, then frost.

Quick Cream Cheese Frosting:
2 (3-ounce) packages cream cheese
1/2 cup butter *or* margarine
4 cups confectioners' sugar
1 teaspoon almond extract

Place cream cheese and butter in a 2-quart casserole. Microwave on LOW (30 percent) for 1-1/2–2 minutes or until softened. Stir in the sugar and almond extract until well-blended. Beat mixture until spreading consistency. Spread on tops of cooled cones. Garnish with nuts and cherries, or as desired.

Marie Fusaro, Manasquan, N.J.

NUT BRITTLE
Makes 1-1/4 pounds

1/4 cup water
1 cup sugar
1/4 cup light corn syrup
1-1/2 cups salted *or* unsalted nuts, coarsely chopped
1 tablespoon margarine
1 teaspoon vanilla
1 teaspoon baking soda

Note: I use mixed salted nuts.

Grease large cookie sheet; set aside. In a 2-quart microwave casserole combine sugar, syrup and 1/4 cup water. Stretch sheet of microwave plastic wrap over 3/4 of top of casserole. Cook on 100 percent power, HIGH, for 10–1 minutes until small amount of candy mixture dropped into very cold water separates into hard, brittle threads. Stir in nuts; cook on HIGH power for minute longer.

Mixture will foam and bubble up. Carefully stir in margarine, vanilla and baking soda. Work quickly. Pour mixture onto greased cookie sheet, spreading rapidly to edges. Pull ends to make brittle fairly thin. Let stand 45 minutes until hard and completely cooled. Break cooled brittle into pieces. Store in air tight container; will keep up to 3 weeks.

Flo Burtnett, Gage, Okl.

PEANUTTY CEREAL TREATS

4 tablespoons unsalted butter
1/2 cup peanut butter
3 cups miniature marshmallows
4 cups dry, crunchy cereal
1 cup dry roasted peanuts

Place butter, peanut butter, and marshmallows in an 8-to 12-cup measure. Microwave on HIGH for 2-1/2 to 3-1/2 minutes. Stir until smooth. Stir in cereal and peanuts. Blend well. Press in a 9-inch square pan. Cool.

HOT GERMAN POTATO SALAD

Serves 4–6

- medium potatoes
- strips bacon
- tablespoons flour
- /4 cup sugar
- -1/2 teaspoons salt
- /2 teaspoon celery seed
- /8 teaspoon pepper
- cup water
- /2 cup vinegar

Wash and pierce potatoes through with fork. Place on paper towel in microwave oven. Microwave on HIGH for 10–12 minutes, turning over and rearranging after 4 minutes or until tender. Remove from oven; cool slightly; peel potatoes and cut in 1/8-inch slices to make about 4 cups.

In 2-quart casserole cut bacon in small pieces. Cover with paper towel. Microwave at HIGH for about 6 minutes, stirring after 3 minutes, until crisp. With slotted spoon remove bacon to paper towels to drain. set aside.

Stir flour, sugar and seasonings into bacon fat until smooth. Microwave on HIGH for 1–2 minutes until bubbly, stirring after 1 minute.

Add water and vinegar to flour mixture. Microwave on HIGH for 4 minutes, or until mixture boils and thickens, stirring after 1 minute. Remove from oven and stir. Add potatoes and bacon; stir gently so potatoes hold their shape. Cover casserole and let stand until ready to serve.

Karen Waldo, Mendota, Ill.

CHICKEN KIEV APPETIZERS

Makes 28 appetizers

2 chicken breasts, boned, skinned, and cut lengthwise

1/4 cup butter *or* margarine in a stick
2 tablespoons chopped parsley
1/2 teaspoon onion salt
Butter *or* margarine, melted
Paprika
Seasoned salt

Pound chicken until 1/4-inch thick. Cut butter lengthwise into 4 sections. Place 1 piece of butter at narrow end of *each* chicken breast. Sprinkle with parsley and onion salt. Fold over sides to cover butter. Roll up in jelly-roll fashion starting at butter end. *Refrigerate for 1-1/2 hours*. Cut into bite-size pieces and secure with toothpicks. Place in a baking dish. Brush with melted butter. Sprinkle with seasoned salt and paprika. Cover with waxed paper.

Microwave on HIGH (100 percent power) for 3–4 minutes. Allow to stand 3 minutes before serving. Arrange on a platter with dates *or* apple slices between each piece of appetizer before serving. Set toothpicks in an attractive holder next to platter and it's ready for guests!

Marie Fusaro, Manasquan, N.J.

BUTTERFLIED WIENERS

1 pound wieners
1/4 cup honey
1 (20-ounce) bottle of your favorite barbecue sauce

Cut wieners crosswise in 3 pieces. Cut each piece in half lengthwise to make 6 pieces. Slit each piece through ends, leaving 1/4-inch joint in center. Set aside. Mix honey and barbecue sauce in 1-1/2-quart casserole. Cover lightly with plastic wrap or waxed paper. Microwave 1 minute on HIGH. Stir. Add wieners. Cover lightly. Microwave 3 minutes on HIGH, or until ends of wieners curl. Serve with cocktail picks.

Ann Elsie Schmetzer, Madisonville, Ky.

VEGGIE MUFFIN MELTS

Serves 4–6

1	cup sliced, fresh mushrooms
1½	cups shredded zucchini (1 medium)
2	green onions, sliced
3	tablespoons mayonnaise *or* salad dressing
½	teaspoon tarragon leaves
⅛	teaspoon salt
	Dash pepper
3	English muffins, split and toasted
1	medium to large tomato
6	slices Monterey Jack cheese

Combine mushrooms, zucchini and onions in 4-cup glass measure. Cook on HIGH for 3–4 minutes, or until almost tender, stirring once; drain well. Mix in mayonnaise, tarragon, salt and pepper. Arrange muffins, cut side up, on glass serving plate. Cut tomato into 6 slices; place a slice on each muffin; top with zucchini mixture. Cut cheese into small pieces and place over top, allowing some of the vegetables to show. Cook on HIGH for 1–1½ minutes, or until cheese starts to melt, rotating plate once.

Mrs. A.S. Warren, Charlotte, N.C.

DRIED BEEF DIP

Serves 8

1 (8-ounce) package cream cheese
2-1/2-ounce package dried beef, finely chopped
2 tablespoons onion, finely chopped
2 tablespoons Worcestershire sauce
3/4 cup sour cream
Dash liquid hot sauce

In a 4-cup glass measuring cup, soften cream cheese on MEDIUM for 2 minutes. Mix other ingredients with cheese; microwave on MEDIUM for 4 minutes; stir halfway through cooking time. Serve with assorted crackers.

Gwen Campbell, Sterling, Va.

MICROWAVE BUN BARS

Makes 60 bars

1 (12-ounce) package (2 cups) semisweet chocolate chips
1 (12-ounce) package (2 cups) butterscotch chips
2 cups peanut butter
2 cups salted peanuts
1 cup margarine *or* butter
1 (3-1/8-ounce) package vanilla *or* milk chocolate pudding and pie filling mix (not instant)
1/2 cup evaporated milk
1 (2-pound) bag (7-1/2 cups) *sifted* confectioners' sugar
1 teaspoon vanilla

Butter 15 x 10-inch jelly roll pan. In medium microwave-safe bowl, combine chocolate chips and butterscotch chips. Microwave on MEDIUM for 6–7 minutes, stirring every 2 minutes. Stir until smooth. Stir in peanut butter; mix well. Spread half of mixture into prepared pan; refrigerate. Stir peanuts into remaining chocolate mixture; set aside.

In large microwave-safe bowl, place margarine. Microwave on HIGH for 15–60 seconds, or until melted. Stir in pudding mix and evaporated milk; blend well. Microwave on HIGH for 45–60 seconds, or until hot. DO NOT boil. Stir in confectioners' sugar and vanilla. Carefully spread over chocolate layer. Refrigerate 30 minutes to set. Drop remaining chocolate-peanut mixture by tablespoonfuls over chilled pudding layer. Carefully spread to cover. Refrigerate until firm; cut into bars. Store in covered container in refrigerator.
Note: I prefer the vanilla pudding but for an extra-chocolaty bar, you can use milk-chocolate pudding instead of vanilla.

Marilyn J. Hoffmann, Oostburg, Wis.

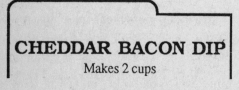

CHEDDAR BACON DIP

Makes 2 cups

6 slices bacon
1 (8-ounce) package cream cheese
1-1/2 cups (6 ounces) shredded sharp cheese
1/4 cup whipping cream
1 teaspoon Worcestershire sauce
1/4 teaspoon dry mustard
1/8 teaspoon onion powder
1/8 teaspoon hot sauce (I use 1 teaspoon)
Parsley

Place bacon on a rack in a 12 x 8 x 2-inch baking dish; cover with paper towels. Microwave on HIGH for 3-1/2–4-1/2 minutes or until done. Crumble bacon and set aside.

Place cream cheese in a 1-quart casserole. Microwave on HIGH for 1 minute, or until melted. Stir in shredded sharp cheese and next 5 ingredients. Microwave at MEDIUM HIGH for 2-1/2 minutes, or until cheese is melted and mixture is heated, stirring once.

Stir in crumbled bacon, reserving 1 tablespoon to sprinkle on top. Garnish with a parsley sprig. Serve with apple wedges on crackers and raw vegetables.

Carolyn Griffin, Macon, Ga.

BERRY NICE STREUSEL

Serves 5–6

1 (21-ounce) can blueberry *or* cherry pie filling
1/2 package (18-1/2-ounce size) yellow cake mix
1/4 cup chopped nuts
2 tablespoons brown sugar
1/2 teaspoon cinnamon
1/3 cup butter *or* margarine

Spread filling in ungreased round glass baking dish, 8-inch size. Sprinkle dry cake mix over filling. Mix nuts, sugar and cinnamon in a small dish; sprinkle over cake mix. Microwave butter on HIGH to melt, about 30 seconds. Dribble over mixture in dish. Microwave, uncovered, for 7 minutes on HIGH. Turn dish 1/4 turn. Microwave on HIGH until mixture bubbles and topping is almost firm, 7–9 minutes. Serve warm or cool.

Barbara Penland, Goshen, Ind.

CARAWAY CABBAGE AND KIELBASA

Serves 4–6

4 cups shredded green cabbage
2 cups chopped tart apple
1 small onion, chopped
2 tablespoons white wine *or* water
1 teaspoon instant beef bouillon
1 teaspoon caraway seeds
1 pound cooked kielbasa

Combine cabbage, apple, onion, wine, bouillon and caraway seeds in a deep 2-quart casserole. Cover and cook on HIGH for 12–14 minutes, or until tender-crisp, stirring once. Cut kielbasa into 1-inch pieces; add to cabbage mixture and stir lightly. Cover and cook on HIGH, or until completely heated through.

Mrs. A.S. Warren, Charlotte, N.C.

VEGGIE MUFFIN MELTS

Serves 4–6

1 cup sliced, fresh mushrooms
1-1/2 cups shredded zucchini (1 medium)
2 green onions, sliced
3 tablespoons mayonnaise *or* salad dressing
1/2 teaspoon tarragon leaves
1/8 teaspoon salt
Dash pepper
3 English muffins, split and toasted
1 medium to large tomato
6 slices Monterey Jack cheese

Combine mushrooms, zucchini and onions in 4-cup glass measure. Cook on HIGH for 3–4 minutes, or until almost tender, stirring once; drain well. Mix in mayonnaise, tarragon, salt and pepper. Arrange muffins, cut-side-up, on glass serving plate. Cut tomato into 6 slices; place a slice on each muffin; top with zucchini mixture. Cut cheese into small pieces and place over top, allowing some of the vegetables to show. Cook on HIGH for 1–1-1/2 minutes, or until cheese starts to melt, rotating plate once.

Mrs. A.S. Warren, Charlotte, N.C.

CHERRY CRUNCH
Serves 6–8

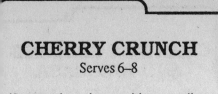

(9-ounce) package white *or* yellow
  single-layer cake mix
/2 cup chopped *or* ground nuts
 tablespoons brown sugar, packed
 teaspoons cinnamon
(21-ounce) can cherry pie filling
/4 cup butter *or* margarine, melted

In a bowl combine cake mix, nuts,
rown sugar and cinnamon. In an 8-
nch glass baking dish, spoon cherry
ie filling into bottom. Sprinkle cake
mix mixture evenly over pie filling.
Drizzle melted butter or margarine over
op. Cook on HIGH for 12–14 minutes,
r until topping is no longer doughy
rotate dish during cooking if cake does
ot appear to be rising evenly). Let
tand 5 minutes. Serve warm with
whipped cream or vanilla ice cream.

Ann Elsie Schmetzer, Madisonville, Ky.

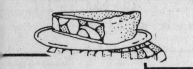

CARAMEL NUT
CRUNCH
Makes 8 cups

/2 cup packed brown sugar
/2 cup dark corn syrup
/4 cup butter *or* margarine
/2 teaspoon salt
 cups toasted oat cereal
/2 cup pecan halves
/2 cup dry roasted peanuts
/2 cup slivered almonds

Combine sugar, syrup, butter and
salt in 2-quart mix-and-pour bowl.
Microwave on HIGH, uncovered, 3–4
minutes, or until mixture boils, stirring
once. Stir well, then microwave on
HIGH for 1-1/2 minutes longer. Combine cereal and nuts in large buttered
microwave-safe bowl; pour hot mixture over all and mix until evenly coated.
Microwave on HIGH for 6–8 minutes,
r until cereal is toasted, stirring *thoroughly* every 2 minutes. Spoon onto

buttered foil. Cool 5–7 minutes, or until
it starts to set. Break into pieces; cool
completely. Store in covered container.
Mrs. A.S. Warren, Charlotte, N.C.

HOT BANANA SPLIT
Serves 1–2

1 firmly ripe medium banana, peeled
2 tablespoons creamy peanut butter
2 tablespoons milk-chocolate pieces
2 tablespoons miniature marshmallows

Using a table knife, cut banana down
the center lengthwise into 2 halves.
Place cut side up in shallow, microwave-safe serving dish. Spread cut sides
with peanut butter. Gently press chocolate pieces and marshmallows into
peanut butter. Microwave on HIGH for
20–30 seconds, or until chocolate and
marshmallows begin to melt. Serve with
a scoop of ice cream for an extra-spe-
cial treat.
*Note: Recipe may be doubled or tripled,
if desired.*

Mrs. A.S. Warren, Charlotte, N.C.

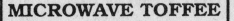

MICROWAVE TOFFEE

1/2 cup chopped pecans
1 cup sugar
1/4 cup water
1/2 cup butter
1 teaspoon salt
4 ounces milk-chocolate chips

Sprinkle pecans in a 9-inch circle on
a greased cookie sheet and set aside.
Rub the inside top 2 inches of a glass
mixing bowl with butter and place
remaining butter in bowl. Pour sugar
directly onto butter (avoid getting on
the sides of bowl). Add salt and water,
but do not stir. Microwave on HIGH for
about 8–10 minutes. Candy is done
when it is the color of brown sugar.
Pour hot candy over nuts. Top with
chocolate, spreading to frost when
chocolate melts. Break into pieces when
cooled.

Jan Ramsey, Quitaque, Texas

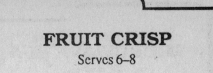

FRUIT CRISP
Serves 6–8

4 cups sliced fruit—apples, peaches,
  pears, *or* a combination, *or* 2 (16-
  ounce) cans fruit cocktail, drained
1/2 cup granulated sugar, sprinkled
  over if fruit is unsweetened
1 (7–8-ounce) package dry blueberry
  muffin mix *or* other muffin mix
1/4 cup diet margarine
1/4–1/2 cup sliced nuts—almonds,
  pecans, black walnuts

Place fruit in greased or Pam-sprayed
8-1/2 x 11-inch dish. Sprinkle sugar, if
needed. Sprinkle dry muffin mix over
fruit. Cut up margarine and dot dry
mixture. Sprinkle nuts over top.

Microwave on HIGH for 12–14
minutes. Turn 1/4 turn after 6–8 minutes. Serve warm or cold with ice cream,
whipped cream or whipped topping.
May also drizzle with chocolate *or*
butterscotch sauce.

This is so easy for unexpected guests.
The pears with ice cream and chocolate
topping are especially good. I've also
used raspberries, blueberries and other
muffin mix, gooseberries, cherries—
really whatever is on hand.

Mrs. J.C. Mantel, Orange City, Iowa

MEXICAN CHEESE PIE
Serves 2

1/2 cup jalapeño peppers, seeded
  and sliced
1 (10-ounce) package longhorn
  cheese, grated
4 eggs, slightly beaten
1/8 teaspoon paprika

Line bottom of greased 1/2-quart
glass ring mold with peppers. Sprinkle
with cheese; mix eggs and paprika;
pour over cheese; cover completely.
Microwave on HIGH for 6 minutes;
turn every 2 minutes; let stand 5 minutes.

Gwen Campbell, Sterling, Va.

SLOPPY JOES
Serves 6–8

1-1/2 pound ground beef
2/3 cup finely chopped onion
1/2 cup diced celery
1/4 cup diced green pepper
1/2 cup ketchup
1 tablespoon Worcestershire sauce
1/2 teaspoon salt
1/8 teaspoon pepper

In 1-1/2-quart casserole crumble beef. Add onion, celery and green pepper. Cover. Microwave on HIGH for 6 minutes, stirring after 3 minutes. Drain meat well.

To cooked meat mixture, add ketchup, Worcestershire sauce, salt and pepper. Cover. Microwave on HIGH for 5–6 minutes, stirring after 3 minutes, until hot. To serve, spoon onto buns.

Karen Waido, Mendota, Ill.

HOT AND HEARTY CASSEROLE
Serves 6

1 (15-ounce) can corned beef hash
1 (16-ounce) can pork and beans
1/4 cup fresh spinach, chopped
1 (16-ounce) can tiny green peas, drained
1 (6-ounce) can tomato-vegetable juice
1 tablespoon ground nutmeg
2 tablespoons butter *or* margarine, melted
1 cup rye bread crumbs
1/3 cup Parmesan cheese, grated
1/4 cup fresh parsley, chopped

In the bottom of a 2-1/2-quart, microwave-safe casserole spread half the hash. Combine next 5 ingredients; spoon half over hash. Layer remaining hash and vegetables; cover with plastic wrap; vent 1 corner. Microwave on HIGH for 12 minutes; rotate dish twice during cooking. Combine butter, rye bread crumbs, cheese and parsley in a glass pie plate. Microwave on HIGH for 2 minutes; sprinkle on top of cooked casserole.

Gwen Campbell, Sterling, Va.

CHILI BURGERS
Serves 4

1 pound ground beef
1 cup chopped celery
1 cup chopped onion
1/2 cup chopped green pepper
1 (10-3/4-ounce) can tomato soup
1/4 cup ketchup
1 tablespoon brown sugar
1-1/8 teaspoon chili powder
1/2 teaspoon dry mustard
1/2 teaspoon salt
1/8 teaspoon cayenne pepper
1/8 teaspoon pepper
1/8 teaspoon garlic powder
1 tablespoon cornstarch
1 (15-ounce) can kidney beans, drained

In 2-quart casserole combine ground beef and vegetables. Cover and microwave on HIGH for 5–6 minutes, stirring once to break up meat. Drain. Stir in rest of ingredients. Cover and microwave on HIGH for 5 minutes. Reduce power to MEDIUM and cook 7–10 minutes until blended. Serve on steak buns.

Patricia Anderson, Fremont, Neb.

HOT FUDGE PUDDING
Serves 8

1 cup flour
1 teaspoon baking powder
1/4 teaspoon salt
3/4 cup sugar
2 tablespoons cocoa
1/2 cup milk
2 tablespoons oil
1 teaspoon vanilla
1 cup brown sugar
1/4 cup cocoa
1-3/4 cups hot water

In a 3-quart casserole combine flour, baking powder, salt, sugar and cocoa. Stir in milk, oil and vanilla. Sprinkle top with brown sugar and 1/4 cup cocoa, mixed together. Heat water in a 2-cup glass measure in microwave until boiling. Pour over batter. Microwave on HIGH for 9–10 minutes, turning 3 times. Spoon into dishes and top with ice cream.

Ruth Meinert, Davis, Ill.

VANILLA PUDDING
Serves 4–6

1/2 cup sugar
2 tablespoons cornstarch
2 tablespoons flour
1/4 teaspoon salt
2 cups milk
2 eggs, beaten
2 tablespoons butter
1 teaspoon vanilla
1 can drained fruit (fruit of your choice)

In 2-quart microwave-safe bowl combine sugar, cornstarch, flour and salt. Stir in milk. Microwave on HIGH for 8 minutes or until thickened; st every 3 minutes. Stir about 1/2 cup mi mixture into eggs and then add eggs mixture; stir well. Microwave on HIGH for 2 minutes. Stir in butter and vanill. Divide drained fruit in serving bowl pour pudding over top.

Another way, instead of the fru fold in 1–2 sliced bananas in puddin

Elaine Belisle, Red Rock, Ontario, Cana

STUFFED BEEF ROLLS
Serves 1

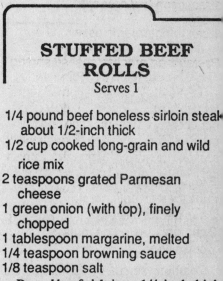

1/4 pound beef boneless sirloin steak about 1/2-inch thick
1/2 cup cooked long-grain and wild rice mix
2 teaspoons grated Parmesan cheese
1 green onion (with top), finely chopped
1 tablespoon margarine, melted
1/4 teaspoon browning sauce
1/8 teaspoon salt

Pound beef sirloin to 1/4-inch thick ness. Mix rice, cheese and onion; spread over beef. Roll up; secure with string Mix remaining ingredients; brush ove beef roll. Place on rack in rectangula dish, 11 x 7 x 1-1/2 inches.

Cover with waxed paper and micro wave on MEDIUM (50 percent) fo 4–6 minutes, turning beef roll over afte 3 minutes, until beef is done. Remov string.

Barbara Nowakowski, North Tonawanda N.Y

Party
FARE

PARTY WEDGE-A-PIZZA
Makes 24

1 1/2 cups corned beef, broken up, or 2 packages corned beef, chopped
5-ounce can tomato paste
1/2 cup shredded cheddar cheese
2 tablespoons minced dehydrated onion or 1/2 cup chopped fresh onion
1 teaspoon leaf oregano
2 eggs
1 can refrigerated crescent dinner rolls
Pasteurized process cheese spread or shredded cheddar cheese

In bowl, combine corned beef, tomato paste, 1/2 cup shredded cheddar cheese, onion, oregano and eggs; mix well. On ungreased baking sheets, separate dough into 8 triangles. Spread each with about 1/3 cup beef mixture. Bake in a preheated 400-degree oven for 20-25 minutes, until edges are golden brown. Cool slightly. Cut each triangle into 3 pieces and garnish with additional cheese. Serve warm or cold.

Mrs. Agnes Ward, Erie, Penn.

YOGURT DIP
Makes 2 cups

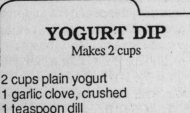

2 cups plain yogurt
1 garlic clove, crushed
1 teaspoon dill
1 teaspoon mint
1 teaspoon minced parsley

Combine all ingredients and chill. Serve with chips, etc.

Mrs. Agnes Ward, Erie, Penn.

WHEAT THINS

1 3/4 cups whole-wheat flour
1 1/2 cups white flour
1/3 cup salad oil
3/4 teaspoon salt
1 cup water

Mix flours; add liquids. Knead as little as possible. Make a smooth dough and roll as thin as possible onto ungreased cookie sheet (not more than 1/8 inch thick). Score with a knife to size desired, but do not cut through. Sprinkle lightly with salt or onion salt as desired.

Bake at 350 degrees until crisp and light brown (about 30-35 minutes). Remove from baking sheet and break into crackers.

Mrs. S.R. Burt, Imlay, Nev.

DEVILED CHEESE DELIGHT

5-ounce jar pimiento cheese spread
2 1/2-ounce can deviled ham
2 tablespoons finely snipped parsley
2 tablespoons mayonnaise
1 teaspoon grated onion
3-4 drops hot pepper sauce

In small bowl combine cheese spread, deviled ham, parsley, mayonnaise, onion and hot pepper sauce. Beat with electric mixer until creamy; chill well. Turn into serving dish, garnish with fresh parsley. Serve with crackers, etc.

Mrs. Agnes Ward, Erie, Penn.

CHEESE DIP DELUXE

1 teaspoon granulated beef bouillon
1 tablespoon hot water
1 large package (8 ounces) cream cheese, softened
1/4 cup milk
1 tablespoon instant minced onion
1/4 teaspoon basil leaves

Combine beef bouillon and hot water, stirring to dissolve. Mix with remaining ingredients. Leave for 20 minutes to allow flavors to mingle. Serve with chips, etc.
Variation:

Add an 8-ounce can of minced clams, or 1/2 cup finely chopped shrimp or crabmeat.

Mrs. Agnes Ward, Erie, Penn.

SPINACH-EGG SPREAD

2 packages frozen chopped spinach, thawed and drained well
1/2 cup chopped onion
1/2 cup diced celery
1/2 cup shredded cheddar cheese
1 1/2 cups mayonnaise
2 tablespoons lemon juice
1 1/2 teaspoons horseradish
4 hard-cooked eggs, chopped
1/8 teaspoon salt

Mix drained, thawed spinach with remaining ingredients. Refrigerate until serving time.

Beatrice Mickelson, Cadott, Wis.

BACON-CHILI DIP

4 strips bacon, fried crisp, drained
  and crumbled
1 large package (8 ounces) cream
  cheese, softened
1 cup sour cream
4-ounce can diced green chilies
1/4 teaspoon garlic salt

Beat cheese and sour cream together
until smooth and fluffy. Fold in chilies
and garlic salt, then bacon. Chill. Serve
with crackers, vegetable sticks, or chips.

Jean Baker, Chula Vista, Calif.

SPICY PUMPKIN SEEDS

Makes 2 cups

1/4 cup oil
1 teaspoon Worcestershire sauce
1/2 teaspoon paprika
1/4 teaspoon each cumin and
  cayenne
2 dashes hot pepper sauce
2 cups hulled pumpkin seeds

Combine all ingredients except
seeds in large skillet. Heat well, stirring to mix. Add seeds and stir to coat
well. Spread in shallow pan. Bake in
preheated 300-degree oven. Stir occasionally. Bake 10 minutes, or until
crisp; cool.

SHRIMP DIP

large package (8 ounces) cream
  cheese, softened
2 tins baby shrimp, drained
3 tablespoons mayonnaise
Salt and pepper
1/4 pound (1 stick) butter, softened
1/8 teaspoon garlic powder
1 tablespoon lemon juice

Beat together lemon juice, cream
cheese, mayonnaise, butter and seasonings until smooth. Fold in drained
shrimp. Serve with raw vegetables,
chips or melba toast.

Mrs. Nan Bomak, Edmonton, Alberta

GRANOLA SNACK

1/2 cup peanut butter (smooth or
  crunchy)
1/4 cup honey
1/4 cup vegetable oil
2 tablespoons firmly packed brown
  sugar
1 package (9 ounces) None-Such
  Condensed Mincemeat®
2 cups quick-cooking oats
1 cup dry-roasted peanuts

Preheat oven to 250 degrees. In a
large saucepan, combine peanut
butter, honey, oil and sugar; blend
well. Break mincemeat into small
pieces and add to peanut butter mixture. Boil briskly, stirring constantly,
for 1 minute. Remove from heat. Add
oats and peanuts and stir well.

Spoon into a 13x9-inch pan. Bake
at 250 degrees for 45 minutes, stirring
every 15 minutes. Cool; break into
chunks. Store in a tightly covered
container.

To re-crisp the snack, place desired amount on a cookie sheet and
heat at 250 degrees for 10 minutes.
Cool.

Agnes Ward, Erie, Penn.

TOASTED SAVORIES

2 egg whites
2 cups unsalted pecans
1 teaspoon salt
1 teaspoon dry mustard
1 teaspoon garlic powder

Cover cookie sheet with foil; grease
and set aside.

Beat egg whites until foamy. Drop
pecans into egg whites and stir to coat
well. Lift with fork or slotted spoon to
drain; place on greased foil.

Mix salt, dry mustard and garlic
powder. Pour into empty salt shaker.
Sprinkle over nuts.

Bake in a 250-degree oven for 25
minutes, or until coating is set. Lift
foil to loosen nuts and break them
apart. Cool. Store in airtight container
or freeze. Keep for 1 week or freeze
for no more than 2 weeks.

MICROWAVE CARAMEL CORN

Makes about 4 quarts

1 cup brown sugar
1/4 pound soft margarine
1/4 cup light corn syrup
1/2 teaspoon salt
4 quarts plain popped popcorn (no
  salt, or butter added)
1/2 teaspoon baking soda

Combine sugar, margarine, corn
syrup and salt in a microwave pan and
bring mixture to boil in a microwave
oven set on "High." Boil for 3 minutes. Remove from oven and stir in
baking soda, mixing well. Pour over
popcorn. Mix to coat well.

Pour caramel corn into a large
brown grocery bag. Fold the top of the
bag down loosely until it will fit in the
microwave oven. Cook on the highest
setting for 3 minutes; shake sack well
every minute during cooking.

Cool the caramel corn on waxed
paper. Store in a 5-quart plastic ice-
cream pail or in other suitable containers.

J. Kopperud, Forest City, Iowa

PARTY POTATO SALAD

Serves 12-14

1 (2-pound) bag frozen hash-brown
  potatoes
1 can cream of potato soup
1 can cream of celery soup
1/2 cup sour cream
1 cup shredded cheddar cheese
1 (8-ounce) package cream cheese
1/2 green pepper, finely chopped
1/2 cup chopped onion
2 teaspoons salt
1/4 teaspoon pepper
1 teaspoon paprika

Combine soups with softened
cream cheese. Add sour cream, green
pepper, onion, and seasonings. Put
potatoes in a 3-quart shallow baking
dish. Pour soup mixture over potatoes
and stir. Spread out evenly; sprinkle
with cheddar cheese. Bake at 325
degrees for 1-1/2 hours.

Laura Braun, Fond du Lac, Wis.

Pies
FESTIVE

SOUR CREAM APPLE PIE

1 cup sour cream
1 cup sugar
1/2 cup flour
1 egg
2 teaspoons vanilla
8 Granny Smith apples, peeled, cored, and sliced
1 deep-dish pie shell

Topping:

1-1/2 cups walnut pieces
1/2 cup granulated sugar
3/4 cup flour
1 tablespoon cinnamon
1/2 cup brown sugar
1/2 cup butter pieces, chopped

Blend all ingredients, except apples, until smooth. Add apples and pour into pie shell. Bake for 45 minutes at 400 degrees or until apples are tender. Mix together all the topping ingredients. Evenly sprinkle the pie with topping and bake pie 15 minutes longer.

This is a very delicious version of apple pie.

June Harding, Ferndale, Mich.

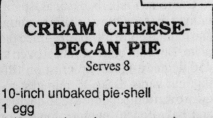

CREAM CHEESE-PECAN PIE
Serves 8

10-inch unbaked pie·shell
1 egg
1 (8-ounce) package cream cheese, softened
1/3 cup sugar

1 teaspoon vanilla
1-1/4 cups coarsely chopped pecans
3 eggs
1 cup light corn syrup
1/4 teaspoon salt
1 teaspoon vanilla

Beat together cream cheese, sugar, 1 egg, and 1 teaspoon vanilla until smooth; spread over bottom of pie shell. Sprinkle pecans over cheese mixture. Combine 3 eggs, corn syrup, salt, and 1 teaspoon vanilla; pour over pecans. Bake at 375 degrees for 40 minutes. Cool.

Lisa Varner, Baton Rouge, La.

GRAPE JUICE PIE

1 (9-inch) pie shell, baked
3/4 cup sugar
1/2 cup cornstarch
1 1/3 cups grape juice
1 egg, beaten
2 tablespoons butter *or* margarine
2 tablespoons lemon juice

Combine sugar and cornstarch; stir in grape juice. Cook over medium heat, stirring until bubbly and thickened; cool 1 minute. Pour small amount of hot mixture into beaten egg, mixing well. Add rest of mixture, stirring constantly. Add butter and lemon juice; return to heat and boil 1 minute, stirring all the time. Pour into the baked shell. Cool. Serve with whipped cream or Cool Whip.

Marjorie W. Baxla, Greenfield, Ohio

FRESH PEACH PIE

5 cups fresh peaches, sliced
1 unbaked 9-inch pastry shell
1/3 cup butter or margarine, melted
1 cup sugar
1/3 cup all-purpose flour
1 egg
1/2 teaspoon cinnamon

Place peaches in pastry shell. Combine remaining ingredients; pour over peaches. Bake at 350 degrees for 1 hour and 10 minutes.

Sarah M. Burkett, Centralia, Ill.

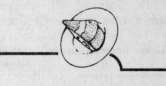

COMPANY PIE

1 (9-inch) pie shell
1/2 cup seedless raisins
1/2 cup chopped walnuts or pecans
1 teaspoon vinegar
1/2 cup butter or margarine
1/4 cup sugar
2 eggs
1/2 teaspoon cinnamon
1/2 teaspoon nutmeg
1/4 teaspoon salt

Bake in a 9-inch pastry shell. Mix raisins, nuts, and vinegar; let stand. Combine butter, sugar, and eggs; beat until thick. Beat in spices and salt. Stir in raisin mixture. Bake at 400 degrees for 30-35 minutes.
Note: Butter bubbles up through the crust, making it flaky and light.

Karin Shea Fedders, Dameron, Md.

PINEAPPLE PINK CHIFFON PIE

Serves 6-8

Crust:
1 inner seal packet graham crackers (finely crushed, 1-2/3 cups)
1/4 cup sugar
1/2 cup flaked coconut
1/4 cup softened butter

Thoroughly blend crumbs, sugar, coconut, and softened butter. Press firmly against bottom and sides of 9-inch pie plate. Bake in 350-degree oven for 8 minutes; cool.

Filling:
1 (3-ounce) package strawberry-flavored gelatin
1 envelope unflavored gelatin
1-1/2 cups boiling water
1 pint heavy cream
1 (1-pound, 4-1/2-ounce) can crushed pineapple, well-drained

Dissolve both gelatins in boiling water. Chill until syrupy. Whip cream; continue beating, adding gelatin gradually. Fold in pineapple. Pile into crust; chill. Garnish with whipped cream and toasted coconut. Chill until firm.

Theresa Rouleau, Cornwall, Ontario, Canada

CRANBERRY PIE

2 cups whole raw cranberries
1½ cups sugar
½ cup chopped nuts
2 eggs
1 cup flour
½ cup margarine, melted
¼ cup shortening, melted
1 (10-inch) unbaked pie shell

Combine cranberries, ½ cup sugar and nuts; place in pastry-lined pie pan. Beat eggs; add remaining 1 cup sugar, flour, melted margarine and shortening. Pour over cranberry mixture and bake 1 hour at 325 degrees.

Sharon McClatchey, Muskogee, Okla.

BANANA MALLOW PIE

Crust:
2 cups shredded coconut
1/3 cup margarine

Combine coconut and margarine in skillet; cook over low heat, stirring constantly until toasted and golden. Press into 9-inch pie pan to form crust. Chill.

Filling:
1 (3 1/4-ounce) package vanilla pudding and pie filling (*not* instant)
1 3/4 cups cold milk
2 cups miniature marshmallows
3/4 cup whipping cream
2 bananas

Follow directions on pudding package. Cook, then refrigerate until cool. Whip cream. Fold into whipping cream the cooled pudding and miniature marshmallows.

Take crust from refrigerator; slice bananas onto bottom of crust. Pour filling over bananas. Chill 3 hours before serving.

Dixie Goodman, Brooklyn, Mich.

SWEET POTATO PIE

1 (9-inch) unbaked pie shell
3 eggs
2 cups sugar
½ stick margarine
1 small can evaporated milk
1 teaspoon vanilla
1 cup mashed sweet potatoes
½ to 1 cup coconut (optional)

Combine all filling ingredients together; pour into unbaked pie shell. Bake at 350 degrees for approximately 1 hour, or until inserted toothpick comes out clean.

Helen Harlos, Ethel, Miss.

MINCEMEAT PECAN PIE

1 (9-ounce) package condensed mincemeat, broken up
½ cup Karo light *or* dark corn syrup
¼ cup margarine
3 eggs, slightly beaten
½ cup coarsely chopped pecans
1 tablespoon grated orange rind
1 unbaked (9-inch) pastry shell
¼ cup sherry

In medium saucepan stir together first 3 ingredients. Stirring constantly, bring to boil over medium heat. Remove from heat. Gradually stir into eggs. Add pecans and rind. Pour into pastry shell. Bake in 350-degree oven for 40–50 minutes, or until knife inserted near center comes out clean. Pour sherry over filling. Cool.

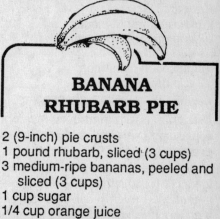

BANANA RHUBARB PIE

2 (9-inch) pie crusts
1 pound rhubarb, sliced (3 cups)
3 medium-ripe bananas, peeled and sliced (3 cups)
1 cup sugar
1/4 cup orange juice
3 tablespoons flour
1/4 teaspoon salt
1/4 teaspoon cinnamon
1/4 teaspoon nutmeg
1 tablespoon butter or margarine

Combine rhubarb, bananas, sugar, orange juice, flour, salt, cinnamon, and nutmeg; turn into pastry-lined pie plate. Dot with butter. Preheat oven to 450 degrees. Place top crust on filling; cut vents. Bake 15 minutes; reduce oven temperature to 350 degrees and bake for 30 minutes longer, or until pie is brown. Cool completely.

Kit Rollins, Cedarburg, Wis.

IMPOSSIBLE CHERRY PIE

This is the pie that's impossibly easy because it makes its own crust, and it's filled with the harvest-fresh goodness of Thank You brand pie filling.

1 cup milk
2 tablespoons margarine or butter, softened
1/4 teaspoon almond extract
2 eggs
1/2 cup Bisquick baking mix
1/4 cup sugar
1 (21-ounce) can Thank You cherry pie filling
Streusel (recipe follows)

Heat oven to 400 degrees. Grease pie plate, 10x1-1/2-inches. Beat together all ingredients, except pie filling and Streusel, until smooth, 15 seconds in blender on high or 1 minute with hand beater. Pour into plate. Spoon pie filling evenly over top. Bake 25 minutes. Top with Streusel. Bake until Streusel is brown, about 10 minutes longer. Cool; refrigerate any remaining pie.

Streusel:

Cut 2 tablespoons firm margarine or butter into 1/2 cup Bisquick baking mix, 1/2 cup packed brown sugar, and 1/2 teaspoon ground cinnamon until crumbly.

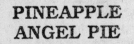

PINEAPPLE ANGEL PIE

1 cup crushed pineapple
1 cup water
1 cup granulated sugar
Pinch salt
2-1/2 tablespoons cornstarch
3 egg whites, stiffly beaten
1 (9-inch) baked pie shell
1 cup cream, whipped
1/2 cup chopped walnuts

1/2 cup coconut
6 maraschino cherries, quartered

Mix together pineapple, water, sugar, salt, and cornstarch. Cook over boiling water in top of double boiler, stirring; cook until thick. Set aside to cool. When cold, fold in stiffly beaten egg whites. Pour into baked pie shell. Cover with whipped cream and sprinkle with nuts, coconut, and maraschino cherries. Chill in refrigerator.

Donna K. Gore, Aztec, N.M.

MISSISSIPPI MUD PIE

3 (1-ounce) squares unsweetened chocolate
1-1/2 cups sifted confectioners' sugar
1/2 cup whipping cream
1/3 cup butter or margarine
3 tablespoons light corn syrup
Dash salt
1 tablespoon vanilla extract
1 (9-inch) graham cracker crust
1 cup chopped pecans, divided
3 cups coffee-flavored ice cream, softened and divided
Sweetened whipped cream

Melt chocolate in a heavy saucepan over low heat; add confectioners' sugar and next 4 ingredients. Cook, stirring constantly, until mixture is smooth. Remove from heat; stir in vanilla and let mixture cool. Spread 1/2 cup chocolate sauce in graham cracker crust; sprinkle with 1/4 cup pecans. Freeze 10 minutes. Remove from freezer and spread 1 cup ice cream over pecans; freeze 20 minutes. Repeat layers twice. Cover pie and freeze at least 8 hours. Drizzle remaining chocolate sauce over pie. Top with whipped cream and sprinkle with remaining pecans.

Edna Askins, Greenville, Texas

HONEY RICE PIE

2-1/2 tablespoons cornstarch
1/2 teaspoon salt
1 cup milk
1/2 cup honey
1 egg, beaten
1 tablespoon butter or margarine
2 teaspoons grated lemon peel
1/4 cup lemon juice
1/2 teaspoon vanilla
2 cups cooked rice

Crust:
3/4 cup saltine crackers
1/2 cup flour
1/4 cup soft butter or margarine
1/3 cup honey
1 teaspoon grated lemon peel
1 (7-ounce) can shredded coconut

Blend cornstarch with salt, milk, and honey. Cook over low heat, stirring constantly until thick. Stir some of the mixture into egg. Blend both mixtures. Add butter and peel. Remove from heat and stir in lemon juice, vanilla, and rice. Cool.

To prepare crust, blend crumbs, flour, and butter. Add honey, lemon peel, and coconut. Press about 3/4 mixture into bottom and sides of 10-inch pie pan. Pour filling into crust. Top with remaining crumb mixture. Bake at 375 degrees for 25 minutes.

Kit Rollins, Cedarburg, Wis.

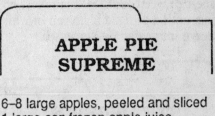

APPLE PIE SUPREME

6–8 large apples, peeled and sliced
1 large can frozen apple juice concentrate
2 tablespoons cornstarch
1 teaspoon cinnamon
1 (9-inch) unbaked pie shell
1 egg white, beaten

Heat juice; add cornstarch. Cook until thick. Add cinnamon and apples. Place in pie shell. Brush top crust with beaten egg white. Bake at 350 degrees for 60 minutes.

Sharon McClatchey, Muskogee, Okla.

MILE-HIGH MINCEMEAT PIE

2 quarts vanilla ice cream
2 cups prepared mincemeat
1/2 cup slivered, toasted almonds
5 egg whites
1/2 teaspoon vanilla
1/2 teaspoon cream of tartar
1/2 cup sugar
10-inch baked pie shell

Let ice cream stand at room temperature to soften slightly. Meanwhile, line a 10-inch pie plate with foil. Combine mincemeat and almonds, mixing well. Into foil-lined plated, spoon ice cream in alternate layers with mincemeat mixture, ending with ice cream. Freeze until ready to use (several hours).

To serve: In large bowl of electric mixer, let egg whites warm to room temperature (for about 1 hour). Mix in vanilla and cream of tartar, and beat mixture at high speed just until frothy. Add sugar, 2 tablespoons at time, beating well after each addition. Continue beating until meringue is shiny and stiff peaks form. Preheat oven to 425 degrees.

Remove foil from bottom of frozen ice cream-mincemeat layer, and place ice cream-mincemeat in baked pie shell. Use metal spatula to spread meringue over the pie, covering the ice cream and edge of crust completely. Make decorative swirls on top of meringue, and place on lowest shelf of oven. Bake 7-8 minutes, or just until meringue is golden brown. Serve immediately. Serves 10.

STRAWBERRY NUT PIE

Serves 6

1   (9-inch) pie shell, baked
1   quart butter pecan *or* vanilla ice cream, slightly softened
2   pints chilled strawberries, sliced
¼   cup light brown sugar
⅔   cup finely chopped toasted nuts

Spoon ice cream into baked crust. Mix together strawberries, sugar and toasted nuts; layer over ice cream. Freeze immediately. Remove from freezer to refrigerator 10 minutes before serving time for easier slicing.
Peggy Fowler Revels, Woodruff, S.C.

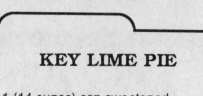

KEY LIME PIE

1 (14-ounce) can sweetened condensed milk
1/2 cup fresh lime juice
3 large egg yolks
1 9-inch baked pastry crust
3 large egg whites
1/4 teaspoon cream of tartar
6 tablespoons sugar

Combine condensed milk and lime juice in medium-size bowl. Blend in egg yolks; turn into cooled crust. Heat oven to 325 degrees. Beat egg whites with cream of tartar in small bowl until soft peaks form. Beat in sugar, 1 tablespoon at a time, until egg whites form stiff, glossy peaks. Spoon over filling; spread to edge of crust to seal. Bake 15 minutes or until golden. Cool on wire rack to room temperature.
Edith Holmes, Brookfield, Mass.

DATE MACAROON PIE

3 egg whites
1/2 cup finely-chopped dates
12 saltines
1 cup white sugar
1/2 teaspoon baking powder
1 teaspoon vanilla
1 teaspoon water

Beat egg whites, water and vanilla together until they form stiff peaks. Crush saltines fine and add remaining ingredients to whites, fold in. Butter 9-inch pie plate and pour mixture into it. Bake in preheated 325 degree oven for 30 minutes. Cut into wedges and serve with whipped cream, garnished with maraschino cherry.
Pearle Goodwin, South Reygate, Vt.

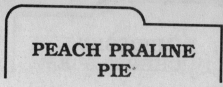

PEACH PRALINE PIE

4 cups fresh peaches, peeled and sliced
1 teaspoon lemon juice
2 tablespoons tapioca
1/4 cup sugar
3/4 cup sugar
1/2 cup flour
4 tablespoons flour
1/2 cup nuts, chopped
1 unbaked pie shell

Mix first 4 ingredients for 10 minutes. Combine next 4 ingredients and sprinkle 1/3 of mixture over bottom of unbaked pie shell. Top with peach mixture, then rest of topping. Bake at 450 degrees for 10 minutes. Reduce heat to 350 degrees and bake 20 minutes more. Serve with ice cream or whipped topping.
Sue Thomas, Casa Grande, Ariz.

LEMON CHIFFON PIE

Makes 1 8- or 9-inch pie

1 (8- or 9-inch) graham cracker crumb crust (reserve 1 tablespoon crumbs for garnish, if desired)
1 (14-ounce) can Eagle Brand sweetened condensed milk (not evaporated milk)
1/3 cup ReaLemon juice concentrate
Few drops yellow food coloring
3 egg whites
1/4 teaspoon cream of tartar
2 cups whipped topping

In medium bowl, combine sweetened condensed milk, ReaLemon and food coloring; mix well. In small bowl, beat egg whites with cream of tartar until stiff but not dry; gently fold into sweetened condensed milk mixture. Pour into prepared crust. Chill 3 hours, or until set. Top with whipped topping and reserved crumbs before serving. Refrigerate leftovers. A dramatic finish to a company dinner!
Theresa McClarrin, Waynesville, N.C.

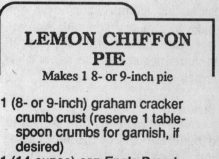

LEMON BUTTERMILK PIE

eggs
/4 cup sugar
tablespoons flour
-1/2 cups buttermilk
/4 cup melted butter or margarine
Grated peel of 1 lemon
tablespoons lemon juice
teaspoon vanilla
(9-inch) pie shell, baked
Cinnamon

Beat eggs and sugar together in large mixer bowl until light and lemon-colored. Beat in flour, buttermilk, butter, lemon peel, juice, and vanilla. Pour into pie shell. Sprinkle lightly with cinnamon.

Bake in preheated oven of 375-degrees for 20-30 minutes, or until knife blade inserted near center comes out clean. Cool on rack, then serve.

Mrs. L. Mayer, Richmond, Va.

STRAWBERRY-SOUR CREAM PIE

2 cups strawberries, crushed
3 tablespoons sugar
1/2 cup sour cream
1 (8-ounce) container Cool Whip, thawed
1 Easy Crumb Crust (recipe follows)

Mix ingredients in order given. Place in crust and chill 4 hours, or freeze until firm. Garnish with more strawberries.

Easy Crumb Crust:
Use either fine graham cracker, chocolate or vanilla wafer, shortbread or gingersnap crumbs.

1 1/4 cups crumbs
1/4 cup melted margarine

Press on bottom of a 9-inch pie pan; chill 1 hour.
A must when strawberries are in season!

Betty Brennan, Faribault, Minn.

JAMAICAN COCONUT PIE

1-1/3 cups Baker's Angel Flake Coconut
1 unbaked (9-inch) pie shell
3 tablespoons butter or margarine
1/2 cup sugar

3 eggs
1 cup dark corn syrup
1/8 teaspoon salt
1 teaspoon cinnamon
1 teaspoon nutmeg
1 teaspoon vanilla
2 tablespoons dark rum

Sprinkle coconut in pie shell. Cream butter; gradually beat in sugar. Add eggs and beat well. Blend in remaining ingredients. Pour over coconut in pie shell. Bake at 350 degrees for 50 minutes, or until slightly puffed on top. Cool to room temperature.

Diantha Susan Hibbard, Rochester, N.Y.

MINCEMEAT APPLE PIE
Makes 9-inch pie

9-inch unbaked pastry shell
2 cooking apples, pared and sliced
6 tablespoons flour
1 (28 ounce) jar ready-to-use mincemeat
1/4 cup firmly-packed light brown sugar
2 teaspoons ground cinnamon
2 tablespoons margarine or butter
1/4 cup chopped nuts

Preheat oven to 425 degrees. Toss apples with 2 tablespoons flour. Arrange in pastry shell. Top with mincemeat. In small bowl, combine remaining flour, sugar and cinnamon. Cut in margarine until crumbly. Mix in nuts. Sprinkle over mincemeat. Bake 10 minutes, reduce oven temperature to 350 degrees and continue baking 25-30 minutes or until browned. Serve warm or cold with vanilla ice cream.

Melba Bellefeuille, Libertyville, Ill.

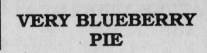

VERY BLUEBERRY PIE

1/4 cup cold water
5 tablespoons flour
Pinch of salt
4 cups fresh *or* dry-pack frozen blueberries, rinsed and drained
1 cup sugar
1/2 cup water
1 (9-inch) baked pie shell

Make a smooth paste of the water, flour and salt. Boil 1 cup of the blueberries with sugar and water. Add the flour paste and stir until it thickens. Remove from stove and cool. When cool, add the remaining blueberries and put into baked pie shell. Refrigerate. When cold, garnish with sweetened whipped cream or whipped topping.

North American Blueberry Council, Marmora, N.J.

DISTINCTIVE RHUBARB PIE

3 eggs, separated
1-1/4 cups sugar
1/4 cup soft butter *or* margarine
3 tablespoons frozen orange juice concentrate
1/4 teaspoon salt
1/4 cup all-purpose flour
2-1/2 cups rhubarb, cut in-2 inch pieces
1/3 cup chopped pecans
1 unbaked 9-inch pie shell

Beat egg whites in a bowl until stiff. Gradually add 1/4 cup sugar, beating well after each addition. Add butter *or* margarine and orange juice concentrate to egg yolks; beat thoroughly. Add 1 cup sugar, flour, and salt; beat well. Add rhubarb to the yolk mixture; stir well. Gently fold in the beaten egg whites (meringue). Pour into unlined pie shell; sprinkle with pecans.

Bake on bottom rack of oven at 375 degrees for 15 minutes. Reduce heat to 325 degrees; bake 45 to 50 minutes more. Let cool on rack.

Marie Fusaro, Manasquan, N.J.

APPLE-MINCEMEAT PIE

Pastry for 1-crust pie
2 cups prepared mincemeat
2 cups thinly sliced tart apples
1 teaspoon cinnamon or nutmeg
2 tablespoons lemon or lime juice
Grated rind of 1 lemon or lime
1/2 cup flour
1/2 cup brown sugar
1/4 cup butter or margarine, melted

Prepare pie crust. Cover bottom of the crust with mincemeat. Cover the mincemeat with apples. Mix juice, rind and spice and sprinkle mixture over apples. Mix flour, sugar and butter and spread mixture over pie. Bake in a 450-degree oven for 10 minutes; reduce heat to 350 degrees and bake 30-35 minutes more. Serve with cheese wedges, hard sauce, or flavored whipped cream or whipped topping.

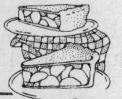

CHOCOLATE CHEESECAKE PIE

1 ready-made chocolate pie crust
12 ounces cream cheese, softened
½ cup sugar
2 eggs
2 teaspoons vanilla
Dash of salt
½ cup semisweet chocolate chips, melted

Preheat oven to 325 degrees. Beat cream cheese and sugar together until smooth. Add eggs, vanilla and salt. Beat until well-blended. Put crust on baking sheet and pour filling into crust. Drop melted chocolate by teaspoonfuls onto filling. Swirl chocolate into filling with tip of knife. Bake on sheet for 25–30 minutes, or until knife inserted in center comes out clean. Cool and chill about 3 hours.

Suzan L. Wiener, Spring Hill, Fla.

CRANBERRY CHIFFON PIE

Makes 9-inch pie

1 cup cooked cranberries
2/3 cup sugar
4 eggs, separated
1 tablespoon unflavored gelatin
1/2 teaspoon salt
1 tablespoon lemon juice
9-inch baked pie shell
1/2 cup whipping cream, whipped

Place cranberries in saucepan. Add half as much water. Cook until skins pop. Strain through a sieve. Measure 1 cup. Place cranberries, 1/3 cup sugar and egg yolks in top of double boiler. Cook over hot water for 8 minutes or until thickened and smooth, stirring constantly. Soften gelatin in 1/4 cup cold water in large bowl. Pour cranberry mixture over gelatin, mix well. Beat in salt and lemon juice. Beat egg whites until soft peaks form. Add 1/3 cup sugar gradually, beating until stiff. Fold into cranberry mixture. Pour into baked pie shell. Chill until firm. Top each serving with whipped cream.

Melba Bellefeuille, Libertyville, Ill.

CRUSTLESS APPLE PIE

6 apples, pared and sliced
1/8 teaspoon nutmeg
1/2 cup sugar
1 tablespoon butter
1 tablespoon water
1 cup brown sugar
2/3 cup flour
1/2 cup shortening
Hard sauce or whipped cream

Mix nutmeg with 1/2 cup sugar. Put apples in baking dish, sprinkle with sugar and nutmeg mix. Dot with butter. Add water. Mix brown sugar with flour and shortening. Blend mixture to crumb texture. Cover apples in baking dish with crumb mixture. Bake at 325 degrees for 30 minutes or until apples are soft. Serve with hard sauce or whipped cream.

Bea Comas, Portland, Maine

PINTO PIE WITH CORNMEAL CRUST

Serves 6–8

2 cups yellow cornmeal
½ teaspoon salt
3 tablespoons vegetable oil
Reserved bean cooking water
2 tablespoons butter
1 onion, chopped
½ cup carrot, chopped
½ cup celery, chopped
1 cup dried pinto beans, cooked and drained (save cooking water)
Dash pepper
1 teaspoon chili powder
Salt to taste
1 cup shredded sharp cheddar cheese

Mix the first 3 ingredients together along with enough of the reserved bean cooking water to make a batter. Press mixture into the bottom and sides of a greased 9-inch pie plate. Set aside.

Melt butter in skillet; add onion, carrot and celery; sauté until tender-crisp. Stir in beans, pepper, chili powder, ¼ cup reserved bean cooking water and salt to taste. Pour mixture into cornmeal crust. Sprinkle top of pie evenly with cheese. Bake at 350 degrees for 30 minutes, or until cheese begins to brown. Cut in wedges to serve.

TAFFY PIE

2 eggs
2 teaspoons water
1 tablespoon melted butter
2 teaspoons vanilla

1 1/2 cups dark brown sugar
8-inch gingersnap or graham cracker crust

Place ingredients in blender and mix well for a few seconds. Add 1 cup pecans and blend until chopped. Pour mixture into an 8-inch gingersnap or graham cracker crust. Bake at 350 degrees for 30 minutes, or until firm.

Agnes Ward, Erie, Pa.

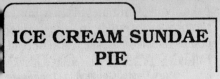

ICE CREAM SUNDAE PIE

1 Ready Crust Chocolate flavored pie crust
1 quart ice cream
1 (12-ounce) jar chocolate fudge topping
Whipped cream
Maraschino cherries
Walnuts

Allow ice cream to soften or stir with spoon until pliable. Spoon into pie crust. Cover and freeze until firm, about 3 hours. Serve pie wedges with fudge topping, whipped cream, and cherries. Add nuts, if desired.

Annie Cmehil, New Castle, IN

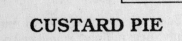

CUSTARD PIE

4 slightly beaten eggs
1/2 cup sugar
1/4 teaspoon salt
1/2 teaspoon vanilla
2-1/2 cups scalded milk
9" unbaked pastry shell
Nutmeg or 1/2 cup flaked coconut

Blend eggs, sugar, salt and vanilla. Gradually stir in milk. Pour into pastry shell. Sprinkle lightly with nutmeg or coconut. Bake in moderate oven at 350 degrees for 35 to 40 minutes, or until knife inserted halfway between center and edge comes out clean. Cool on rack, then chill.

Elsie Abeln, Traverse City, MI

CARROT CUSTARD PIE

1/2 cup sugar
2/3 cup milk
1 teaspoon vanilla
1 tablespoon cornstarch
1-1/2 cups mashed, cooked carrots
1 unbaked 9 inch pie shell
2 eggs, beaten
1 tablespoon lemon juice
1/4 teaspoon cinnamon

Combine sugar and cornstarch. Add eggs, milk, carrots, lemon juice, and vanilla. Mix well; pour into pie shell. Sprinkle with cinnamon. Bake at 375 degrees for 45 minutes or until custard is set. Serve warm or cooled. "Really delicious!"

Agnes Ward, Erie, Pa.

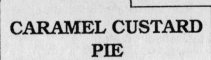

CARAMEL CUSTARD PIE

3 cups milk, scalded
1/3 cup caramelized syrup (below)
4 eggs, well beaten
1/3 cup sugar
1/2 teaspoon salt
1 teaspoon vanilla
Baked 10-inch pie shell

Blend together milk and caramelized syrup. Combine beaten eggs, sugar, salt, and vanilla. Slowly stir egg mixture into milk. Bake in a buttered 10-inch pie plate in a 350 degree oven for 40 minutes, or until a knife inserted in center comes out clean. Cool. Loosen edges of custard carefully with spatula. Shake gently to loosen bottom. Slide custard from pie plate into cooled pie shell.

Caramelized Syrup:

2 cups sugar
1 cup boiling water

Pour sugar into heavy skillet that heats uniformly. Melt over low heat, stirring constantly with wooden spoon to prevent scorching; the lumps will melt away.

When sugar becomes a clear brown syrup, remove from heat. Stir in boiling water slowly so that it does not splatter. Return to low heat, and stir until syrup is smooth again. Cool. (What you don't use can be put into a clean pint jar and stored in refrigerator for several weeks.)

Mrs. S. R. Burt, Imlay, NV

OLD-FASHIONED VANILLA CUSTARD PIE

Serves 6

1 (9 inch) pie shell, unbaked
3 eggs
4 tablespoons granulated sugar

1/8 teaspoon salt
3 cups scalding hot milk
1-1/4 teaspoons vanilla extract
1/4 teaspoon freshly grated nutmeg

Beat eggs until thoroughly mixed and bubbly. Add sugar and salt; mix well. Add 3 tablespoons of the scalding hot milk to egg mixture; mix well. Add egg mixture to the milk; stir in vanilla. Beat gently until all is evenly mixed; pour into unbaked shell. Bake 400 degrees for 12 minutes; reduce heat to 350 degrees and bake 25 minutes or until tested done in middle. Remove from oven; cool; refrigerate at least 2 hours before cutting.

Gwen Campbell, Sterling, Va.

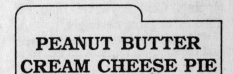

PEANUT BUTTER CREAM CHEESE PIE

Pecan crust:

1-1/2 cups pecans, toasted and finely chopped
1/2 cup sugar
1/4 cup butter
1/4 teaspoon cinnamon

To make crust: Mix together all crust ingredients and press into a 9 inch metal pie pan. Freeze.

Topping:

1/2 cup fudge ice cream topping

Filling:

1 cup whipping cream
1-1/4 cups powdered sugar (divided)
1 tablespoon vanilla
1 (8 ounce) package cream cheese at room temperature
1 cup creamy peanut butter
2 tablespoons butter

To make filling: Beat cream with 1/4 cup powdered sugar and vanilla, until stiff peaks form; set aside. In another bowl, beat remaining 1 cup powdered sugar, cream cheese, peanut butter, and butter until fluffy. Fold in half the whipped cream mixture. Spoon cream cheese mixture into reserved crust. Cover and chill 2 hours. Spread fudge topping on pie, leaving a 1 inch border. Rebeat reserved whipped cream mixture and spoon around border. Chill 1 hour.

Leah Maria Daub, Milwaukee, Wis.

PEANUT BUTTER PIE

1 cup "chunky" peanut butter
1 (8 ounce) package cream cheese at room temperature
3/4 cup sugar
2 tablespoons melted butter
1 cup whipping cream, whipped
1 tablespoon vanilla
1 prepared graham cracker crust
1/3 cup melted hot fudge topping

Cream together peanut butter, cream cheese, and sugar. Add butter and vanilla; blend. Fold in whipped cream until well blended. Pour into a graham cracker crust; chill 4-5 hours or until set. Drizzle top with hot fudge topping. Chill anywhere from 30 minutes longer to overnight.

This is very rich! It will serve several, because you only need a tiny slice.　　　Pam Portillo, Culver City, Calif.

DEER MEAT PIE

1 pound ground venison (2 cups)
1-1/2 teaspoons salt of less
1/2 teaspoon pepper or less
1 cup drained canned tomatos
1/2 cup grated or shredded American cheese
1 tablespoon chopped parsley (optional)
1 tablespoon chopped onion or more
1/2 teaspoon dried basil (optional)

Combine ground venison, salt and pepper; spread in 9-inch pie pan, bringing meat up the sides. Cover with drained tomatos. Sprinkle with cheese, parsley, onion and basil. Bake at 375 degrees for 20 to 25 minutes. Pour off fat; cut in wedges and serve hot. Ground beef can be substituted for the venison.

Mary Ann Altobeli, Virginia, MN

MERRY MINCE PIE

1 cup sugar
1/2 teaspoon salt
1/2 teaspoon cinnamon
1/4 teaspoon cloves
1/4 teaspoon ginger
1-1/2 cups finely chopped pared apples
1 cup raisins
1/2 cup jellied cranberry sauce
1/3 cup chopped walnuts
1 teaspoon grated orange peel
1/2 teaspoon grated lemon peel
1/4 cup lemon juice
4 tablespoons butter
Pastry for 2-crust pie

Combine sugar, salt, and spices. Add next seven ingredients; mix well. Pour into pastry-lined 9 inch pie plate. Dot with butter. Apply top crust; cut slits, and crimp edges. Bake in 400 degree oven for 35 minutes. Serve warm.

June Harding, Ferndale, Mich.

APPLESAUCE PECAN PIE

1 unbaked pie shell
2 tablespoons butter
1 cup light brown sugar
1/4 teaspoon cinnamon
3/4 cup dark corn syrup
1/2 cup applesauce
1 cup chopped pecans
3 eggs, beaten

Combine butter, sugar, and cinnamon. Add syrup, applesauce, pecans, and eggs. Blend well. Pour into pie shell. Bake in a 400 degree oven for 15 minutes. Reduce heat to 325 degrees and bake for 25-30 additional minutes. Delicious!

Mrs. Bruce Fowler, Woodruff, SC

BLACK WALNUT PIE

1 cup black walnut halves
2 eggs, slightly beaten
1 cup dark corn syrup
1 teaspoon vanilla
1 tablespoon melted butter
1 cup white sugar
1/8 teaspoon salt
1 unbaked 9-inch pie shell

Mix ingredients, adding black walnuts last. Pour into unbaked pie shell and bake in conventional oven at 400 degrees for 15 minutes. Reduce temperature to 300 degrees and bake about 30 minutes more or until a toothpick inserted in the center comes out clean. Serve warm or cold. Enjoy!

Mary Davis, Cookeville, Tennessee

CHOCOLATE CHIP WALNUT PIE

2 eggs
1/2 cup flour
1/2 cup sugar
1/2 cup packed brown sugar
1 cup butter, melted, cooled to room temperature
1 (6 ounce) package chocolate chips
1 cup chopped walnuts
1 (9 inch) unbaked pie shell

Beat eggs in large bowl until foamy. Beat in flour, granulated and brown sugars until well blended. Blend in melted butter. Fold in chocolate chips and walnuts. Spoon into unbaked pie shell. Bake at 325 degrees for 1 hour or until knife inserted in center comes out clean.

Do not overbake. Serve warm.

Karen Krugman, Tampa, Fla.

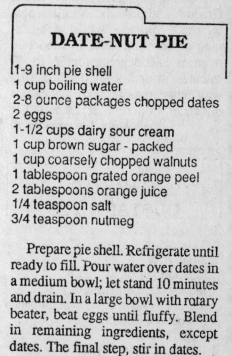

DATE-NUT PIE

1-9 inch pie shell
1 cup boiling water
2-8 ounce packages chopped dates
2 eggs
1-1/2 cups dairy sour cream
1 cup brown sugar - packed
1 cup coarsely chopped walnuts
1 tablespoon grated orange peel
2 tablespoons orange juice
1/4 teaspoon salt
3/4 teaspoon nutmeg

Prepare pie shell. Refrigerate until ready to fill. Pour water over dates in a medium bowl; let stand 10 minutes and drain. In a large bowl with rotary beater, beat eggs until fluffy. Blend in remaining ingredients, except dates. The final step, stir in dates.

Pour into unbaked pie shell. Bake at 375 degrees for 45-50 minutes or until filling is set in center when pie is gently shaken.

Nancy Johnson, Kenosha, WI

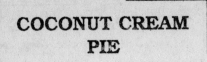

COCONUT CREAM PIE

2 cups milk
1/2 cup granulated sugar
2 tablespoons all-purpose flour
2 tablespoons cornstarch
2 large eggs, separated
1 tablespoon butter
1/2 teaspoon salt
1-1/4 cups shredded coconut
1 teaspoon vanilla

Scald 1-1/2 cups milk in top of a double boiler. Combine sugar, flour, cornstarch, and salt. Stir in remaining 1/2 cup milk and egg yolks. Stir this flour mixture into hot milk; cook until thickened. Remove from heat. Add butter, vanilla, and 3/4 cup coconut. Allow mixture to cool, then pour into baked 9 inch pie shell. Cover with meringue and remaining coconut. Bake at 350 degrees 10-12 minutes, or until meringue browns lightly.

Dorothy E. Snyder, Mifflinburg, PA

CRAZY PIE

1 cup flour
1 teaspoon baking powder
1/2 teaspoon salt
1 tablespoon sugar

Mix well the flour, baking powder, salt and sugar. Blend in:
2/3 cup butter-flavored shortening
3/4 cup water

Beat 2 minutes on medium speed with electric mixer. Pour batter into 9" pie pan. Do not spread. Pour favorite pie filling in center of batter. Do not stir. Bake 45-50 minutes in preheated 425 degree oven.

Lucille Roehr, Hammond, IN

END OF THE LINE PIE

Serves 8

1 (4 ounce package) German Sweet Chocolate

1/4 cup butter
1 (13 ounce can) evaporated milk
1-1/3 cups flaked coconut
3 eggs, slightly beaten
1/2 cup sugar

In saucepan melt chocolate and butter. Gradually add milk and coconut. Combine eggs and sugar, and stir into chocolate mixture. Pour mixture into pie crust. Bake at 400 degrees for 45 minutes. Completely cool before cutting the individual servings.

FOURTH OF JULY PIE

1 (3-ounce) package lemon gelatin
2/3 cup boiling water
2 cups ice cubes
1 (8-ounce) container frozen whipped topping, thawed
1/2 cup sliced fresh strawberries
1/2 cup whole fresh blueberries
1 (9-inch) prepared graham cracker crumb crust

Dissolve gelatin in the boiling water, stirring about 3 minutes. Add ice cubes and stir constantly until gelatin is thickened, about 2 to 3 minutes. Remove any unmelted ice. Using a wire whip, blend in whipped topping and whip until smooth. Fold in strawberries and blueberries. Chill, if necessary, until mixture will mound. Spoon into pie shell. Chill about 2 hours.

HAWAIIAN CHESS PIE

3 eggs beaten
1/4 cup milk
1-1/2 cup sugar
2 tablespoons flour
2 teaspoons lemon juice
1/4 cup melted margarine
1 - 8 ounce can crushed pineapple, with juice
2/3 cup flaked coconut
1 - 9 inch deep dish unbaked pie shell

Combine eggs, milk, sugar, flour, lemon juice, and margarine. Beat until smooth. Add pineapple and coconut. Pour into pie shell. Bake at 350 degrees for 50-55 minutes or until center of pie is set. Cool and serve. Yummy!

Barbara June Ohde, Atkinson, NE

MILLION DOLLAR PIE

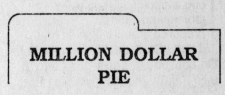

1/3 cup lemon juice
1 can sweetened condensed milk
1 (No. 2 can) crushed pineapple, drained
1 (9 ounce) container frozen dessert topping, thawed
1 cup chopped nuts (reserve some for top to garnish)
1 (8 ounce) package cream cheese, softened
1 large (or 2 small) baked pastry or graham cracker shells.

Mix all ingredients together well and pour into pie shells. Sprinkle with reserved nuts and chill. Cut into small wedges.

Laura Scheer, New Haven, Mo.

NO-FOOL PIE

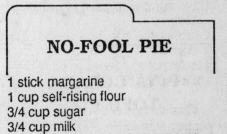

1 stick margarine
1 cup self-rising flour
3/4 cup sugar
3/4 cup milk
1 to 1-1/2 cups fruit, drained (blueberries, peaches, cherries, etc.)

Preheat oven to 350 degrees. Melt margarine in deep 8-inch cobbler pan while oven is preheating; set aside. Combine flour, sugar, and one-half of milk; stir until dry ingredients are moistened. Add remaining milk and stir until smooth. Pour batter over melted margarine. DO NOT MIX! Sprinkle drained fruit over top of this mixture. Do not stir to combine. Bake 30-40 minutes, or until lightly browned and center springs back when lightly touched with finger. Serve hot, with or without ice cream.

Larry Luttrell, Marietta, GA

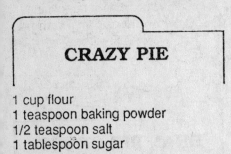

MOM'S CHEESE PIE

Crust:

1 cup sifted flour
1/2 teaspoon baking powder
2 tablespoons sugar
4 tablespoons shortening
1 egg, beaten

Note: Crust dough forms a ball. Do not roll out crust; press into 10-inch lightly greased glass pie plate.

Filling:

1 large and 1 small package cream cheese (11 ounces total)
7 heaping tablespoons sugar
2 heaping tablespoons flour
1 egg
Juice of half a lemon
1 teaspoon vanilla
2 cups milk (regular whole milk is best)

Have cheese, milk, egg and lemon at room temperature; mix together in large bowl. Pour into pie plate. Batter will be watery. Place carefully in oven. Bake in preheated 350 degree oven about 1 hour or until knife inserted in center comes out clean. Sprinkle with cinnamon.

Adele A. Roselli, Longhorne, PA

PINA COLADA TOFU PIE

Tofu makes this a healthy dessert without sugar. Great for people on restricted diets.

1 pie crust (regular or graham cracker)
1 pound tofu cut-up and drained
1-1/2 tablespoons oil
1/3 cup plus 2 tablespoons honey
1-1/2 teaspoons cornstarch
1 teaspoon vanilla
1-1/4 cups drained crushed pineapple
3/4 cups shredded unsweetened coconut

Blend well all ingredients. Bake at 350 degrees for 20-30 minutes. Let cool to set.

Sande Guetthoff, Butler, PA

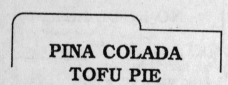

SAWDUST PIE

1-1/4 cup white or brown sugar
1-1/2 cups chopped pecans
1-1/2 cups vanilla wafers or graham cracker crumbs
1-1/2 cups flaked coconut
1/2 teaspoon cinnamon
1/2 teaspoon nutmeg
7 egg whites, unbeaten
1 unbaked 9-inch pastry shell
1 sliced banana
Whipped cream

Combine the first seven ingredients in a large mixing bowl. Stir until just blended. Pour into pie shell and bake at 375 degrees for 35 minutes or until filling is set.

Presentation: Top each slice with a dollop of whipped cream and a slice of banana. Serve warm or at room temperature.

Edna Lawrence, San Antonio, TX

SHOO-FLY-PIE

Combine the following ingredients to make crumbs:

1/4 cup shortening
1-1/2 cups flour
1 cup brown sugar

Liquid filling:

3/4 teaspoon baking soda
1/8 teaspoon nutmeg
Dash of ginger
Dash of cinnamon
Dash of cloves
1/4 teaspoon salt
3/4 cup molasses
3/4 cup hot water

Mix well the baking soda, nutmeg, ginger, cinnamon, cloves, salt, and molasses. Add hot water. In an unbaked pie shell, place crumbs and liquid in alternate layers, with crumbs being on both bottom and top. Bake 15 minutes at 450 degrees; lower heat to 350 degrees and bake for an additional 20 minutes.

Gracie Miesen, Phoenix, Ariz.

TRANSPARENT PIE

4 egg yolks
3/4 cup sugar
1 stick butter
1 cup evaporated milk
1 teaspoon vanilla
1 partially baked pie shell
8 tablespoons of sugar (additional)

Beat together egg yolks and sugar. Place in medium saucepan over low heat. Melt butter in egg mixture, stirring constantly. Remove from heat as soon as butter melts. Add evaporated milk and vanilla. Pour into crust and bake for 15 minutes at 400 degrees. Then reduce heat and bake until custard is set. Cover pie with meringue made form 4 egg whites and 8 tablespoons sugar. Return to oven to brown meringue. (Watch carefully)

Mary Bowles, Killen, AL

BRAN PIE CRUST SHELLS

Makes two 8" or 9" shells

1/3 cup bran
2 cups sifted flour
1/2 teaspoon salt
2/3 cup shortening
6 tablespoons cold water

Crush bran into fine crumbs; mix with flour and salt. Cut in 1/3 cup of the shortening to the consistency of cornmeal. Cut in remaining shortening to the consistency of peas. Sprinkle cold water over top of mixture, a little at a time. Mixing with a fork until dough is just moist enough to hold together. Turn onto a sheet of waxed paper and shape the dough into a ball. Roll out according to directions.

Marcella Swigert, Monroe City, MO

Sandwich
TASTIES

BARBECUED FRANKS
Serves 6

3 tablespoons salad oil
1 medium onion, chopped
1 teaspoon dry mustard
1 teaspoon paprika
1 tablespoon sugar
Salt
Pepper
1/2 cup water
1/2 cup ketchup
1/4 cup vinegar
1 tablespoon Worcestershire sauce
Drop of Tabasco sauce
12 wieners or franks

Simmer onion in salad oil until golden. Add all remaining ingredients, except the wieners; simmer for 15 minutes. Split wieners; place cut side down in shallow baking dish. Pour barbecue sauce over wieners. Bake in preheated oven at 350 degrees for 30 minutes, basting several times.

Leota Baxter, Ingalls, Kan.

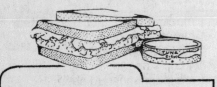

FRENCH TOASTED TUNA SANDWICHES

9 1/4-ounce can tuna, drained and flaked
1/4 cup finely chopped celery
1/4 cup finely chopped onion
1/4 cup sweet pickle relish

1/4 cup mayonnaise
12 slices dry bread
2 beaten eggs
1/3 cup milk
1/2 teaspoon vanilla
2 tablespoons oil

Combine tuna, celery, onion, relish, and mayonnaise. Spread tuna mixture on six slices of bread; top with remaining slices.

Combine eggs, milk and vanilla. Dip sandwiches into egg mixture to coat each side. Brown in hot oil in a hot skillet or on griddle, about 3 minutes on each side.

Charlotte Adams, Detroit, Mich.

SLOPPY JOES
Serves 6

1 pound ground beef
1 (8-ounce) can tomato sauce
1/2 onion, chopped
1/4 cup ketchup
1 tablespoon vinegar
1 tablespoon sugar
1-1/2 teaspoons Worcestershire sauce
1/2 green pepper (use whole, not chopped)

Brown hamburger; drain off fat. Mix remaining ingredients and simmer until hot. Remove green pepper. Put in Crockpot to keep warm. Spoon on hamburger buns.

Betty Slavin, Omaha, Neb.

CONEY ISLAND HOT DOGS
Serves 10

1 package onion soup mix
1 cup hot water
1/2 pound ground beef
2 tablespoons shortening
1 teaspoon chili powder
3/4 cup catsup
1 pound cooked hot dogs or franks
Hot dog buns

Soak onion soup mix in hot water for about 15 minutes. Strain out onion pieces and save liquid. Brown onion pieces and ground beef in shortening in large skillet. Add seasonings, catsup, and liquid drained from onions. Simmer together about 30 minutes. Serve on hot dogs in buns.

Sharon M. Crider, Evansville, Wisc.

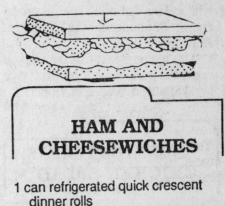

HAM AND CHEESEWICHES

1 can refrigerated quick crescent dinner rolls
4 slices ham
4 slices cheese
Ketchup or prepared mustard

Separate dough into 4 rectangles. Place slice of ham and 1/2 slice of cheese at one end of each. Spread with ketchup or mustard, if desired. Fold over. Bring edges of dough together to cover filling; fork edges to seal. Top with another 1/2 slice of cheese. Bake at 375 degrees for 10–13 minutes. Serve hot.

Shari Crider, Stoughton, Wis.

Seasonal
SALADS

CREAMY CRANBERRY SALAD

1 (6-ounce) package strawberry gelatin
1 cup hot water
1 (1-pound) can whole cranberry sauce
½ cup diced celery
¼ cup chopped nuts
1 (8-ounce) package cream cheese, softened

Dissolve gelatin in hot water. Cool and chill slightly. Break up cranberry sauce with a fork and add to gelatin with celery and nuts. Fold in cream cheese. Pour into an 8x8x2-inch pan. Refrigerate.

This recipe is easy to make and you can make it any time of year. It is nice to take to a covered-dish supper.

Mrs. Albert Foley, Lemoyne, Pa.

SUMMERTIME CHICKEN SALAD
Serves 8

1 cup mayonnaise
1 cup frozen whipped topping, thawed
3 cups cooked chicken, cut into chunks
2 cups sliced celery
1 cup seedless grapes, cut into halves
1 cup slivered, toasted almonds
1/2 cup pimiento-stuffed olives, sliced
Lettuce cups

Mix together mayonnaise and whipped topping. Mix together the rest of the ingredients, except lettuce cups. Pour mayonnaise and whipped topping over chicken mixture; toss lightly but thoroughly. Refrigerate until serving time. Serve in crisp lettuce cups.

Agnes Ward, Erie, Pa.

FROSTY FROZEN FRUIT SALAD
Serves 6–8

1 (8-ounce) package cream cheese, softened
1 cup dairy sour cream
¼ cup sugar
1 (17-ounce) can apricot halves, drained and halved
1 (8¾-ounce) can crushed pineapple, drained
1 (16-ounce) can pitted, dark sweet cherries, drained
1¼ cups miniature marshmallows
Crisp lettuce or watercress

In large mixer bowl, beat cheese until smooth; blend in sour cream and sugar; stir in fruit and marshmallows. Pour into 6–8 individual molds or into 4½-cup mold. Freeze overnight. Ten minutes before serving, unmold on crisp lettuce leaves or watercress.

Gwen Campbell, Sterling, Va.

HOLIDAY SALAD
Serves 10–12

6 cups raw broccoli
1 head raw cauliflower
⅔ cup cheddar cheese, cut up
3 tablespoons raw onion, cut up
3 tablespoons pimiento
Salt and pepper to taste

Dressing:
½ cup mayonnaise
½ cup plain yogurt
1 teaspoon pepper
1 teaspoon Lawry's seasoned salt

Put all cut-up salad ingredients in bowl. Mix all dressing ingredients together and put on salad; toss well.

Katherine V. Frierson, DeLand, Fla.

UNCLE SAM COLESLAW

1 medium head cabbage, grated
1 carrot, grated
1 green pepper, diced
3/4 cup vinegar
1 teaspoon mustard seed
1 1/2 cups sugar
1 teaspoon celery seed

Toss the cabbage, carrot, and pepper in a large salad bowl. In a saucepan combine vinegar, mustard seed, sugar and celery seed. Bring mixture to boil for 1 minute and allow to cool. Pour over cabbage mixture and serve chilled.

TAFFY APPLE SALAD

4 cups chopped Red Delicious apples, un-peeled
1 (8-ounce) can crushed pineapple, drained (re-serve juice)
1 cup salted peanuts
½ cup sugar
1 tablespoon cornstarch
2 tablespoons cider vinegar
1 egg, beaten
1 (8-ounce) container Cool Whip, thawed

Place apples, drained pineapple and nuts in bowl; mix. Combine corn-starch, sugar, vinegar and reserved pineapple juice. Cook over low heat for 1 minute, then add beaten egg. Cook until thick. Cool. When above mixture is cool, stir in apple mixture and mix well. Fold in the Cool Whip. Refrigerate overnight, or at least 6 hours.

This reminds you of eating taffy apples.

Edna Santapoalo, Kenosha, Wis.

SPIRITED POTATO SALAD

3/4 cup mayonnaise
3/4 cup sour cream
1/4 cup beer
6 cups peeled, cubed, cooked potatoes
1/2 cup onions, chopped
3/4 cup celery, chopped
1/2 pound bacon, crisped and crumbled
Salt and pepper to taste

Blend mayonnaise, sour cream, and beer. Toss lightly with potatoes, on-ion, celery, and bacon. Add salt and pepper to taste. Chill 3 hours and serve cold or heat at 275 degrees for 20 minutes and serve hot.

Joy Shamway, Freeport, Ill.

YOGI BERRY SALAD

1 Red Delicious apple, cored and chopped
1 cup halved, seedless green grapes
1 cup sliced strawberries
½ cup sliced celery
¼ cup raisins
½ cup lemon yogurt
2 tablespoons sunflower seeds
Lettuce

In a bowl, combine apple, grapes, strawberries, celery and raisins. Toss gently. Fold in yogurt. Cover and chill. Just before serving, stir in sun-flower seeds. Serve on lettuce leaves.

Kit Rollins, Cedarburg, Wis.

EASTER SOUFFLE' SALAD

Serves 8

3 (3-ounce) packages lemon-flavor gelatin
2 cups boiling water
2-1/2 cups cold water
1 cup dairy sour cream
1-1/2 cups green seedless grapes
1 orange, peeled and sectioned
1 apple, cored and diced
1 cup coarsely chopped walnuts

Dissolve gelatin in boiling water. Add cold water. Chill until partially set. Pour 1-1/2 cups gelatin into 3-quart mold. Chill. Add sour cream to remaining gelatin. Whip until fluffy. Chill until slightly thickened. Fold in fruit and nuts. Pour into mold. Chill until firm.

SUMMER POTATO SALAD

7 potatoes, cooked and cubed
1 tablespoon chopped onion
1 teaspoon salt
1/4 teaspoon pepper
1/4 cup pickle relish
1/4 cup French dressing

1 cup radishes, sliced
1 cup celery, diced
1/2 cup diced carrots
1/2 cup diced cucumbers
5 hard-cooked eggs, sliced
1 cup mayonnaise

Combine the onion, salt, pepper, pickle relish and French dressing with the potatoes. Chill about 1 hour. Fold in vegetables, eggs and mayonnaise for a real treat!

WILD RICE SALAD

Serves 6

2 cups cooked wild rice, chilled
2 large unpeeled red apples, diced
1 tablespoon lemon juice
2 tablespoons brown sugar
2 stalks celery, chopped
½ cup plain, non-fat yogurt
¼ cup low-fat mayonnaise

Toss diced apples with lemon juice and brown sugar. Stir in celery and rice. Blend together yogurt and mayonnaise. Toss with salad ingredients. Chill.

Laura Hicks, Troy, Mont.

CHERRY AMBROSIA

Serves 12

10 large oranges, peeled and sectioned
3 (8½-ounce) cans crushed pineapple, undrained
1 (10-ounce) jar marasch-ino cherries, drained and halved
1 (3½-ounce) can flaked coconut

Combine orange sections and pine-apple in a large bowl; chill 2–3 hours. Just before serving, stir in cherries. Spoon into individual serving dishes; sprinkle with coconut.

This is a family favorite!

Mrs. Bruce Fowler, Woodruff, S.C.

Soups & STEWS

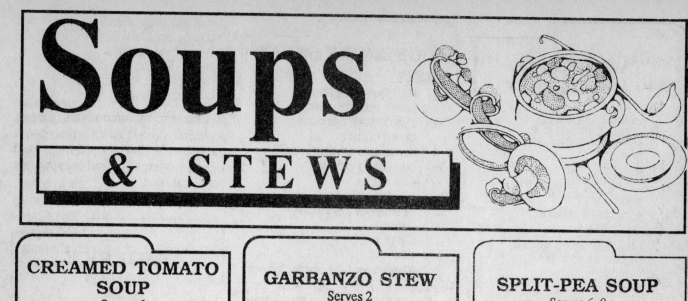

CREAMED TOMATO SOUP
Serves 6

1 (19-ounce) can toma-
   toes
1 large onion, finely
   chopped
   A few celery leaves,
   minced
1 tablespoon sugar
½ teaspoon savory
1 tablespoon cornstarch
2½ cups milk

Simmer first 5 ingredients together for 20 minutes. Mix cornstarch with ½ cup of the milk. Add remaining milk; simmer over medium heat, stirring often, until it comes to a boil. When ready to serve, pour this hot milk over hot tomatoes. Stir quickly. Do *not* boil.

If desired, ½–1 cup cooked rice can be added at the same time as milk.
Agnes Ward, Erie, Pa.

GARBANZO STEW
Serves 2

1 tablespoon olive oil
2 onions, thinly sliced
2 cups shredded cabbage
1 (1-pound) can gar-
   banzos
¾ pound kielbasa sau-
   sage, cut into chunks
½ teaspoon oregano
   Pitted ripe olives for
   garnish

Heat oil in a large skillet over medium heat; add onion and cabbage; cook, stirring, until vegetables are limp and lightly browned. Stir in garbanzos and their liquid. Cut kielbasa into 2-inch chunks and add to garbanzo mixture. Cover and simmer for 35 minutes. Stir occasionally. Skim and discard fat if desired. Add oregano; cook 2 minutes longer. Garnish with sliced, pitted olives. Serve hot.
Marie Fusaro, Manasquan, N.J.

SPLIT-PEA SOUP
Serves 6–8

1 pound dried split peas
6 cups water
1 meaty ham bone
½ to 1 cup chopped
   celery, carrots and
   onions
   Salt, pepper and cloves
   or allspice to taste

Rinse peas, but do not soak. Put all ingredients in a large pot. Cook 1–2 hours, stirring occasionally. When peas have cooked up and soup looks like "mush," it is done.

SPINACH–RICE SOUP
Serves 6-8

2 medium yellow onions, peeled
   and coarsely chopped

2 tablespoons butter or margarine
4 (13-3/4-ounce) cans chicken broth
1/4 cup uncooked rice
2 (10-ounce) packages frozen
   chopped spinach, thawed
2 teaspoons salt
1/4 teaspoon nutmeg
1/4 teaspoon pepper

Stir-fry onions in butter in a large saucepan over moderate heat, 8-10 minutes, until golden. Add broth and bring to a boil. Stir in rice and boil, uncovered, 10 minutes, until rice is about half done. Add remaining ingredients and simmer 12-15 minutes longer, until rice is done.

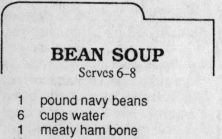

BEAN SOUP
Serves 6–8

1 pound navy beans
6 cups water
1 meaty ham bone
½ cup *each* chopped
   onion, celery and carrot
   Pepper to taste

Soak beans in water to cover overnight. Rinse. In large pot put all the ingredients. Simmer until beans are soft, several hours. In a Crockpot cook for 6–8 hours at a medium setting.

HAMBURGER SOUP

2 medium-size potatoes
½ pound hamburger
1 small onion
   Salt and pepper to taste

Cut potatoes into small chunks. Roll hamburger into small balls. Finely chop onion. Place all ingredients in pan; cover with water. Add salt and pepper. Cook for 30 minutes over medium heat.

Fast and easy!!
Dorothy Bohl, Mason, City, Iowa

MEATBALLS IN ONION SOUP

- 1 pound hamburger
- ¾ cup rolled oats
- 1 egg
- ½ cup milk
- 1 teaspoon salt
- ⅛ teaspoon pepper
- ½ teaspoon tarragon
- ⅓ cup flour
- 2 tablespoons fat
- 1 package onion soup mix
- 2¼ cups water
  Shredded Parmesan cheese

Combine first 4 ingredients. Add salt, pepper and tarragon. Blend. Shape into 18 medium-size balls, and roll lightly in flour (save excess flour). Melt fat and brown meatballs. Dissolve soup mix into 2 cups of water and add to meatballs. Cook, covered, over low heat for 20–25 minutes. Mix remaining flour and water to paste. Stir into onion soup and meatballs. Sprinkle with Parmesan cheese just before serving.

Gladys V. Keel, Oklahoma City, Okla.

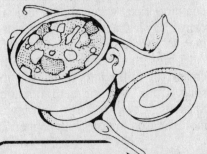

BEEF CORN STEW
Serves 4

- 1 pound ground beef
- ½ cup fresh or frozen chopped onion
- 3 large potatoes, peeled and diced
- 1 (17-ounce) can cream-style corn
- 1 (10½-ounce) can beef broth
- 1 teaspoon salt
  Dash of pepper

In large skillet brown beef and onion; drain off fat. Add remaining ingredients; mix well. Cover; cook over low heat for 20–25 minutes, stirring occasionally.

Annie Cmehil, New Castle, Ind.

CREAM OF ASPARAGUS SOUP
Serves 6

- 1 (16-ounce) can asparagus (cuts and tips)
- 1 medium onion, chopped
- ¼ cup butter or margarine
- ¼ cup flour
- ½ teaspoon salt
- ¼ teaspoon nutmeg
  Milk
  Croutons or shredded Swiss cheese for garnish

Drain asparagus; reserve liquid. Sauté onion in butter until tender. Stir in flour and seasonings; cook and stir until blended. Add milk to reserved asparagus liquid to make 1 quart. Gradually add to flour mixture; cook and stir until slightly thickened. Purée three-fourths of asparagus in blender or food processor; add to milk mixture with remaining asparagus; heat thoroughly. Garnish, as desired.

Joy B. Shamway, Freeport, Ill.

BROWN 'N WILD RICE SOUP
Serves 6

- 6 tablespoons butter or margarine
- ½ cup sliced green onions, including tops
- ½ cup shredded carrots
- ½ cup all-purpose flour
- 4 cups chicken broth
- 2 cups brown rice, cooked
- ½ cup wild rice, cooked
- ½ cup minced ham
- ¼ teaspoon ground white pepper
- ¼ teaspoon thyme
- 1 cup half-and-half (cream and milk)

- 1 tablespoon dry sherry (optional)
- ¼ cup toasted, slivered almonds (for garnish)

Melt butter in large saucepan or Dutch oven; cook onions and carrots until tender-crisp. Blend in flour; gradually stir in broth. Cook, stirring constantly, until mixture comes to a boil; boil, stirring, 1 minute. Stir in brown rice, wild rice, ham, pepper and thyme; simmer, uncovered, for about 5 minutes. Stir in half-and-half and sherry. Garnish each serving with almonds.

Hollie Rogers, Columbus, Ohio

GERMAN LENTIL SOUP

- 2 quarts beef or chicken stock
- 1 cup lentils
- ½ cup chopped carrots
- ½ cup chopped celery
- ½ cup chopped onion
- 1 teaspoon pepper
- 1 orange, quartered
- 3 sprigs parsley
- 1 teaspoon thyme leaves
- 1 bay leaf
- ½ pound bacon
- 2 tablespoons flour
- ½ cup sour cream
- 2 tablespoons dry sherry
- 6 cooked sausages (gray bratwurst), cut into ¼-inch slices

Combine broth, lentils, chopped vegetables and pepper in large pot. Tie orange, parsley, thyme and bay leaves in cheesecloth bag. Add to saucepan. Bring to a boil; reduce heat and simmer 45 minutes. Fry bacon until brown; pour off all fat, except save 2 tablespoonfuls. Reduce heat; stir in flour and cook, stirring constantly, for 2 minutes. Add to lentil mixture and continue simmering 15 minutes. Discard cheesecloth bag. Can be made ahead to this point. Combine sour cream and sherry; stir into soup. Add sausage and heat through.

Debra Hahn, Annandale, N.J.

CREAM OF CARROT SOUP

Serves 4 to 6

1 bunch of carrots
1 small onion
Sprig of parsley
1/4 cup of rice
2 tablespoons butter or drippings
1-1/2 teaspoons. salt
Few grains of cayenne
2 cups water
2 cups scalded milk
2 tablespoons flour

Chop enough carrots to make 2 cups; cook in water until tender. Press through sieve, saving cooking water. Cook rice in milk in double boiler. Cook onion in butter or fat; add flour and seasonings. Mix carrots with rice and milk, add butter or drippings, flour and water in which carrots were cooked. Bring to boiling point; serve. If too thick, thin with milk.

Ms. R. Ohlsen, Utica, NY

CREAMED ZUCCHINI SOUP

Serves 6-8

Here is a great way to use wonderful zucchini. We are always looking for new serving ideas.

2 cups grated zucchini
2 cups water
1 tablespoon dried minced onion
2 chicken bouillon cubes
Grated pepper
1 teaspoon garlic powder
1 teaspoon dillweed
1/2 teaspoon nutmeg
1(13-ounce) evaporated milk
1/2 cup water
2 tablespoons cornstarch

In a 2-quart casserole combine zucchini, water, onion, bouillon cubes, pepper, garlic powder, dillweed, and nutmeg. Microwave for 8 minutes on HIGH. Puree in blender. Pour back into bowl.

In a small dish combine the cornstarch with the 1/2 cup water; mix well. Pour into the puree, add the can of milk, and microwave the entire mixture until thick, for 5-8 minutes on HIGH. Refrigerate to cool. Serve as a cold soup with garnish of paprika and parsley.

CREAM OF WILD RICE SOUP

Serves 4

1/2 cup wild rice
10-3/4 ounce can condensed chicken broth
1 cup water
1/4 cup chopped onion
1 small bay leaf
1/2 teaspoon dried basil, crushed
4-ounce can sliced mushrooms, drained
1/4 cup fresh parsley, snipped or 1/8 cup dried
2 cups of light cream or milk
1 tablespoon flour
1/4 cup shredded carrot

Rinse rice. In 3-quart saucepan, combine rice, water, broth, onion, carrot, bay leaf and basil; cover, simmer 45 minutes. Remove bay leaf. Add mushrooms and parsley. Stir cream (or milk) into flour; add to soup. Cook and stir until mixture thickens. Cook and stir 1 minute more. Season to taste with pepper.

Joy Shamway, Freeport, IL

CREAM OF SPINACH SOUP

Serves 8

2 tablespoons butter
1 leek, chopped, or 6 to 8 green onions, cut in 1-inch pieces
1 clove garlic, cut in half
1 can (13-3/4 ounce) chicken broth
2 packages (10-ozs. each) fresh spinach, cleaned
1 medium potato, shredded
3 cups milk
1 teaspoon salt
1/8 teaspoon nutmeg
Pepper

Dairy sour cream (optional)

In a 5-quart dutch oven, melt butter over medium heat; sauté leek and garlic until tender, but not browned. Add 1/2 cup of chicken broth, spinach and potato. Simmer, covered, over medium heat, stirring occasionally, about 15 minutes. In bowl of food processor, place chopping blade; add spinach mixture. Process just until blended. Carefully return spinach mixture to Dutch oven. Add remaining chicken broth, milk, salt and nutmeg; stir until blended. Cook, covered, over medium heat for 15 minutes or until hot. Season with salt and pepper as desired. Garnish with dollop of sour cream.

Sue Hibbard, Rochester, NY

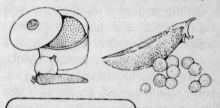

ORIENTAL CHICKEN NOODLE SOUP

Serves 6

6 chicken thighs, (about 1-1/2 pounds)
6 cups water
1 cup frozen green peas
2 medium eggs
2 (3 ounce) packages dried ramen or Oriental noodles for soup
Soy sauce or salt

In 5-quart Dutch oven, heat chicken thighs and water to boiling. Cover; simmer chicken over low heat until fork-tender, about 20 minutes. Transfer chicken to bowl; cool until easy to handle. Skim off and discard all fat from surface of broth. Remove and discard skin and bones from chicken. Tear chicken into pieces. Add peas to broth; cook for 1 minute. In cup, beat eggs lightly, just to break yolks. Drizzle eggs into soup. Add noodles and seasoning packets. Cook just until noodles soften. Stir in chicken. Add soy sauce or salt to taste.

Leona Teodori, Warren, Mich.

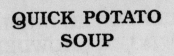

QUICK POTATO SOUP

1 medium potato, peeled and cubed
1 medium onion, peeled and chopped
2 cups milk
1 teaspoon chicken flavor bouillon granules, or one cube
1 tablespoon sugar
1 cup dried potato flakes
Pinch white pepper
2 slices bacon, diced
1/4 cup smoked ham or diced, boiled ham
2 quarts of water (more or less)

In saucepan, fry bacon until partially cooked, *not* crisp. Drain off most fat; add chopped onions. Cook until transparent. Add water, ham, chicken flavor bouillon, to hot bacon. Simmer until all is tender, about 15 minutes. Add sugar, pepper, and half of dried potato flakes, stirring well until all is mixed. Simmer an additional 10 minutes. Add rest of potato flakes, stirring well, then all milk. Simmer another short time until soup is well thickened. Add diced potato; cook until soft.

Note: If a thinner soup is wanted, add additional milk. Skim milk powder, or canned milk works well, as long as it is added slowly and never boiled, only simmered.

If a brighter soup is wanted, add cubed red pepper, or a few canned or frozen sweet peas at the same time as the potato flakes. When checking for taste, a bit of salt can be added, but as the ham, bacon, and chicken bouillon are cooked, salt may not be needed.

George B. McCroskey, Oregon, OH

POTATO SOUP

Serves 4-6

2 (10-1/2 ounce) cans of chicken consommé
1 soup can water
2 cups diced potatoes
2 scallions, chopped
1 soup can milk
1 teaspoon Worcestershire sauce
1/2 cup sour cream

Combine consommé, water, potatoes, and scallions in a large saucepan; bring to a boil. Reduce heat; simmer until potatoes are tender, about 12 minutes. Blend smooth in a blender; return to saucepan. Stir in milk and Worcestershire sauce; heat. Stir in sour cream. Can be eaten hot or well chilled.

Joy Shamway, Freeport, Ill.

IRISH CREAM OF POTATO SOUP

Serves 6

4 stalks celery and leaves
2 medium onions
1 medium carrot
1-1/2 cups water
2 chicken bouillon cubes
1-1/2 cups cooked, mashed potatoes
1 tablespoon butter
2 cups half-and-half

Chop celery, onions and carrot; add water and simmer 30 minutes. Strain through sieve (large tea strainer will work). Stir bouillon cubes into strained vegetable-water. While hot, pour over potatoes, stirring until dissolved. Rub through strainer to make sure no lumps remain. Add butter and half-and-half; heat. Sprinkle paprika and parsley flakes on top.

If you have never tried bisques, you do not know what you have missed. The definition of a bisque is a thick, rich creamy soup with shellfish as its base. Bisques always have been popular in the southern states, most of which border a waterway. But today, all regions enjoy their own variety of this thick soup. We will wager that the official definition does not match the taste of this hearty soup which is served both as a first course at dinner or as lunch, all by itself.

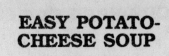

EASY POTATO-CHEESE SOUP

Serves 6

1 package au gratin potatoes
1 (#303) can chicken broth
3 cups water
1/4 cup carrots, finely diced
1/4 cup celery, finely diced
1 small can Pet milk
Chopped parsley

Combine contents of potato package, including cheese sauce mix, broth, water, carrots, and celery in a 3-1/2 quart saucepan. Bring to a boil, stirring occasionally. Reduce heat and simmer, covered, for 15 minutes or until potatoes are tender. Remove from heat; add milk. Garnish with parsley.

Agnes Ward, Erie, Pa.

HAMBURGER SOUP

1 pound hamburger
1 cup chopped onion
1 cup celery
1 cup diced potatoes
1 quart tomatoes
2 large carrots, grated medium
1 tablespoon salt
1 bay leaf
1/4 teaspoon basil
1/4 teaspoon thyme
1/4 teaspoon fresh ground pepper
2 tablespoons beef bouillon
6 cups water
2 small cans whole kernel corn
1 small can yellow wax beans
1 cup frozen peas

Fry hamburger with onion until done. Add everything else except corn, beans, and peas. Simmer 30 minutes. Add last 3 ingredients and simmer another 5 minutes. A really great "hurry up" meal, tastes like it took hours to prepare.

Linda Taylor, New Lenox, IL

BEEF STEW

2 pounds beef chuck roast
2 medium onions, peeled and quartered
1 pound carrots
16-ounce can tomatoes
2 cups water
1 tablespoon basil
1 teaspoon pepper
5 potatoes, peeled and quartered

Cube beef; sauté in small amount of fat; slice onions and sauté in fat. Place beef, onions, carrots, tomatoes, basil, pepper and water into large covered pot. Bring to boil; simmer 2 hours. Add potatoes the last 45 minutes.

June Harding, Ferndale, MI

GREEN PEPPER STEW

Economy dish, serves 4

1 onion, chopped
4 tablespoons shortening
2 cups water
2 green peppers, chopped
2 tomatoes, chopped
1 teaspoon salt
1/2 teaspoon black pepper
4 medium sized potatoes, diced
2 tablespoons flour

Brown onion in shortening. Add water, peppers, tomatoes, salt and pepper. Cook for 20 minutes. Add potatoes and cook until potatoes are soft but not mushy. Mix flour with small amount of water. Add just enough to vegetables to thicken.

Elizabeth, S. Lawson, Delbartow, WV

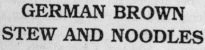

GERMAN BROWN STEW AND NOODLES

50 years old

1-1/2 pounds stew beef, cubed
2 tablespoons Crisco
1 large apple, pared and shredded

1/2 cup carrots, shredded
1/2 cut water
1/2 onion, sliced
1 clove garlic, minced
2 beef bouillon cubes
4 tablespoons cornstarch
1/4 cup cold water
1/4 teaspoon Kitchen Bouquet

Brown meat in Crisco; drain. Add apple, carrots, onion, 1/2 cup water, salt, pepper, garlic and bouillon cube. Place in saucepan; bring to boil; simmer about 2 hours. Combine cornstarch with 1/4 cup cold water and Kitchen Bouquet; add to meat mixture. Stir until thick and serve over hot noodles.

Marie Kerber Sherwood, Staten Island, NY

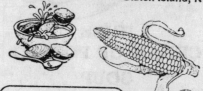

SEAFARER'S TOMATO CLAM CHOWDER

Makes 10 cups

3 slices bacon, chopped
1 onion, chopped
2 ribs celery, chopped
1 clove garlic, minced
2 cups tomato juice
2-1/2 cups potatoes, diced
1 (28 ounce) can whole tomatoes, undrained and cut
1/4 teaspoon salt
1/2 teaspoon dried whole thyme
1 (8 ounce) bottle clam juice
2 (6-1/2 ounce) cans minced clams, undrained
4 tablespoons cornstarch

In a Dutch oven, cook bacon until lightly browned. Add onion, celery, and garlic; sauté until tender. Add tomato juice and next 5 ingredients. Cover; cook 25 minutes or until potatoes are tender. Drain clams; reserve liquid. Mix cornstarch and clam liquid; stir until smooth. Carefully stir clams and cornstarch mixture into vegetables. Gently boil about 2 minutes, stirring constantly, until slightly thickened.

Gwen Campbell, Sterling, Va.

CHASE THE CHILLS WINTER CHOWDER

1 pound dried lima beans
1 large onion, chopped
2 large ribs celery, chopped
1/4 cup butter
1/4 cup flour
1 teaspoon salt
Pepper to taste
3 cups heavy cream
16-ounce can Italian plum tomatoes
16-ounce can corn
1/4 pound sharp Cheddar cheese, grated

Rinse dried lima beans and soak in 6 cups water for 6 hours or overnight. Drain and cook beans for about 1 hour in large pot with 6 cups fresh water. In large saucepan, sauté onion and celery in butter until slightly tender. Thoroughly blend in flour, salt and pepper. Add cream and bring to a gentle boil. Add beans and their liquid; add remaining ingredients. Bring again to a boil; adjust seasonings before serving.

Mrs. Gwen Campbell, Sterling, VA

SMOKY CORN CHOWDER

Serves 6

1/2 cup chopped onion
1/4 cup margarine or butter
1/4 cup all-purpose flour
1 teaspoon salt
1/8 teaspoon pepper
4 cups milk
1 (17 ounce) can whole kernel corn, drained
1 (12 ounce) package fully-cooked smoked sausage links, sliced
1 (8-1/2 ounce) can Lima beans, drained

In saucepan cook onion in margarine or butter until tender, but not brown. Blend in flour, salt, and pepper. Add the milk all at once; cook and stir until thickened and bubbly. Stir in corn, sausage, and Lima beans. Simmer 10 minutes.

Marcella Swigert, Monroe City, Mo.

CHICKEN SOUP

1 large chicken, cut up
2 eggs
Juice of 2 lemons
2 teaspoons salt
8 cups water

Boil chicken* and salt in water about 2 hours. Remove chicken from broth; skin and debone; dice.

Beat eggs until light. Slowly add lemon juice; add 1 cup warm broth very slowly. Add to remaining broth with diced chicken and continue to heat through.

*For a different taste add finely chopped carrots, celery, and onion to the chicken when originally cooking.

A wonderfully-flavored and hearty soup such as this one needs only warm bread with butter, a tossed salad, and a dessert to make a filling meal.

Soups date back to prehistoric man when he combined bones, meat, water, and hot rocks in animal skin bags to produce a tasty brew. In ancient Roman cookbooks, the first known printed cookbooks contained recipes for soup. Both Queen Elizabeth I and Queen Victoria drank a cup of mutton broth to begin each day. The first soup "restorative" (later to be known as restaurant, and serve other foods) was established in Paris in 1750.

George Washington deserves credit for increasing the popularity of soup in our country. He requested that his personal cook, with few provisions, create a warm meal for his troops at Valley Forge. But it was our European ancestors who brought with them their favorite soups, and over the years, these soups have been adapted and blended to use local ingredients to suit a variety of tastes.

CHILI-BEEF SOUP
Serves 6

1/2 pound ground beef
1/2 cup chopped onion
1/2 cup chopped celery

1 (16-ounce) can stewed tomatoes
1 (10-1/2 ounce) can condensed beef broth
1 soup-can water
1 teaspoon chili powder
1/2 teaspoon salt
1/2 teaspoon Worcestershire sauce
1 cup cooked peas

Brown meat in large, heavy Dutch oven or kettle. Drain off fat. Add onion and celery; cook until vegetables are done. Stir in tomatoes, beef broth, water, chili powder, salt, and Worcestershire sauce. Cover and cook until all is tender, about 15 minutes. Stir in peas; heat through.

HOT DEER CHILI
Serves 4-6

2 pounds coarsely ground venison
3 tablespoons chili powder
1 teaspoon black pepper
1 medium onion, chopped
1 bell pepper, chopped
1/2 teaspoon chopped jalapeño pepper
1 small can tomatoes (already seasoned with peppers, or regular tomatoes if others are unavailable)
1 (20-ounce) can tomato juice
1/2 teaspoon garlic salt
1/4 teaspoon salt
1 tablespoon oil
1/2 cup water

Sauté onion, bell pepper, and jalapeño pepper in oil in large skillet or pan until onion is clear; add meat and cook until meat loses its redness; add chili powder and black pepper. Mix well and cook 2 minutes, then allow it to set for 3 minutes. Add tomatoes, tomato juice, and salts. Heat to boiling, then simmer for 1 to 1-1/2 hours. Add water, as needed.

Note: You may use beef instead of venison.

AMERICAN CHILI
Serves 8

2 pounds stewing beef, cut in 1/2-inch cubes

2 tablespoons cooking oil
2 cups chopped onions
2 cloves garlic, minced
1 (1-pound) can tomatoes, cut up
1 beef bouillon cube
2 tablespoons chili powder
1-1/2 teaspoons salt
1 teaspoon dried oregano leaves
1 teaspoon ground cumin
2 (15-ounce) cans pinto or kidney beans

Brown meat in hot oil in Dutch oven. Add onion, garlic, tomatoes, bouillon cube, chili powder, salt, oregano, and cumin. Cover and simmer 1-3/4 hours. Add undrained beans; simmer 15 minutes.
Barbara Beauregard-Smith, SouthAust.

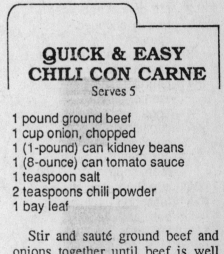

QUICK & EASY CHILI CON CARNE
Serves 5

1 pound ground beef
1 cup onion, chopped
1 (1-pound) can kidney beans
1 (8-ounce) can tomato sauce
1 teaspoon salt
2 teaspoons chili powder
1 bay leaf

Stir and sauté ground beef and onions together until beef is well done. Add kidney beans, tomato sauce, salt, chili powder, and bay leaf. Cover and cook slowly for 1 hour.

Suzan L. Wiener, Spring Hill, Fla.

BEEF STEW WITH DUMPLINGS
Serves 6

2 (24-ounce) cans beef stew
1 cup water
2 cups Basic Campers' Mix
1 cup milk

Combine canned stew and water. Bring to a boil. Combine Basic Campers' Mix and milk. Spoon onto hot stew. Cook, uncovered, over low coals for 10 minutes; cover and cook 10 minutes longer.

Vegetable DELIGHTS

SPINACH SQUARES
Makes 7 dozen

2 (10-ounce) packages frozen, chopped spinach
3 tablespoons margarine
1 small onion, chopped
¼ pound fresh mushrooms, sliced
4 eggs
¼ cup fine dry bread crumbs
1 can cream of mushroom soup
¼ cup Parmesan cheese
⅛ teaspoon *each,* pepper, basil and oregano leaves

Put spinach in strainer and rinse under hot water to thaw. Press out water. Melt butter; add onion and mushrooms. Cook until onion is limp. In bowl beat eggs, then stir in bread crumbs, soup, 2 tablespoons cheese, pepper, basil, oregano leaves, spinach and onion-mushroom mixture. Blend well. Put into a well-greased, 9-inch square pan. Sprinkle with remaining cheese. Bake, uncovered, at 325 degrees for 35 minutes. Cool slightly.Cover, then refrigerate. Cut into 1-inch squares.

Laura Hicks, Troy, Mont.

BAKED-COATED VEGETABLES
Serves 8

1 (10-ounce) package frozen broccoli
2 cups zucchini, sliced

2 tablespoons oil
2 tablespoons water
1 envelope Shake 'n Bake Seasoning and Coating Mixture Original Recipe for Chicken

Thaw frozen vegetables under cold running water just enough to separate. Moisten vegetables with mixture of oil and water; shake off excess. Empty seasoning and coating mixture into plastic shaker bag. Shake vegetables, a few at a time, in the bag until evenly coated. Place in ungreased, shallow baking pan. Bake at 400 degrees for 15 minutes.

Teresa Bridge, Lima, Ohio

OLD SETTLERS BAKED BEANS

1/2 pound bacon
1/2 pound hamburger
1/2 cup chopped onion
1/2 cup bell peppers
3/4 cup (scant) brown sugar
1/4 cup ketchup
1/4 cup barbecue sauce
2 tablespoons mustard
1/2 teaspoon pepper
1/2 teaspoon chili powder
1 teaspoon salt
1 can kidney beans
1 can butter beans
1 (31-ounce) can pork and beans

Fry bacon and drain. Brown onions and pepper with hamburger. Add remaining ingredients along with bacon, and mix. Bake for 1 hour at 350 degrees. This can be prepared ahead and kept refrigerated or frozen.

Marie Walder, Beeville, Texas

MUSHROOM RICE PILAF
Serves 8

1/2 cup onion, minced
1/2 cup celery
1/4 cup butter
1-1/2 cups uncooked regular long-grain rice
1 (6-ounce) can mushroom buttons, drained
1 teaspoon salt (optional)
1/2 teaspoon crumbled thyme
3-1/2 cups chicken broth

Cook onion and celery in butter until tender; add rice and cook until golden. Add mushrooms, salt and thyme. Stir in chicken broth. Bring to boil; reduce heat and simmer, covered, for 20 minutes. At this point spoon into greased 2-quart baking dish. Bake at 325 degrees for 30 minutes.

M. Monson, Castle Rock, Wash.

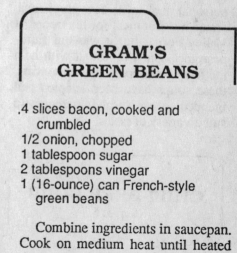

GRAM'S GREEN BEANS

.4 slices bacon, cooked and crumbled
1/2 onion, chopped
1 tablespoon sugar
2 tablespoons vinegar
1 (16-ounce) can French-style green beans

Combine ingredients in saucepan. Cook on medium heat until heated through.

Helen Weissinger, Levittown, Pa.

MINTED CAULIFLOWER

Serves 2

1 teaspoon vegetable oil
2 cups cauliflower florets, blanched
1/4 teaspoon mint flakes crushed
1/8 teaspoon salt
1/8 teaspoon pepper
2-3 teaspoons lemon juice

In 8-inch skillet, heat oil. Add cauliflower, mint, salt, and pepper; saute until cauliflower is tender-crisp, about 5 minutes. Sprinkle with lemon juice and saute for 2 minutes longer.

Mrs. Robert T. Shaffer, Middleburg, PA

BROCCOLI-CHEESE SQUARES

3 tablespoons butter, softened
2 (10 ounce) packages frozen chopped broccoli
3 large eggs
1 cup milk
1 cup flour
1 tablespoon baking powder
1 teaspoon salt
4 cups mild shredded Cheddar cheese
2 tablespoons finely chopped onion
Seasoned salt

Grease 13x9-inch dish with the butter. Steam broccoli until partly cooked, about 3 minutes; cool and press dry. Beat eggs and milk until frothy. Thoroughly mix flour, baking powder, and salt; stir into egg mixture; mix well. Fold in broccoli, cheese, and onion. Spoon into baking dish; spread evenly. Sprinkle with seasoned salt. Bake in 350 degree oven for 35 minutes.

Pauline Dean, Uxbridge, Mass.

BROCCOLI SUPREME

Serves 12-14

2 (10-ounce) packages frozen chopped broccoli, cooked and drained. Place in 2-quart casserole and add:

1 cup mayonnaise (not salad dressing)
1 small onion, chopped
1 can cream of mushroom soup
1 can cream of chicken soup
2 cups grated Cheddar cheese
2 eggs, beaten slightly

Cover and bake at 350 degrees for 1 hour.

Mrs. Hobert Howell, Waco, Texas

BROCCOLI PUFF

Serves 6

1 (10-ounce) package frozen broccoli
1 can condensed cream of mushroom soup
2 ounces sharp American cheese, grated
1/4 cup milk
1/4 cup mayonnaise or salad dressing
1 beaten egg
1/4 cup fine dry bread crumbs
1 tablespoon butter or margarine

Cook broccoli as directed, omitting salt; drain thoroughly. Place cuts into a 10 x 6 x 1-1/2-inch baking dish. Stir soup and grated cheese together. Gradually add milk, mayonnaise, and beaten egg to soup mixture; stir until blended. Pour over broccoli. Combine bread crumbs and melted margarine; sprinkle evenly over soup mixture. Bake in moderate oven of 350 degrees for 45 minutes until crumbs are lightly browned.

Peggy Fowler Revels, Woodruff, SC

BROCCOLI RING

Serves 10-12

3 eggs
2 tablespoons flour
1 cup half and half
1-1/2 cups chopped and cooked broccoli
1/2 cup chopped onion
3 tablespoons chopped sweet red pepper
1 teaspoon salt
1/8 teaspoon pepper
1/8 teaspoon paprika
Dash of nutmeg

Preheat oven to 350 degrees. Beat eggs slightly. Make a paste with flour and a small amount of water. Put all ingredients in bowl and mix. Add mixture to a greased 1 quart ring mold. Place mold in a pan of hot water and bake at 350 degrees, for 45 minutes or until firm. Turn mold out on plate and garnish with parsley and cherry tomatos; center of the ring may be filled with drained corn (mixed with butter) or any vegetable desired. Pimentos may be substituted for red pepper.

Betty Perkins, Hot Springs, AR

LO-CAL GINGER CARROTS

Serves 2, 48 calories per serving

3 medium carrots, cut in 3 x 1-1/4" strips
1 teaspoon reduced calorie margarine
1 teaspoon brown sugar
1/8 teaspoon ground ginger

Cook carrots in a small amount of boiling water until crisp and tender. Drain and set aside. Melt margarine in a saucepan. Stir in sugar and ginger. Cook over low heat, stirring constantly until sugar melts. Add carrots, cook stirring gently, until carrots are well coated and hot.

Agnes Ward, Erie, PA

DELICIOUS DILLED CARROTS

Fresh carrots, peeled and sliced into strips
Dill weed, to taste
Sugar to taste
1 stick butter
1/2" water in pan bottom

Place water in pan. Add butter and heat to melt. Add remaining ingredients. Bring to a boil. Cover and lower heat. Simmer until tender.

Cynthia Kannenberg, Brown Deer, WI

SCALLOPED CARROTS

5 cups raw carrots, sliced or diced
1 onion, sliced
1/2 cup butter
1/2 pound Velveeta cheese
12 Ritz crackers

Cook carrots until done; drain. Sauté onion in butter. In baking dish, layer carrots and cheese. Pour onions and butter over top. Break up Ritz crackers and sprinkle over top. Bake at 350 degrees for 30-40 minutes.

Evelyn Eckhart, Alexandria, Minn.

GREEN BEAN AND CARROT COMBO
Serves 6-8

1 pound can green beans, drained
1 pound can sliced carrots, drained
1/2 teaspoon sugar
1/4 teaspoon salt
1/4 teaspoon onion powder
1 can cream of celery soup
1/4 cup milk

Combine all ingredients; mix well. Place in greased casserole and bake for 25-30 minutes at 350 degrees.

Sharon Crider, Evansville, Wis.

GLAZED CARROTS WITH BACON 'N ONION
Serves 4

1 pound carrots, scraped and sliced
    diagonally
3 slices bacon
1 small onion, chopped
3 tablespoons brown sugar
1/8 teaspoon pepper

Cook carrots, covered, in small amount of boiling water for 15 minutes or until crisp tender; drain. Cook bacon in skillet until crisp; crumble. Reserve 1 tablespoon drippings in skillet. Sauté onion in drippings. Add

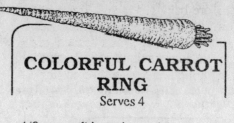

brown sugar, pepper, and carrots. Cook until heated; sprinkle with crumbled bacon.

Edna Askins, Greenville, Texas

COLORFUL CARROT RING
Serves 4

1/2 cup soft bread crumbs
3 eggs
1 small onion
1/4 cup parsley
1 tablespoon butter or margarine,
    melted
1/4 teaspoon cinnamon
1/4 teaspoon salt
1/8 teaspoon pepper
2-1/2 cups carrots, cooked
1 tablespoon brown sugar or
    maple syrup

Place all ingredients in food processor; process 1 minute or until carrots are cut very fine. Turn into an 8-inch ring mold; set in a shallow pan of water; bake at 375 degrees for 30 minutes or until set and firm. Unmold on serving plate; fill center with tiny peas.

Gwen Campbell, Sterling, Va.

POTATOES AND MUSHROOMS

8-10 small, new potatoes
1/4 cup butter, melted
2 tablespoons green onions or
    chives, chopped
1/2 pound mushrooms, chopped
1 cup meat stock
2 egg yolks
1 teaspoon lemon juice
Salt and pepper

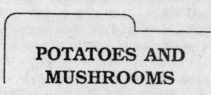

Cook potatoes in jackets until tender. Drain and dry. Place in a casserole, adding butter and chopped onion. Beat egg yolks and add lemon juice, mushrooms, and meat stock. Season with salt and pepper. Pour over potatoes in casserole. Bake uncovered in preheated 350 degree oven for 30-40 minutes.

Betty Perkins, Hot Springs, AR

SWISS POTATOES

1-1/2 cups large baking potatoes,
    thinly sliced
1 teaspoon salt
1 teaspoon minced dried onion
2 eggs, beaten
1-1/2 cups milk, scalded
1/4 pound Swiss cheese, grated

Mix together all above ingredients, saving some grated cheese to sprinkle on top. Place into medium-sized, lightly-buttered casserole. Sprinkle top with reserved cheese. Place in preheated 350 degree oven and bake for 1 hour.

Recipe can be doubled easily.

Agnes Ward, Erie, Pa.

POTATO CELERY SUPREME
Serves 4

4-6 medium potatoes, cut into small
    pieces
Salt and pepper to taste
1/3 stick margarine
1 can cream of celery soup
1/2 cup water

Put cut potatoes into greased casserole; add salt and pepper, margarine, soup, and water. Stir lightly. Bake covered in a 350 degree oven for 1-1/2 hours.

Edna Askins, Greenville, Texas

COUNTRY-FRIED POTATOES

2 tablespoons butter or margarine
2 tablespoons bacon drippings (or
    shortening)
6 cooked, pared, thickly sliced
    potatoes
1 medium onion, chopped
Salt and pepper to taste

Melt butter and drippings or shortening in heavy skillet. Add sliced potatoes and chopped onions to hot skillet. Season with salt and pepper. Cook over low fire until bottom crust is brown; turn, and brown other side.

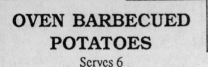

OVEN BARBECUED POTATOES

Serves 6

2 cups (8 ounces) Cheddar cheese, grated and divided
1 (10-3/4 ounce) can cream of mushroom soup
1/3 cup milk
1/4 cup barbecue sauce
1/4 teaspoon salt
1/4 teaspoon oregano
1/8 teaspoon pepper
4 medium potatoes, unpeeled and thinly sliced
1/2 teaspoon paprika

In large bowl combine 1-1/2 cups cheese, soup, milk, barbecue sauce, oregano, salt and pepper; blend thoroughly. Add potato slices; toss until well coated. Spoon mixture into a greased 9-inch square pan; cover with foil and bake at 350 degrees for 45 minutes. Remove foil; bake about 30 minutes longer or until tender. Remove from oven. Sprinkle remaining cheese and paprika on top. Let stand 5-10 minutes before serving.

Agnes Ward, Erie, PA

POTATO-CHEESE LOGS

2 medium potatoes, diced
2 tablespoons cream
2 tablespoons butter
1 egg, beaten lightly
1/2 teaspoon salt
1/8 teaspoon pepper
Dash cayenne pepper
1 clove garlic, crushed
3 tablespoons Parmesan or Romano cheese, grated
1 tablespoon parsley, minced
1/2 cup fine bread crumbs or cornflake crumbs

Boil potatoes until soft; drain and mash with cream and butter and whip until fluffy. Beat in egg, salt, pepper, cayenne, and garlic. Fold in cheese and parsley. Wet hands and shape into rolls, 2 inches long by 1 inch in diameter. *Roll in crumbs. Bake at 400 degrees for 15-20 minutes.

*To freeze, place on baking sheet immediately after rolling in crumbs and before baking. Place in freezer until firm; then pack in container and return to freezer. When needed, place frozen logs on lightly greased baking sheet and bake uncovered for 30 minutes at 400 degrees, turning once.

Eleanor V. Craycraft, Santa Monica, Calif.

BAKED CREAMED POTATOES

2 tablespoons butter or margarine
2 tablespoons flour
1 teaspoon salt
1/8 teaspoon white pepper
1-1/2 cups milk
1/2 teaspoon celery salt
1/4 cup chopped parsley
3-1/2 cups diced cooked potatoes (4 to 5 medium potatoes)
1 cup soft bread crumbs
2 tablespoons butter or margarine, melted

Preheat oven to 375 degrees. Butter a 1-1/2-quart casserole. Melt 2 tablespoons butter in a large saucepan. Sprinkle in flour, salt, and pepper; let it bubble up. Remove from heat and add milk all at once and stir to blend. Return to heat and stir until boiling, thickened, and smooth. Remove from heat and stir in celery salt, parsley, and potatoes. Pour into prepared casserole.

Combine bread crumbs and melted butter; sprinkle over all. Bake at 375 degrees for about 20 minutes or until hot and well-browned. These can be prepared ahead and then heated.

Lillian Smith, Montreal, Quebec, Canada

POTATOES RIO GRANDE

Serves 4

1-1/3 pounds (4 mid-size) potatoes, cut into 3/4 inch cubes
2 teaspoons vegetable oil
1 medium green (or red) bell pepper, seeded and cut into strips
1 (4-ounce) can diced green chiles
1 large clove garlic, pressed
1 (16-ounce) can stewed tomatoes
1/4 teaspoon pepper
Salt to taste
1/2 cup shredded Cheddar cheese
2 tablespoons chopped parsley

Continued on next page

Cook potatoes, covered, in 2-3 inches boiling water in 3-quart saucepan until not quite tender (about 12 minutes). Meanwhile, heat oil in large skillet. Add green pepper; toss over high heat, 5 minutes. Add chiles and garlic; cook and stir, 2 minutes. Stir in tomatoes and pepper. Cook to reduce liquid by half. Drain potatoes; add to skillet. Gently cook; stir to heat through. Stir in salt. Sprinkle cheese over potato mixture; cover to melt cheese. Sprinkle with parsley.

Judie Betz, Lomita, CA

SCALLOPED POTATOES AND GREEN TOMATO BAKE

8 medium-size unpeeled potatoes, thinly sliced
3 large green tomatoes, thinly sliced
1 medium-size onion, diced
1 cup flour
1 pound Cheddar cheese, grated
1/4 pound bacon, browned and crumbled
Salt and pepper to taste
1/2 cup milk

Butter a large baking dish. Put a layer of potatoes on the bottom. Cover with a layer of green tomatoes. Sprinkle on a little bit of onion, flour, Cheddar cheese, bacon, salt, and pepper. Continue layering until dish is full; end with layer of cheese. Pour milk over the top; bake at 350 degrees for 1 hour or until potatoes are cooked and bubbling brown on top.

Gwen Campbell, Sterling, VA

CHEESE POTATO CRISPS

3 tablespoons melted margarine
4-5 medium potatoes
Salt to taste
1-1/2 cups shredded American cheese
2 cups crushed crisp-rice cereal
Paprika

Brush melted margarine over bottom of jelly roll pan. Cut potatoes in lengthwise slices, about 1/4 inch thick. Arrange slices in single layer, turning once to coat both sides with margarine. Sprinkle potatoes with salt, then with cheese. Top with crushed cereal. Sprinkle with paprika. Bake at 375 degrees for about 20 minutes. Delicious!!

Cheryl Santefort, Thornton, Ill.

CHEESE DIP FOR BAKED POTATOES

1 (8-ounce) package cream cheese
4 tablespoons milk
1 tablespoon minced onions
1 teaspoon salt
1/4 teaspoon garlic powder

Soften cream cheese to room temperature. Mix all ingredients together. If too thick, add more milk. Serve over baked potatoes in place of sour cream.

Melanie Knoll, Marshalltown, Iowa

SLOW POT POTATOES

Serves 4 - 6

1/4 pound bacon, chopped
2 onions, thinly sliced
4 potatoes, thinly sliced
1/2 pound Cheddar cheese, thinly sliced
Salt and pepper
Margarine

Line your slow pot with aluminum

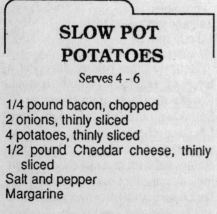

foil and leave enough to cover potatoes before cooking. Put half of of the bacon, onions, potatoes and cheese in layers in slow cooker. Season with salt and pepper; dot with margarine. Repeat layers. Again put salt and pepper and dot with margarine. Cover with foil. Place cover on slow pot; cook on low overnight (10 to 12 hours) or cook on high for 3 to 4 hours.

Mrs. Jodie McCoy, Tulsa, OK

CRUMB-COATED BAKED POTATOES

Serves 3-6

6 new red potatoes
1/4 cup butter or margarine
1/2 cup herb-seasoned bread crumbs
1 teaspoon garlic salt
1/8 teaspoon pepper
1/4 teaspoon chopped chives
1/8 teaspoon paprika

Scrub potatoes; leave on skin. Melt butter in an 8 x 8 x 2-inch baking pan; roll potatoes in butter, then in bread crumbs to coat. Sprinkle with seasonings; place in baking pan. Bake, uncovered, 45 minutes or until potatoes are fork tender.

Gwen Campbell, Sterling, Va.

OVEN FRIED POTATOES

Cut 4 potatoes (unpeeled) in wedges and place in shallow baking dish. Mix together and pour over potatoes:

1/4 cup cooking oil
1/4 cup water
2 tablespoons grated cheese (Romano or Parmesan)
1 teaspoon salt
1/2 teaspoon garlic powder
1/4 teaspoon paprika
1/8 teaspoon pepper

Bake at 375 degrees uncovered for 45 minutes. Baste occasionally.

Betty Cleri, Endicott, NY

POTATO SUPREME

Serves 6

1 cup sour cream
2 cups cottage cheese
2 teaspoons salt
2 tablespoons grated onion
1 clove garlic, minced
6 medium-sized potatoes, cooked and diced
1/2 cup shredded American cheese
Dash paprika

In a bowl, thoroughly mix sour cream, cottage cheese, salt, onion, and garlic. Gently fold in potatoes. Pour into buttered 1-1/2 quart casserole. Sprinkle evenly with cheese and lightly with paprika. Bake at 350 degrees until heated through and lightly browned, 40-45 minutes.

Mrs. E. O'Brien, Richmond, Va.

POTATOES WITH A ZIP

6 large baking potatoes
1 cup shredded sharp Cheddar cheese
1/2 cup tomato juice
1/3 cup sour cream
Paprika
Butter or margarine
Salt and pepper

Preheat oven to 375 degrees. Scrub potatoes and rub with butter or shortening. Prick several times with a fork. Bake 1 hour 15 minutes, or until tender. Increase oven temperature to 400 degrees. Slice each potato in half; scoop out inside, leaving a thin shell.

In large mixer bowl, mash potatoes; gradually beat in cheese, tomato juice, and sour cream. Fill potato shells with potato mixture. Garnish with paprika. Bake 15-20 minutes or until tops are lightly browned. Serve with butter. Refrigerate any leftovers. Can be prepared ahead and frozen. If frozen, bake at 350 degrees for 35 minutes.

Diantha Susan Hibbard, Rochester, N.Y.

FRIED GREEN TOMATOES

6 green tomatoes
3 tablespoons flour
1-1/4 teaspoons salt
Pepper to taste
4 tablespoons bacon fat
1 cup evaporated milk
1-1/4 teaspoons sugar

Wash tomatoes, but do not peel. Cut in half crosswise. Mix flour, salt, sugar, and pepper. Roll tomatoes, one at a time, in flour mixture. Brown on both sides in hot bacon fat. Remove to serving dish and keep warm. Add evaporated milk to same frying pan. Boil slowly, stirring constantly until thickened (about 2 minutes). Pour over tomatoes before serving.

Joy Shamway, Freeport, Ill.

BROCCOLI-TOMATO LOAF

2 cups broccoli, cooked
2 eggs
1 cup canned tomatoes
1 cup onion
1/2 cup celery
3 tablespoons butter or margarine
1/4 teaspoon salt
1/8 teaspoon pepper
1/4 teaspoon sugar
1 cup coarse cracker crumbs
Quick Cheese Sauce (recipe follows)

In a food processor or blender, chop and mix first 9 ingredients; stir in crumbs. Bake in a greased loaf pan at 350 degrees for 40 minutes. Serve with Quick Cheese Sauce.

Quick Cheese Sauce:

1/3 cup milk
1 cup Cheddar cheese, cubed
2 tablespoons flour
1/8 teaspoon salt
1/2 teaspoon Worcestershire sauce

In a saucepan over low heat, blend all ingredients until hot, thickened, and cheese has thoroughly melted.

Gwen Campbell, Sterling, Va.

GOLDEN MERINGUE TOMATOES

4 large tomatoes
2-1/2 tablespoons butter, softened
4 eggs, separated
Salt and pepper to taste
1/3 cup grated Romano cheese
2 tablespoons chopped parsley or chives

Stand tomatoes upright; cut a slice from the top of each tomato. Scoop out pulp; finely chop and mix with softened butter, egg yolks, salt, and pepper. Add half the cheese and half the herbs. Put the mixture into tomato shells. Place tomatoes in an ovenproof dish; cook 12 minutes in 350 degree oven. Beat egg whites until stiff; fold in remaining cheese and herbs. Remove tomatoes from oven; top each with the meringue. Bake also at 350 degrees for about 6 minutes, or until meringue is set, puffed, and golden.

Mrs. Gwen Campbell, Sterling, VA

GARDEN SALAD STUFFED TOMATOES

6 firm red tomatoes
1/2 teaspoon salt
1/8 teaspoon pepper
1/4 cup peas, cooked
1/4 cup lima beans, cooked
1/4 cup carrots, raw julienne strips
1/4 cup asparagus tips
1/4 cup zucchini, grated
2 hard-cooked eggs, chopped

Cut a slice from the stem end of each tomato; scoop out pulp; set aside; discard seeds. Sprinkle shells with salt and pepper; invert on rack to drain for 15 minutes. Combine all vegetables and tomato pulp with enough mayonnaise to form a firm mixture; fill tomato shells. Top each shell with chopped hard-cooked eggs.

Gwen Campbell, Sterling, VA

FRIED TOMATOES
Serves 4

6 or 8 firm (or green) tomatoes
1 egg
1 tablespoon water
Fine bread or cereal crumbs
Salt and pepper to taste

Wash the tomatoes; remove the stem end, and slice into 1/2-inch slices. Beat the egg slightly; mix water in; dip tomato slices in this mixture and then roll in crumbs seasoned with salt and pepper. Set aside.

Heat oil in heavy skillet and place tomato slices in hot oil. Brown on one side; turn carefully, and then reduce heat so tomatoes can cook thoroughly before browning.

Lift from skillet onto heated platter and serve immediately.

If you are from the country (or wish you were), and aren't counting calories, you'll pour hot, creamy gravy over the top.

TOMATO-CUCUMBER MARINADE
Serves 6

2 medium tomatoes, sliced
2 cups cucumber, peeled and thinly-sliced
1/2 medium onion, thinly-sliced and separated into rings
1/2 cup salad oil
1/4 cup white wine vinegar
1 teaspoon salt
1 teaspoon basil
1 teaspoon tarragon
1/8 teaspoon pepper
Shredded lettuce

Alternate layers of tomato, cucumber, and onion in shallow glass dish. Combine other ingredients except lettuce; beat well with electric mixer. Pour over layered vegetables; chill covered, for 5-6 hours. Drain, reserving marinade. Arrange marinated vegetables on shredded lettuce. Pass reserved marinade for individual servings of dressing.

Diantha Hibbard, Rochester, NY

Home Cooking

INDEX

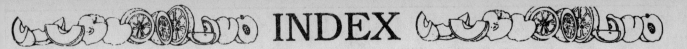

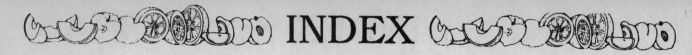

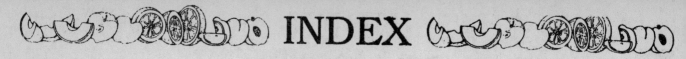